Mastering
Counselling skills

Information, help and advice
in the caring services

Jennie Lindon
and
Lance Lindon

MACMILLAN

First published 2000 by
MACMILLAN PRESS LTD
Houndmills, Basingstoke, Hampshire RG21 6XS
and London
Companies and representatives
throughout the world

ISBN 0–333–76005–0

A catalogue record for this book is available
from the British Library.

This book is printed on paper suitable for recycling and
made from fully managed and sustained forest sources.

10   9   8   7   6   5   4   3   2   1
09   08   07   06   05   04   03   02   01   00

Printed and bound in Great Britain by
Creative Print & Design (Wales), Ebbw Vale

◾ ⍌ Contents

Acknowledgements   vii
Introduction   ix

1 **Essentials of good practice**   1
   1.1   Helping in context   1
   1.2   Boundaries and objectives   5
   1.3   Standards for behaviour   9
   1.4   Attitudes towards clients   14
   1.5   Client records   17
   1.6   Anti-discriminatory practice   20

2 **Effective communication**   26
   2.1   The communication framework   26
   2.2   The importance of attention   29
   2.3   Awareness of body language   36
   2.4   Using verbal communication well   41
   2.5   Responding to clients' feelings   49

3 **First contact and short exchanges**   54
   3.1   Clients' first impressions   54
   3.2   Positive short exchanges   59
   3.3   Dealing with mistakes and complaints   64

4 **Sharing information and offering advice**   68
   4.1   Information services for clients   68
   4.2   Writing your own material   75
   4.3   Electronic communications   80
   4.4   From information to advice   84
   4.5   Referrals   87

5 **Help over the telephone**   92
   5.1   Telephone helping services   92
   5.2   Good practice for telephone helplines   96

6 **Helping other people: a positive framework**   108
   6.1   Background knowledge for counselling skills   108
   6.2   Essentials in counselling   109
   6.3   Personal styles in helping   115
   6.4   Setting the scene to use counselling skills   121

7 **Understanding and extending the perspective of clients**   130
   7.1   Stage One: using counselling skills to understand clients   130
   7.2   Stage Two: exploring alternative perspectives   144

8 Goal setting and action planning   **155**
  8.1 From problems to realistic goals   155
  8.2 Dealing with dilemmas   160
  8.3 Stage Three: action planning   164
  8.4 Stage Four: plans into action   168
  8.5 The end of a helping relationship   170

9 Helping through group work   **170**
  9.1 The nature of group work   172
  9.2 Planning a group   175
  9.3 The role of group leader   181
  9.4 Learning in the group   187

10 Running a group   **193**
  10.1 The development of a group   193
  10.2 The first session   197
  10.3 Working with group dynamics   201
  10.4 Activities in the group   212
  10.5 The end of a group   218

11 Specific applications in brief   **220**
  11.1 Mediation or conciliation   220
  11.2 Advocacy   221
  11.3 Bereavement and loss   222
  11.4 Crisis and trauma   224
  11.5 Helping children and young people   226
  11.6 Helping in health-care settings   227
  11.7 Disability and chronic health conditions   229
  11.8 Work with couples or families   231
  11.9 Work with elderly clients   232
  11.10 General resources   233

12 Safe practice for yourself, your team and your clients   **234**
  12.1 Health and safety issues   234
  12.2 Handling stress   240
  12.3 Working well together   247
  12.4 Personal development   251

13 Final thoughts   **254**

Appendix   256
Index   257

▼ Acknowledgements

We have learned a considerable amount from our colleagues and clients and the wide range of people from public services and business to whom we have taught counselling skills. It would be impossible to name everyone, so we would like to express our appreciation of the many ideas, suggestions and constructive feedback over the years.

As we were writing this book, the following individuals were generous with their time and further contacts: Sarah Johnston, Jessica Johnson, Diana Renard and Kath Kelly. All the organisations mentioned in the book have been helpful over the telephone or in sending written material about their work. We would especially like to thank the Women's Nationwide Cancer Control Campaign (WNCCC), the Advice and Mediation Services at the National Foster Care Association, the Kingston Friends Workshop Group and the Samaritans.

The diagram of the counselling model (page 122) was adapted and developed from the idea of the four diamonds in Gerard Egan and Michael Cowans, *People in systems: a model of development in the human-service professions and education* (Brooks Cole, 1979). The diagram of themes and outcomes in work teams (page 174) was adapted from John Adair, *Effective leadership: a modern guide to developing leadership skills* (Pan, 1983). The diagrams of levels of communication (page 26), the communications process (page 28) and the listening and questioning funnel (page 44) have been adapted from material that has been available for some years among professionals working in the area of communication. Despite our efforts, we have been unable to identify the originator of these diagrams and would be pleased to make an appropriate acknowledgement in future editions. The illustration of two ears, two eyes and one mouth (page 31) was originated by Lance, who also developed and adapted the remaining diagrams. In addition, the authors and publishers would like to thank the following illustration sources: Steve Redwood for photographs on pages 8, 32, 126, 241; Bill McKenzie for that on page 57; ChildLine, RNIB and Relate for that on page 76; NCH for that on page 173 and Peter Hayman for that on page 248, ChildLine for that on page 100. Other photos were supplied by Jennie and Lance Lindon. Every effort has been made to trace all copyright-holders, but if any have been overlooked the publishers will be pleased to make the necessary arrangement at the first opportunity.

To **Nick Georgiades** *and* **Brich Wilkinson**
who set us on this path

▾ Introduction

Objectives and focus of the book

Many people within the caring professions are involved in helping relationships with the users of their service, whether short- or longer-term. This book is specifically designed for readers who are in the position of offering support to clients. Primarily these roles will be through information or advice and sometimes direct help through supportive conversations with individuals or work with groups.

Use of skills in communication is essential for even the shortest exchanges with clients. Good communication can make a crucial difference in how clients then use, or choose not to use, your own or other services within an organisation.

The bedrock of effective daily communications within a service comes from the basic skills in counselling. As such, an understanding of counselling skills has become essential for the majority of workers in health, education, social services, careers advice and voluntary helping organisations. Professionals and volunteers in these settings need to understand and use counselling skills to improve their effectiveness even though they are not, nor are they intended to be, full-time counsellors.

A reader's guide

In response to the wide-ranging use of communication skills in helping professions, this book starts with general approaches to good practice in any setting and the important communication basics underpinning how to share information. Chapters 1–5 offer practical advice and explanation that is applicable to many settings. Chapters 6–8 cover more specific application of counselling skills to the caring professions. Chapters 9 and 10 cover working with groups. Chapter 11 highlights in brief a range of applications to different kinds of help or to groups of clients. Chapter 12 considers safe practice and personal well-being for helpers in any profession.

The content of the book includes both information and explanation but also offers a wide range of suggested activities to undertake on your own, as well as in discussion with colleagues or within a team meeting, or with fellow students during a training course or session. In many cases each chapter is complete in itself, although Chapters 6–8 on counselling skills and 9–10 on group work are designed to be read in the given order.

Terms used

Given the wide variety of readers, our choice of words and phrases was not straightforward. We decided to use the term 'client' rather than change words depending on the example being used at the time. Both clients and service providers may be female or male. We resolve this potential problem of style by using the plural, as in 'clients . . . they'. Sometimes we use 'she or he' and names are given in examples.

☑ ∎ Essentials of good practice

1.1 Helping in context

Helping services and organisations

A wide range of public services, commercial organisations and charitable groups offer some kind of help to their clients. For example:

- Health services may offer support and information to clients whilst some health centres make counselling services available. Health visitors make personal contact with families, and some health authorities are part of outreach services that offer advice and support. Specialist units and clinics deal with children, young people, adults and their families.
- Social Services and Housing offices offer information and advice as well as direct client support through the social work system.
- Educational services have increasingly found that parents welcome advice and information. Pastoral care systems, offering support to children and young people, have been effective in some schools for many years. Some educational authorities are part of home visiting schemes, perhaps in collaboration with Social Services or voluntary organisations.
- Careers guidance for secondary school pupils and for college students combines information and advice.
- Early years care and education settings have increasingly offered support and advice to parents, in addition to facilities for the children. Some playwork settings offer similar services.
- Some children's and family centres have support and counselling as an integral part of their work. Community and drop-in centres can deal with a very wide variety of requests for help.
- Youth services may also offer information, advice or group work to young people on the range of issues that concern them.
- Commercial companies sometimes offer support services to their employees, either as a regular part of the Human Resources function or in response to particular events, such as redundancy.
- Citizens' Advice Bureaux offer advice or information to people who visit or telephone.
- There are a considerable number of helping organisations, some with charitable status and some with a membership structure. Some offer a very

broad base of help, while others have more specific concerns and therefore a more focused client base.

Different types of help

There are broad differences between the kinds of help to clients that are covered in this book, although many of the same skills remain important.

Information

Some organisations have a primary role in offering an information service. Some start with such information and then add further services as these are requested by clients. Information may be given through clear explanations for clients, for instance, of the possible forms of child care or the implications of particular legislation. Information might also be offered about other individuals, groups or organisations who could help further.

Advice

In some services clients reach their own decisions based on the information provided. However, other services help clients to weigh up the implications of this information. Advisers may suggest that one course of action would be more appropriate or realistic, given a client's wishes or needs, for instance, in the choice of possible child care.

Guidance

Use of information and advice plays a larger part in guidance than in less directive helping. Clients make their own decisions but help is offered with a view to the realities of a client's situation, for instance, about study and careers choice or dealing with a serious health condition. Helpers use their expertise and experience to guide clients towards realistic options rather than leaving clients to discover these alone.

Support

Some helping services aim to support clients so that they feel confident there is someone who will give them attention and empathy. Support may be offered through a sympathetic listener over the telephone or face to face, a friendly place to find company or by providing a companion to attend a stressful meeting or consultation. Befriending services offer personal contact, face to face or over the telephone, and non-judgemental support.

Counselling

Genuine counselling includes an explicit offer of time and expertise to a client, which is accepted by the client without any pressure. The use of counselling skills is essential for many helping relationships – not just those of full-time counsellor and client. The counselling approach covered in this book depends on qualities of warmth, genuineness and empathy and includes effective skills of communication, positive and respectful challenge and joint problem-solving.

Mediation or conciliation

This use of counselling skills is focused on helping people in conflict to reach a resolution in a non-confrontational way. Mediators provide a neutral place for clients, for instance, couples in the process of separating, to discuss difficulties and reach important decisions without increasing resentment. Mediation skills have also been successfully taught to children.

Advocacy

Support through advocacy represents more active involvement for helpers, since an advocate speaks up on behalf of clients. Advocacy supports clients who are sufficiently young, daunted by authority or unable to express their views and preferences so as to be heard.

Self-help

Some services have an explicit objective that clients will be enabled to help themselves, and perhaps also to support others in a similar position. The services offered might include information so that clients can plan and act from a strong base, or groups in which clients help one another. An organisation might offer basic counselling or a group facilitator to support clients to the point where self help is a realistic option.

Clients' acceptance of help

Within Britain there has been a long tradition of asking for advice or support from within the family, from close friends, from the immediate local community and from respected figures such as the local priest or doctor. These sources of support have not disappeared and some social and cultural groups still place a great deal of emphasis on dealing with difficulties within the family or immediate community without involving strangers. However, public services and specific organisations have increasingly developed to meet a need for help when people either feel they cannot speak with family or friends or are seeking information or advice that they cannot find from their personal circle.

Certain kinds of help have been socially acceptable in Britain for a long time. Advice and information on specialist areas, such as careers guidance, financial advice or health information, have generally been viewed as sensible consultation with experts. There has been considerably more reservation about seeking help for personal difficulties.

One source of resistance seems to be a cultural outlook that equates asking for help on personal problems as an admission of failure, though this is changing gradually. In contrast, the United States experienced a widespread acceptance of therapy and counselling long before Britain. Another source of resistance is the fear that talking will only make matters worse – a view summed up by the cliché 'least said, soonest mended'. The belief persists that even very distressing experiences will fade away and talking will only make matters worse. This view is not, of course, universal but is expressed in connection with seriously distressing experiences for children, young people and adults. There now seems to be rather more acceptance that talking through problems and difficulties can be useful and that it does not imply incompetence or mental breakdown. However, a level of wariness remains.

Activity

Over several weeks, collect examples that highlight common views about seeking advice, information or help with personal problems. You could cut out items from newspapers or magazines. Or listen in to everyday conversation.

- What range of views are emerging?
- Can you see a different outlook depending on the type of help sought?

Common misunderstandings about helping

A number of beliefs persist about the process of helping and such misunderstandings can affect both clients and inexperienced helpers, in any of the different types of help.

Helpers always solve people's problems

Even very experienced helpers do not resolve all the issues put to them. Some queries or difficulties do not have an easy or quick answer. A helper should be able to draw on past experience to support the person currently seeking help. However, that experience does not provide a certain list of reliable solutions to common problems. Sometimes helpers enable clients to come to terms with the realities of their situation or to learn to live with a situation that cannot easily be changed.

Helpers solve problems quickly

Swift answers do not work because the 'quick fix' approach depends on reducing clients' individuality and pushing them into a ready-made category, such as, 'It's a mid-life crisis', or, 'Just like the housing problem I solved last week.' An effective helper uses skills of good communication, including listening, to understand what clients are expressing. Even relatively straightforward information or advice cannot be given effectively for a client unless you have listened and understood in the first place.

Helping means telling people what to do or how to think – giving answers

A common belief about being helpful is that the apparently more experienced person tells the less experienced person what he or she should be doing or not doing. If you listen to everyday conversations, you will hear a lot of telling masquerading as help. Another kind of unhelpful telling is through premature explanations or forced interpretations. Comments may be made like, 'You know what this is really about', or, 'I know you don't want to face it, but what's actually going on is . . .'. The intended help is more likely to be experienced as patronising and intrusive.

In order to help other people, you need age and wisdom

Of course, age in increasing years does not necessarily bring wisdom. Sometimes it just brings a greater conviction of being correct, of having the right to tell younger people what to do and define their priorities. Genuinely effective helpers draw on appropriate skills, as well as experience gained over time. Furthermore, grown-ups are not the only helpers. Children and young people can be very supportive and genuinely helpful to each other.

You can't help unless you've been through the same experience

If this belief were true, the helping services would be very fragmented. Effective helpers listen, so that they can understand what this individual client has experienced, whether or not the helper has experienced something similar. Relevant experience can contribute both to the practical help that is offered and to an understanding of emotions, but the helper still has to draw on appropriate learned counselling skills.

In order to help other people you need lengthy training

Effective helping does require preparation and training. You need opportunities to practise and improve the skills needed for the kind of help that you will offer to clients. Some types of counselling and therapeutic intervention do have training courses that spread over years, but this type of study is not necessary for all kinds of helping intervention. Experienced helpers continue to learn and to take opportunities that extend their skills, as well as reflecting on their own approach and reactions.

Helpers never have problems themselves

An enduring myth is that people who offer help or advice to others avoid any personal problems or doubts, but even very experienced helpers will have some difficulties in their own life. It can be especially hard if you experience personal difficulties in the very area in which you are a professional helper.

1.2 Boundaries and objectives

Any service that offers help to clients needs to be organised with a clear understanding of the nature of the service.

- What kind of help is being offered?
- Is help on offer to anyone who makes contact or only to certain groups of people?

- Is it clear if your organisation offers a specialised kind of help and who might benefit?
- What are the boundaries of the service, in terms of the kinds of help or time available? Identifying boundaries is not a criticism of a helping service. All organisations will have some boundaries because help can never be limitless.
- How does the organisation ensure that potential clients understand what is offered and what is not?

Everyone within a team should be able to explain to clients, or to other agencies, in simple and accurate terms, what the organisation offers and its boundaries (what it does not do). So, a new team member has to be fully briefed during the early days and weeks to build common understanding and commitment. This induction period is equally important for volunteers, who are sometimes overlooked, but who are just as crucial as paid employees in promoting an accurate and positive view of the organisation.

Any team with a positive outlook will discuss the direction of the service: whether it continues to meet the needs of clients or should be adjusted in some way. Every service that offers help should give room for initiative and flexible response by individual workers, but some areas of what is offered and in what way will not be negotiable. Every team needs opportunities to talk and listen to each other, so that possible improvements and 'what if' scenarios can be covered.

Review and change of direction

A healthy service is both open to review and ready to change in response to changing circumstances. Organisations which have been in existence for many years have often taken a constructively critical look at the reasons why they were originally started, the current request for services and changes in society as a whole and adjusted accordingly. A change in focus or in the breadth of what is offered is frequently signalled by a change in name for an organisation.

For example, the organisation Relate was first established as the National Marriage Guidance Council in 1938 and changed in 1987. Relate developed from an organisation focused on marriage and associated values to one concerned more broadly with relationships. Their work also expanded to help clients with the breakdown of any relationship as much as supporting people, not always couples, to live together peaceably.

Activities

1 Explore the ways in which your own service or organisation promotes a shared understanding of your objectives and boundaries to team members. For instance:
   - What were the details of your early days and weeks with this team?
   - Looking back, what was most useful in the induction period?
   - On the basis of your current experience, what would you add to, or take away from, the induction programme?

2 If your service or organisation has experienced a change in direction over the years, explore how this arose and how the change was managed:
   - You could talk with team members who were involved in the discussions about change.
   - You could also look at any written material about the refocusing of the service.

If you are part of a relatively new organisation, then you could look at written material from organisations of longer standing. Some have leaflets describing the life of the service. For example, Action for Sick Children, previously the National Association for the Welfare of Children in Hospital, has a leaflet about the organisation's history in its student pack. Contact them at 300 Kingston Road, Wimbledon Chase, London SW20 8LX. Tel: 0208 542 4848. Fax: 0208 542 2424.

Monitoring a service

Any service needs to be monitored, to check both the nature and extent of the service offered and the quality of the work. There are two broad approaches: making a service audit and quality assurance.

1 The aim of a service audit is to identify who uses a service and how resources are allocated within that service. An audit has to use methods of systematic data collection and analysis. This approach could include some socio-demographic details of service users, such as gender, ethnic group or self-described disability. This audit is typically designed to track the characteristics of clients. So, clients' names may not be required and even counselling services would not break confidentiality.
2 Quality assurance relates the service provided closely to established standards. The aim is to assess the extent to which the service meets those required standards. It is therefore essential that clear and specific standards have been agreed in the first place.

In your own service it may not yet be feasible to undertake a comprehensive audit or establish a quality assurance system. However, there will always be opportunities to monitor at least parts of your service.

Log of requests to your service

Do you have a system for keeping track of the kind of enquiries you receive? Effective monitoring requires simple and appropriate categories, for instance, the different kinds of enquiry to a health information line or the numbers of pupils or students who ask about particular kinds of higher education courses. You can monitor your service in this way even when exchanges with clients are brief or over the telephone.

If your service is open to a wide spectrum of people, then it will be appropriate to keep track of the range of clients in terms of broad social and ethnic group categories. This kind of monitoring should be self-determined by clients because it is not your role to decide on a client's ethnic group or whether they consider themselves to be disabled. So, the monitoring has to work by asking clients themselves to complete short information forms that ask for gender, ethnic group or any disability. This information can help you to address those not using the service and find possible reasons for the gap. You might need to make the service, or its publicity, more appealing to some groups, or work harder to reach them in the first place.

Ask clients for their views

All services should be open to feedback from clients. You need to listen to what is said, even if clients do not express their comments in a flattering way, and learn from the feedback. A more organised survey of client views can be helpful so long as this is done with care. Clients need an accurate idea of why they are being asked and the likely result. Much like isolated customer charters, a regular canvassing of opinion about a service with no visible consequences tends to create cynicism. You might organise a questionnaire survey, perhaps followed by some interviews with clients. If your services are available to children and young people, make sure that you invite their opinions too, rather than just canvassing their parents.

Activity

Find out how your own service is monitored. What methods are used and what kind of information is gathered? If your service is not monitored, then collect any customer questionnaires or feedback forms that you receive as a service user.

1.3 Standards for behaviour

Any helping service should take an ethical approach to clients. This requirement means that everyone within the service must be clear about appropriate standards of behaviour towards clients.

The importance of trust

A valid helping relationship between clients and your service is based on trust. Clients should be enabled to have confidence in your organisation, from a basic reliance on the information that you give, all the way through to a safe setting in which to confide very personal issues.

Genuine helping, even of the most short-term kind, needs to be based firmly in what clients ask or explain about their situation. Effective helpers stand back from their own assumptions and personal preferences about what people should do in similar situations. Any information or advice should be given in an even-handed way and not direct clients towards options in which the helper has any kind of vested interest, or personal or business involvement.

Codes of practice

All helping organisations should have clear and public standards for the behaviour of anyone offering the help. These standards should be described in specific terms, so that it is possible for the team members and clients to recognise when standards are being met and when they are not.

In your organisation you may talk about standards, a code of conduct or good practice guidelines. You may refer to the ethics of the service or relate the expected behaviour of helpers to the underlying core values of the service. Regardless of the exact words or phrases used, any helping organisation should have a clear view, communicated throughout the whole team, about how you should all act: in some cases what you should do and some instances of what you definitely should not do.

Written codes of practice lay out a framework in which the service should be offered. They help to ensure that any actions are even-handed, objective and genuinely helpful. A set of standards or a code can guide a team, but cannot foresee and cover every possible situation or dilemma. For this reason, every team within a helping service should have opportunities to discuss issues or dilemmas that arise and to learn from them.

Clear ethical standards for behaviour can become especially important when you use counselling skills with clients or work with groups. Clients often draw on other life experiences to judge the quality of a walk-in information service and a telephone helpline. However, clients may be much less certain about suitable boundaries in a counselling relationship or within a group. Clients who are at a vulnerable point in their life are at risk from poor use of counselling skills or group work. Clients placed under inappropriate pressure, or who feel unsafe in a group, may doubt the validity of their concerns. Perhaps they feel their discomfort or distress is their own fault or that they have to experience this level of emotional pain in order to improve their life. Safe use of counselling skills can help clients to face areas of their life that they find hard to handle. However, neither the individual nor the group experience should make clients feel worse, nor should they create new distress and problems.

Personal and professional

An effective helping relationship will be friendly but you are not forming a friendship. Neither short-term nor long-term help should be guided by how much you warm to the client. All clients should be treated professionally, which means with equality. Any problems that arise because of difficulties in forming an appropriate, courteous relationship need to be tackled rather than allowing your feelings of like or dislike to shape the amount and quality of help you give.

A close relationship can develop when you use counselling skills over several sessions, or run groups, but your relations with clients have to remain at a professional level. It is contrary to codes of practice for counsellors or group workers to become personally involved with individual clients. You will lose your objectivity if you become close friends or intimately involved with a client. There is also a serious risk of exploitation of vulnerable clients because, however well-intentioned the counsellor or group worker, the relationship is one of uneven power and privilege.

Given the large numbers of people involved, it is inevitable that some counsellors or group workers will be personally attracted to some clients. The professional response is to postpone any personal involvement until the professional relationship is completely finished. Alternatively, if feelings are very strong and appear to be reciprocated by the client, then the professional part of the relationship must end and, if necessary, the client referred to someone else.

Concerns are most often expressed about intimate relationships between a client and counsellor or group worker. However, any kind of non-professional involvement brings a risk of confusing the boundaries of the professional relationship. For example, it is unwise to enter any kind of business relationship with a client, such as buying a car or inviting the client's expertise for your financial affairs. You should talk in confidence with a colleague or supervisor if you face a blurring of the boundaries between personal and professional relationships with clients.

Confidentiality

Few services will be totally confidential in the sense that what any client tells any helper will never go beyond that conversation. There must, however, be clear guidelines about any limits to confidentiality and these must be understood by all the team and communicated to clients. Such boundaries are just as important in information and advice services as in more personal counselling relationships.

Clients' concerns remain within the service

Clients have the right to expect that their use of a service and any conversations are kept within professional exchanges inside the boundaries of your service.

- What clients have said, their questions, concerns and experiences should never fuel light conversation or be the source of 'good stories' exchanged with anyone else.
- Personal information about clients should not be repeated, as a kind of professional gossip, within an organisation.
- If you give examples within a training or workshop context, then these should be anonymous and with no detail that could possibly identify the individual client.
- This emphasis on confidentiality and honesty with clients applies in work with children and young people just as much as in work with adults. Children's confidences should never be routinely broken with the justification of 'the good of the child'. Your own issues and concerns for the child should be shared with them in appropriate language.
- Helpers may discuss a client with their supervisor or seek specific support from a colleague in dealing with a complex situation, but the boundary to confidentiality should be drawn clearly at that point. In services where support and supervision is an important part of working with individual clients, then those clients should be told at the outset that you may discuss their situation with your supervisor and the client's agreement should be gained before you do so.

The confidentiality guidelines apply to the providers of a service. If clients want to talk with friends or anyone else about what they have discussed or asked, then that is their decision. They have the right to discuss their situation or confide in anyone else, if they wish.

Ethical problems and confidentiality

The only valid reason for breaking confidentiality is the genuine risk that the client is currently damaging or is likely to damage someone else, especially if this other person is young or for some other reason unlikely to be able to protect themselves.

Some services face this possibility more often than others, for instance, children's services who all have an obligation to child protection. These limits to confidentiality should be made clear in any written material about the service and directly to clients themselves. When children disclose abuse, the helper has an obligation to support the child but cannot agree to keep secrets that endanger that child.

Services that work with clients under great stress or who are very depressed will face the dilemmas raised by individuals who sound suicidal or who express feelings and plans about self-harm. You must be clear about the approach that your organisation takes over such ethical dilemmas and should follow those guidelines. Additionally, you need access to support and supervision in order to discuss the strong feelings that can be aroused even in experienced helpers.

Inappropriate requests for information

Your own organisation may have a clear understanding about your confidentiality, but you may have contact with other professionals who take a different view. For example:

- An employer asks you to give personal details of employees who have asked for advice.
- Teachers expect to be briefed on confidential pastoral or careers guidance sessions with pupils.
- Parents expect to be told about what their children or teenagers have discussed with you.

You can be placed in a difficult position by such requests, especially if you have not explained the situation beforehand. You may have assumed that your work will be confidential, but did not check the assumptions of other people involved. Perhaps the employer has paid you, or your organisation, and assumes that his or her briefing is part of the service. The teacher or parent has assumed that they have a right to know what is happening with the child or young person.

Good practice in confidentiality requires that you:

- Explore other people's assumptions about confidentiality when your service could be seen to have more than one client in the situation.
- Tell your clients of any limits to the confidentiality of what they discuss with you. It is crucial to be clear and explicit about what is, and what is not, confidential.

The situation regarding help for children and young people is uncertain. On the one hand, some legal principles, for instance, the 1985 *Gillick* ruling, have established that under-sixteens can make medical decisions for themselves if they are judged to have sufficient understanding. On the other hand, adults like parents and teachers are responsible for children in their care. Genuinely caring individuals may benefit from understanding a child's problems. If your service is offered to children and young people you need to have discussed this issue in detail, be clear about how you work and communicate your stance to both the children and adults involved.

Inappropriate use of personal material

No detail of a client's situation, no matter if it appears very minor, should be used without their clear and informed consent. This limit applies to using examples in the written material of your service or if you write magazine articles or books. Clients should never be put in the position of having to agree to the use of their personal information in order to receive help. So it would be unacceptable to push clients into an agreement to:

- Be featured as a case study or training material.
- Take part in a research project or experimental trial.
- Be taped – audio or video.
- Accept the presence of trainees or students in a session.

Clients may sometimes agree to any of the above, so long as they are asked in a respectful way and the reasons or benefit to them are explained. Clients should have time to consider the request and not be pressured with, 'It's alright if we . . . isn't it?' Clients have the right to refuse such requests and still receive the full service with no reservations.

Examples

In the following examples consider:

- How a team might explain their actions.
- The reasons that such situations are not good practice.

1 Alice went for help at her local child guidance centre because her 8-year-old son was refusing to attend school. In the first meeting, Alice was told that the clinic's policy was to video-record all guidance sessions for use as training material. She felt pressured to agree and was doubtful that any further help would be given if she refused. She attended one session with her son but felt very uneasy and did not return for the next appointment. Her son's school head telephoned the clinic and was told that there was no pressure and that Alice could have refused to be videoed.

2 Jake was taking his daughter, Siobhan, to the local out-patients' clinic for a minor health condition. After three visits, the condition appeared to be better but Jake was asked to make another appointment. When questioned, the doctor confirmed that there was no concern about Siobhan. However, the consultant was undertaking a research project on this condition and wanted to monitor any children who had been seen. Jake said that Siobhan could join the project, but that the researchers would have to visit her at home after school hours. The doctor said that was impossible; patients had to come into the clinic.

3 A group of first-year students agreed to complete a very personal questionnaire and were assured that the information would remain with a named college project. A year later they found that the questionnaire information was part of a large computer database to which many researchers had easy access. The group demanded a meeting with the original project leader who was unwilling to apologise, saying that they had overreacted and that this would block valuable research.

1.4 Attitudes towards clients

What do you call clients?

Commercial organisations use the term 'customer' or 'end user'. Public services generally only use the word in reference to customer care and charters. Different service traditions have led to different terms:

- 'Client' has been the preferred term in social work, for most counselling services and is often used in training and consultancy services.
- In educational services, one set of customers are called 'parents' and the second set may be called 'pupils', 'students' or 'children'.
- Medical services, and any therapy or counselling services with medical links, are most likely to refer to 'patients'.
- Some community and voluntary services have chosen the term 'service user'. However, the word can carry negative overtones in services where there is a tradition of selecting people on the basis of defined need and priority. People who are believed to work the system, or to be manipulative, are said to use the service for their own ends.

To think about

- What are the users of your service called? What are the associations of the word – positive and negative?
- Think about this issue yourself but also gather the opinions of colleagues and of some service users.
- When you are a service user, how do you feel about the term used to describe you? For example, how does it feel to be a 'patient'?

It matters what you call the users of your service because the term chosen conveys a message, which can be more or less positive. Some years ago one of us worked with a large educational day centre for young people with learning disabilities. The head had taken the decision that every young person was to be called a 'student', regardless of the programme of study followed or whether this led to any paper qualification. This positive term for the young people contributed to an atmosphere of learning and of respect.

Customer charters

The 1990s saw an extensive development of customer charters within public services and a wide range of commercial organisations. Charters are grounded in the belief that users of any service have a right to accurate information about what they can expect from the service and how they will be treated. Charters do not in themselves create good customer service; they only work as part of an integrated approach.

If implemented well, charters can contribute to a positive relationship between the service provider and the user. However, charters, not surprisingly, raise expectations that clients will experience treatment consistent with the promises. Dashed expectations and dismissive treatment create resentment and cynicism. Clients, who were previously resigned to an indifferent quality of service, become angry and ready to take action. Irritation is further fuelled by heavy use of slogans in charters and related material or frequent use of the word 'care' by a service whose employees manifestly fail to show this quality.

Develop a positive outlook on clients

You need to see each client as an individual and, even within brief exchanges, to attend to what the client wants and may need. Various attitudes can block a respect for and valuing of clients and you may need to acknowledge and deal with your own personal outlook. However, dismissive attitudes can also develop within a service and they then become part of the working atmosphere and have to be tackled within the whole team.

Without a clear direction and positive supervision in helping services, a team may develop the negative outlook that short encounters do not deserve their attention. There may be a view of, 'What's the point, I never see clients again.' Or a 'half-empty bottle' philosophy may be expressed as, 'If I had a lot more time, I could help.' Every team involved in helping needs to focus on what can be offered to clients and what can be done, with an outlook determined by respect for clients and the type of courteous treatment that you yourself would wish to receive.

Address negative views

Clients will not be valued by a team who share firm views about how clients should behave, perhaps that:

- Patients of a medical service should not question or express doubts. The ones who question are troublemakers.
- Parents whose children attend educational facilities should acknowledge that teachers have more expertise than parents ever could.
- Young people attending a drop-in facility should be appreciative and not criticise the behaviour of workers who give their time without any payment.

A team, or an individual, with rigid views about how clients should behave can develop two approaches depending on whether these are 'good' or 'bad' clients. The good ones deserve attention, whereas the bad ones can be pushed through the service and out again as fast as possible. Overall negative outlooks about clients can develop, that they are difficult, manipulative or generally troublesome. Such attitudes are often developed from (and then justified by) a few bad experiences with clients. These experiences are then generalised to the whole group of clients. Experiences with clients that fit the stereotype are logged as further evidence. However, clients who do not behave in the expected negative way are seen as exceptions, perhaps as 'good' clients who stand out from the rest.

Finally, it can be that much harder to value clients if you feel seriously undervalued yourself. Organisations sometimes treat their staff poorly and yet still expect that dismissive treatment should not affect the quality of service to clients.

Expertise of clients

Sometimes clients are already knowledgeable about the area in which they are seeking some help. Certainly never assume that clients are inexpert. Clarify their level of expertise first. Clients may through necessity have become experts on their own health condition or that of a member of their family. Parents of disabled children can be very knowledgeable about the disability of their own child and how it affects him or her, as well as the reality of the condition for their family.

Workers in helping organisations can feel threatened by expert clients, particularly if those workers have a firm belief that they should always know more than their clients. However, genuine help builds on joint problem-solving – which includes a recognition of clients' knowledge and skills. It is not helpful to believe (even if only privately) that clients will always be less knowledgeable and to resent or challenge any evidence to the contrary.

Friendly but not friends — an example

A common misunderstanding is that customer service in helping organisations means getting to know clients very well as individuals. So, if your service offers short and irregular contact with clients, then good customer service is judged to be impossible.

A worker in a walk-in library and information service expressed this view to us during a conversation about possible improvements in how the team behaved towards clients. It would indeed have been difficult, if not impossible, to keep track of the many people who came and went during a week. However, the constructive criticism of some workers' behaviour was in no way linked to their making a close, personal relationship with clients.

Some of the team failed to greet clients in any way, left them waiting at the counter with no acknowledgement and chatted with colleagues while ignoring the waiting client. Some workers failed to make eye contact or say anything at all, if an exchange could be completed without words. None of the workers were actively rude in what they said, although the body language was often dismissive. However, the overall message was discourteous, that there was no point in spending time on people who were just passing through the service.

● In your organisation how have you clarified the difference between being 'friendly' and 'being friends'?

1.5 Client records

A database on clients

Technical advances in collection, storage and accessing of information have led to a society in which many people experience regular requests for personal information, often linked with a purchase or application for financial services. Some of the information requested is necessary for the commercial service, but a proportion is of benefit only to the organisation and not to the customer.

The result of this common experience is that many people answer a series of questions without resistance, until questions become very intrusive. However, another consequence is that, overloaded with unnecessary questions, some people have become more assertive, either asking for a rationale for the questions or refusing to answer beyond a point that seems appropriate to them.

Activity

Over a month, keep track of all the requests made to you for personal information: face to face, over the telephone or through the mail.

- What was the context and rationale for the questions?
- How far do you judge that answering the questions was of real benefit to you as a service user or purchaser?
- How did you feel about being asked very personal questions and were there any questions that you declined to answer?
- What reaction did you receive if you challenged someone's need to ask you?
- What have you learned that could be applied to your contact with clients?

Clients have a right to privacy on the personal information that you hold, specifically that:

- Their names, with or without details, are never passed to third parties without the explicit informed consent of the individual client – ideally their written consent.
- Clients' data should not be added to other databases, unless you have their specific, informed consent.

This good practice holds even if you genuinely believe that the client could benefit from contact with another individual or organisation, from a book, pamphlet or any other product. Ask before you pass on a client's name. See also page 87 on referrals.

Good practice in keeping records

Written records are only as good as the care taken in setting up a record and adding relevant information.

- Information must be accurate and any mistakes in personal details of clients should be corrected promptly.
- Care needs to be taken in hand-written records; these must be clear and legible. Entering information on a computer database needs just as much care to check that the information has been entered correctly.
- Any records should clearly distinguish facts from any opinions. Your opinions can be valuable but should always be supported by observations and reasons.

Any records should be stored securely. The nature of the records and the location of your service might lead to higher levels of security, for instance, if you are working in an area that has many break-ins. If your records are on computer then you need secure systems with password access only.

Written files and records should be easily accessible for workers to consult, but kept secure from people who have no right of access. Good practice often involves simple precautions such as putting files away when you have finished, never leaving a file on a desk or countertop and not leaving a client's file on the computer screen in full view of anyone who passes. These restrictions apply as much to fellow professionals who visit your service as to the general public. Other helping professionals must have a sound reason for consulting the records.

Informing clients about records

Your organisation needs to establish and maintain good practice in collecting information on clients of your service:

- Be clear about your organisation's reasons for collecting the information that you request and explain the rationale simply to clients.
- Be ready, with no resistance or surprise, to answer specific queries from clients about details that you ask, any forms to be completed or the notes you make.
- Deal with clients' questions courteously, even if they ask in an abrupt or confrontational way. Clients may feel uneasy about challenging your information systems and this unease can emerge in an apparently unfriendly way.
- It is important that your entire organisation commits to a view that clients have a right to understand why information is requested. Clients are not being awkward, unduly anxious or paranoid. They are exercising a basic civil right to ask, 'What do you want to know that for?'
- Explain in a straightforward way how clients can access their own information, and the extent to which their information is available to others in the organisation.

Clients' right of access

Policy, practice and the legal situation about written records has changed considerably since the 1970s. At that time, clients were very unlikely to be able to see their own records and a request to do so was likely to be met with surprise as well as refusal. The climate has changed towards a far greater recognition of anyone's basic right of access to their own records. Parents, and other adults *in loco parentis*, have right of access to records on their children. Legal changes underpin and enforce good practice, for instance:

- The Access to Personal Files Act 1987 applied to Social Services and gave clients right of access to their own files.
- Since 1990 all parents of pupils under 18 years and all pupils of 16 years and older have right of access to the pupils' own education record held by the school.
- The Access to Health Records Act 1990 gave right of access of individuals to their own health records written after 1 November 1991.

It is accepted good practice to remove third party information, that is, letters or reports from professionals outside your service, before clients have access to their files, unless those people have given permission. You would also remove, or make anonymous, any references to other individuals within a file. Some local authorities and organisations follow a policy, made explicit on all correspondence, that any material is open in a file to the person about whom the file is written, unless third parties make a specific request that their letters or reports are to be removed. Make sure you are clear about the policy of your service.

The Data Protection Act 1984 entitled individuals to be informed about the existence of records about themselves stored on computers and the right to inspect them. The Data Protection Act 1998 will extend some of these rights. If an organisation holds personal data on computer, then, with few exceptions, you have to be registered with the Data Protection Registrar.

Further information on computer records

You can contact the Data Protection Registrar and get more information from Wycliffe House, Water Lane, Wilmslow, Cheshire SK9 5AF, information line 01625 545 745 or web site at http://www.open.gov.uk/dpr/dprhome.htm.

Descriptive personal notes

If you undertake work with individual clients or groups, there are advantages in keeping a descriptive record. Short notes are often appropriate because:

- Clients of some services may not be seen by the same professional each time. A written record should contain essential personal information so that clients do not have repeat themselves each visit.
- Brief records of repeat telephone callers can be important if different people are likely to answer the help line.

Descriptive notes will be valuable if you use counselling skills with clients individually or in groups over a series of sessions.

- A written summary of a session can help you to identify themes, to organise your thoughts and to think ahead to the next session.

- If you are working with a number of individuals or groups, your written notes will be important in helping you to keep the work clearly separate.
- Keep records that are only as detailed as you need; the aim is not to produce large files that you rarely consult. Useful notes will cover the scope of a session and where the work finished. Notes for group work can additionally cover attendance, the objectives of a session, planned activities and how those activities were received by the group.
- You should write up notes promptly after working with an individual or group. You would not normally take notes during a session.
- Records also help you to monitor and evaluate your own work and can sharpen up your powers of reflection and observation.
- Records place your work in the context of the organisation to which you belong and help to make you more accountable.

You should let individuals or a group know if you keep notes and explain your reasons. You would not normally share your personal notes with an individual client or group. However, you should nevertheless ensure that any notes are either factual or your well-supported opinions and do not contain offhand remarks about clients.

1.6 Anti-discriminatory practice

Any service has to ensure that it is operating well, so that:

- All clients, and potential clients, are treated in an equal way.
- Practice is free of direct or indirect discrimination towards any groups in society.
- Prejudiced actions, words or assumptions form no part of how the team works.
- The whole team is able to challenge assumptions and beliefs in a constructive way and so ensure an improving and seasitive practice.

Legislation

Legal requirements will affect aspects of how your service works: employment of team members, advertising of your service, access to your building and behaviour towards clients. Anti-discriminatory practice is more than just following the law, but legal changes have established that no service or organisation can act in a way that is prejudicial to sections of the population.

The Sex Discrimination Acts 1975 and 1986

This legislation makes it illegal to discriminate against people on the grounds of their sex and the Equal Opportunities Commission monitors these Acts. Although the law was introduced in response to employment and pay discrimination against women, the requirements apply equally to males and females. For instance, your service cannot choose that a new team member is specifically male or female unless the sex of a worker can be justified as a genuine occupational qualification. Treating anyone less favourably just because of their sex is called direct discrimination and is illegal. Indirect discrimination is also illegal and often less obvious, because conditions are in force that mean that one sex is considerably less likely to be able to meet the condition and so is treated unfairly.

The Race Relations Act 1976

The Act made it unlawful to discriminate on racial grounds, which cover skin colour, race, nationality including citizenship, and ethnic or national origins (but not religious affiliation). The Commission for Racial Equality monitors the application of this Act. The law covers both direct and indirect discrimination, as well as victimisation and segregation. This legislation does not explore individual motives or intentions; the focus is entirely on what happens as a result of behaviour or organisational rules put into practice.

Disability legislation

This range of laws has helped to create a generally more positive atmosphere in which the needs of disabled adults, young people and children are harder to overlook and may affect your own service directly. A series of Employment and Education Acts have affected work for disabled adults or young people and requirements for children's education. The Chronically Sick and Disabled Persons Act 1970 and the Disabled Persons Act 1981 included requirements to make buildings more accessible to disabled people.

Further information

If you need detailed information on the legal situation, then contact the following organisations:
- On sex discrimination legislation: Equal Opportunities Commission, Overseas House, Quay Street, Manchester M3 3HN. Tel: 0161 833 9244.
- On race discrimination law: Commission for Racial Equality, Elliot House, 10–12 Allington Street, London SW1E 5EH. Tel: 0207 828 7022.
- For disability legislation and civil rights: RADAR 12 City Forum, 250 City Road, London EC1V 8AF. Tel: 0207 250 4119.

Good practice

How your service operates

As discussed on page 6, some services are tailored to specific groups in order to respond to a defined need. Under these circumstances it is appropriate to guide some potential clients away from the service because it will not be right for them. Many other helping services are open to a much wider range of potential clients within the population.

Within the boundaries of the service, it is essential that team members remain open-minded about potential clients. Discriminatory assumptions or prejudices mean that you fail to meet clients' needs. It will be important that:

- All your promotional material about a service makes clear the potential client base and any specific needs that are being addressed. The material needs to be produced in the main community languages.
- Everyone on the team understands any boundaries and expresses these in a positive way to potential clients. You can suggest other possible services, when your own is not appropriate, but any referral should also be made on the basis of what you have learned about a client and not on assumptions.

Even in a service with a clearly defined client base, all the team still has to be open to discussion about their own assumptions and possible prejudices. Such a discussion needs to be positive and constructive. Improvements in practice will not emerge from a team whose members only criticise each other with negative labels like 'racist', rather than listening and working through any assumptions.

Promotion of your service

What messages are given by any written material on your service? Does it imply that the service is for particular groups of people and is this accurate? Check out whether any case examples, descriptions and illustrations suggest inaccurate restrictions, for example, that:

- None of your clients are ever disabled, when your service would be equally relevant for people with disabilities.
- Most of your clients are young and white, when they could just as well be older and from any ethnic group.
- Most of your team are female when you also have male workers.

Reception and welcome to clients

What impression do clients form when they first walk into your building or make their first telephone call?

- What implicit message is given by any posters or pictures on the walls? Can clients see themselves in any illustrations?
- How easy is it for clients to get into your building or office if they have a disability that affects mobility? Or if a parent is visiting with young children and a buggy?
- Can a client in a wheelchair see you clearly, or is the view blocked by a high desk or a restricting access window?
- Does your service have a text telephone facility ('Minicom' is the brand name) for deaf clients who cannot hear a voice at the end of the phone and need to write their inquiries?
- In a service that anticipates clients with young children, are the baby changing facilities easily available to fathers as well as mothers?

Some clients may appreciate practical help at this early stage, for instance, a client may be visually disabled. Useful help starts with questions, 'How may I help?', or, 'Would you like me to walk with you to the reception desk?' It is discourteous to seize the arm of visually disabled clients or to start talking for them as if they are not present.

Assumptions within the team

Unspoken assumptions affect the quality of service that you offer clients. Some assumptions will be offensive, but others may simply be an inaccurate generalisation that will reduce the help you offer to the client. For instance, there may be unchecked assumptions that:

- A physically disabled young woman will also have difficulties in communication.
- A smart, well-spoken young man will not have any literacy problems; he may be dyslexic.
- A older women who is widowed will lack confidence in money matters, because her late husband will have handled the family finances.
- Young male clients know their way around computers and so will not need support in accessing information, whereas female clients will want help.
- Men are less likely to be distressed by bad news and so are supposed to calm a female partner who will get upset.
- An Asian client will have to consult her husband before making a major decision.

You need to be open in checking your own assumptions and help to create a positive atmosphere in the team. Make it easier to explore beliefs and challenge assumptions in a constructive way.

- Describe what you have noticed in a specific way. You might ask, 'Are you aware that you addressed all the health care advice to Mrs Parkinson? You scarcely talked with her husband.' Descriptions increase the chance that colleagues will listen and learn.
- Avoid guessing about underlying motives or applying critical labels. Colleagues are likely to defend themselves against blunt accusations of, 'That was a really sexist thing to say', or, 'I would never have thought you'd be so racist.'
- Raise issues as a matter of general concern within the team rather than accusing individuals. For instance, you might say, 'I'm concerned that most of our posters show white clients. There are hardly any black or Asian people', rather than, 'Why hasn't anybody ever done anything about these biased posters?' You might raise as a general issue, 'People keep saying "We have to treat disabled clients the same as anyone else." ' Well surely then we're not treating the clients as individuals. Their disability may be exactly what brings them here as our client.'
- Acknowledge positive changes within team practice or individuals; do not just speak up for negative observations.

Dealing with assumptions of clients

Sometimes you will need to deal with unhelpful beliefs of the clients about who should help them and how. For example:

- Speaking with a female team member, the client assumes that a nearby male worker will be the more senior and can make a decision about the current disagreement.
- A white client is resistant to sitting down with a black worker and says, 'No offence really but I'd rather speak with somebody who's English.'
- One of your team is in a wheelchair. Some clients look surprised when she moves out from behind her desk.

Activity

It can be valuable for a team to discuss a range of 'what if' scenarios. Work through the following examples, ideally with colleagues. Discuss and try to decide whether the requests are:

- Acceptable because . . .
- Unacceptable because . . .
- Would only be appropriate when . . .

1 Is it acceptable for a female client to express a preference to speak with a female worker rather than a male?
2 Is the reverse all right? Can a male client say he would rather speak with a fellow male, and if not, why not?
3 A client, who is less confident in English than her home language, makes a request for a worker who is also bilingual.
4 An English-speaking client asks not to be assigned your Nigerian colleague in the future on the grounds that she and her child have difficulty in understanding the worker's accent. And if a similar request is made about your Irish colleague?
5 A client in his fifties asks to be passed on to someone with more experience. The current worker is in her twenties.
6 What if a black teenager asks if he can talk with a black worker? And if a white teenager expresses a preference for a white worker?
7 A client is changing places in the queue, apparently in order to avoid the next available help desk run by a disabled worker, who has one foreshortened arm and missing fingers on the other hand.
8 A gay client asks if you have a team member who is also gay. And if a heterosexual client wants to move on from the current worker on the grounds that the worker is gay?

To think about

Meaningful anti-discriminatory practice is part of continuing discussion and reflection in your work. There should never be any sense of, 'Right, we've fixed that then!'

For instance, during the second half of the 1990s there was some refreshing thinking about anti-sexism, including a challenge to the assumption that this approach should only focus on the needs of girls and women. You will find a good example of addressing the imbalance in *Let's hear it for the boys*, edited by Gill Lenderyou and Caroline Ray (National Children's Bureau, 1997). This report looks at the response of educational and youth services to supporting sex and relationships education for boys and young men. The report is a stimulating read whether or not you are involved in this area yourself. The contributors offer a full view of the services, including the image promoted by leaflets and posters, creating a positive setting, preparing and training staff, consulting with and learning from the boys and young men and informed group work.

☑ 2 Effective communication

2.1 The communication framework

Communications by people in any kind of helping service need to convey acceptance and welcome to clients, a message of the genuineness of your response, a basic sense of empathy (fellow feeling) with the client and a respect for service users. These qualities are shown, or fail to be conveyed, through all aspects of your communication and cannot be faked.

Levels of communication

Communication between people can be seen as a hierarchy (see the diagram below). As a helper you need to be aware of the subtle rules and levels of communication, many of which are influenced by cultural tradition.

At the most basic level, communication is in the form of ritual exchanges. For example, within British culture, the greeting of 'How are you?' is supposed to be followed by the response of 'Fine, thanks', 'Alright' or 'Not too bad'. This ritual

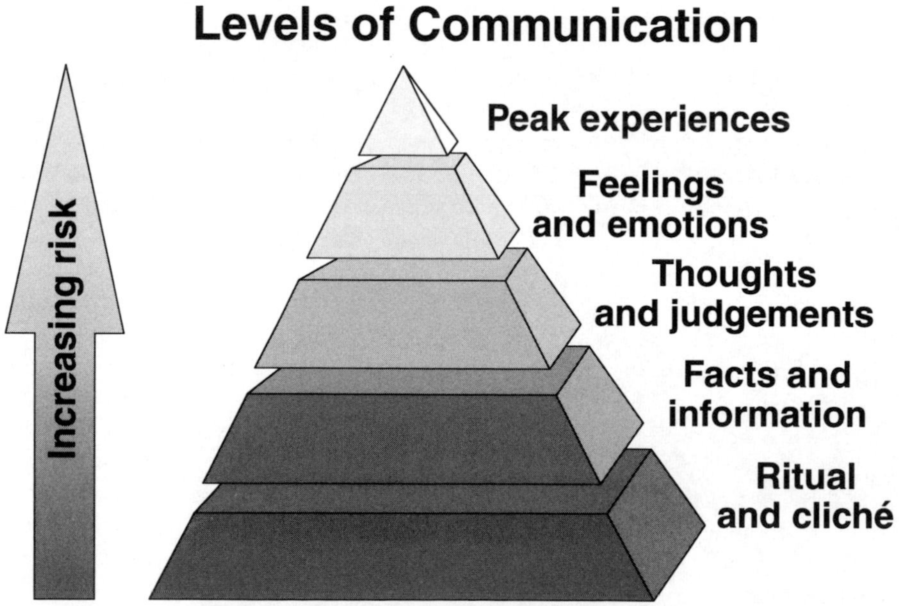

Levels of Communication

Increasing risk

Peak experiences

Feelings and emotions

Thoughts and judgements

Facts and information

Ritual and cliché

question is not supposed to be taken literally and followed by details of the other person's skin problems or family worries. People use ritual and cliché to acknowledge each other and not to convey deep meanings or personal concern. When people are genuinely interested in the details of 'How are you?', their additional words and body language flag this message. As communication moves up the levels, the level of risk also increases:

- An exchange of information or a request for facts is slightly more risky than ritualised communication. Some clients may be wary of showing that they do not know something or concerned that you will think them ignorant.
- Sharing thoughts entails a higher level of risk since someone else may disagree with either your way of thinking or your conclusions. As you get to know people better you are more likely to share your opinions and views yet will be most wary about potentially contentious areas like politics or religion.
- Sharing emotions involves a greater level of risk since very personal inner feelings and reactions are communicated. People are unlikely to communicate at this level unless they trust the other person.
- Very important experiences, highs and lows in personal life, are the most risky kind of communication, since a negative response or use of cliché will be experienced as a deep rejection.

You will tend to move towards the upper levels of communication with people whom you know well and trust. Ritual and cliché will be more usual in trivial interactions with acquaintances. Some people will always be more private than others, some are more outgoing. Cultural and social traditions also affect beliefs about the appropriateness of expressing thoughts and feelings and to whom. In a helping relationship with clients you broadly move through the levels as clients feel more able to trust you. It will not be good practice to push clients faster than they wish to move.

Clients may start at different levels of communication when they contact you and you need to match their level. At the information-seeking level, the risks are relatively low since the exchange is usually emotionally neutral, although clients can still experience good or poor practice in a service. When clients wish to share emotional issues then they are very likely to resent clichés in response because they will feel dismissed and their worries trivialised. Ritualised responses can provoke annoyance because they feel impersonal (see page 56).

In working with clients, it is crucial to base your work on facts and information communicated by the clients. This material forms the basis of shared understanding and provides the details of the query, problem or situation that you are helping the client to address. For many helping services covered by this book, the factual level of communication is the basis of the enquiry anyway. When clients become emotional, it is important to acknowledge and deal with the feelings so that they and you can better process the relevant information. You constantly return to the communication level of facts and information so that you can give objective and practical help.

The potential for misunderstanding

Even without any mismatch in levels, communication with others inevitably brings the risks of misunderstanding and misinterpretation. The diagram below sums up what can happen.

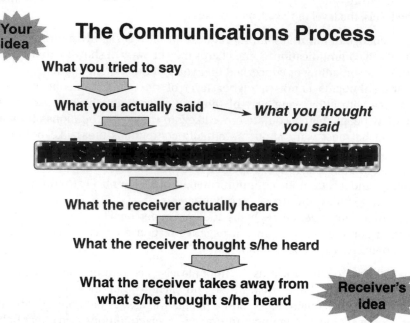

The Communications Process

Your idea

What you tried to say

What you actually said → *What you thought you said*

What the receiver actually hears

What the receiver thought s/he heard

What the receiver takes away from what s/he thought s/he heard

Receiver's idea

Communication is a social process. Inevitably, everyone starts to make sense of the communication of another person as soon as the exchange starts. Everybody interprets to some extent, fills in the gaps of what is implied, but not said, and starts to anticipate what may come next. If you are puzzled by what you hear, part of your attention is working through in your head some of the possibilities of what the other person means. You do not communicate with a completely blank sheet, because your past experience provides a set of expectations, assumptions and ways of making meaning out of the words you hear and the gestures you see. An advantage is that this selective perception helps you to focus your attention on key areas of interest. The disadvantage is that it can block important information outside your focus and which fails to support your assumptions or views.

Because everyone works to make meaning from what they hear, there is always some scope for misunderstanding, even with people who know each other well. There is more to communication than just 'I send you a message' and 'You receive it'.

Any communication starts with an idea, however brief. Imagine that you are talking with a colleague:

- You have some idea of what you want to say, a message that you try to get across.
- You speak to your colleague or communicate in some way (the channel of communication).

- You have a memory of what you are sure that you said, which may be slightly or very different from what you actually said.
- The reception process of communication starts with what your colleague actually hears. This may not be everything that you said, because she was not listening to the beginning of your sentence, or there was a distracting noise.
- However, your colleague forms a clear thought about what she is sure that you said.
- Then she builds an understanding from what she is sure that she heard from you, becoming an idea in her mind as a result of your communication.

Sometimes the process of communication is very clear with few misunderstandings. More often a wider gap develops along the way between your original idea and the idea that has now lodged in the mind of the other person. The communication is easily shaped by:

- Your mood and that of the other person.
- All the expectations and assumptions that are based in past experience between the two of you and outside this relationship.
- Factors that block communication, such as a delay in starting to listen, other people talking and background noise.
- Lack of flexibility in either person, such as insisting that 'what I thought you said' definitely is 'what you said to me'.

The channel of communication also creates or blocks possibilities. Face-to-face communication offers the most information, since you have visual as well as auditory feedback. Telephone communication loses the visual element, although this loss is sometimes an advantage if callers do not wish to see the other person and their reaction, for instance to bad news.

Any kind of one-way communication prevents immediate interaction and clarification of the message. Letters, email and voice mail offer the advant-age of thinking about the communication and rephrasing it but also bring the disadvantage that miscommunications may not be known, since the person on the receiving end may not express confusions or misunderstandings to you.

2.2 The importance of attention

Attending to others

Whenever you are in a discussion with someone else you effectively make a choice to give greater importance either to what you want to say or to what the other person is trying to communicate. When you attend fully to someone else, you are choosing to value that person and what she or he wishes to say to you. Full attention is crucial in your work with clients, at all levels of communication. Good attention involves both looking and listening:

- Awareness of the body language of your clients: what you can see in their behaviour.

- Awareness of your own body language: what they can see in your behaviour.
- Listening to what clients say and how they say it.

Without attention, a dialogue between two people fails to be a give-and-take exchange and works more like a double monologue, a parallel communication. It is almost impossible to make someone believe that you are really attending when you are not. Your lack of attention will show in two ways:

- Your body language will betray you. Your eye contact will wander or you will fidget; perhaps you will often glance at your watch.
- What you say in reply will demonstrate that you have not been listening. For instance, your words will show that you do not understand what has been said and are not trying to understand. Or what you say may bear little relationship to what you should have heard.

You cannot attend properly while half your mind and your eyes are interested elsewhere. The ability to look and listen is absolutely central to good practice in any of the helping services, including those in which your contact with clients is brief. If you attend well then:

- Clients feel respected. They feel that you are giving them time and attention and that their concerns matter to you.
- You will hear and be better able to understand the reasons why clients have come to your service, or have contacted your telephone help or information line.
- You will be in a much stronger position to provide clients with appropriate information or advice that meets their concerns in a way that will genuinely help them.
- You will be able to judge whether your service is likely to be able to help a client and, if not, to make sensible suggestions about who may be more appropriate.

In contrast, if you do not attend properly, then:

- You fail to show respect for the client as a person because you are unwilling to give appropriate time and attention.
- You cannot know what kind of help clients may require. You can only make broad assumptions. You are reduced to guessing what clients want or shaping their needs in the direction that suits what your service offers.
- You will be less helpful than you could be and may even be actively unhelpful. You may undermine the confidence of a client who found it hard to come and ask for help. Maybe you give misleading, inappropriate or plain wrong advice. Even worse, perhaps your lack of attention discourages clients from seeking help again, from you or other agencies.

Giving clients your full attention may lead to spending slightly more time with each client. However, in many short contact services your time per client will not be greatly extended. This avoids more work later because clients have been wrongly referred or have become irritated with the lack of proper attention.

Two ears,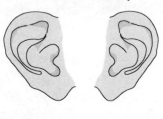

two eyes,

one mouth...

we sometimes forget this!

Activity

How do you judge when somebody is paying you full attention? Note down experiences over the next couple of weeks when:

- You felt that the other person was fully aware of you and listened well. What made you sure that you had his or her attention?
- You felt that the other person was not listening, or was distracted from what you were saying. What exactly led you to this conclusion?
- What can you learn for your own practice from what you noticed about other people's attentive behaviour, or lack of it?

How to listen well

Some people are probably better natural listeners than others but everyone can improve their listening skills. You need to:

- Value clients enough to give your time and attention. Valuing the client is just as possible, and important, in brief exchanges as in longer-term helping relationships. In a conversation as short as a few minutes, clients should feel confident that they have your undivided attention.
- Plan how to listen well in your setting and draw on those communication skills that you already have.
- Pay attention to what seems to distract you from listening well to clients and work to improve those areas within your control.
- Practise your listening skills.

Focus on the client

Give clients your full attention, with your eyes and your ears. It is easier to listen well to another person when you:

- Are close enough that neither of you has to strain to hear.
- Face one another directly rather than looking from an angle. If you are sitting down, you should be able to look directly at each other.
- Maintain regular eye contact but do not stare. A friendly and attentive gaze is broken from time to time; an unwavering stare is likely to be experienced as intimidating.
- Are aware of your own body language and make changes towards greater attentiveness. Perhaps you need to stop hair, beard or jewellery twiddling, fiddling with your pen, drumming your fingers or crossing and uncrossing your legs. You are definitely not trying to be a robot, just peaceful and focused on the other person.
- Create a comfortable open space between the two of you, as far as your work environment allows. See also physical barriers on page 34.

Activity

Work with another person to explore the kinds of behaviour that help you to listen and those that do not.

- Decide who will be the talker (A) and who will be the listener (B). Person A talks about any lightweight topic for two minutes at the most. If you cannot think of a topic, pick one of the following: 'my ideal weekend', 'my worst holiday ever' or 'what I would do if I won the lottery'.

- For two minutes, person A talks. Person B says nothing but shows, in any way that makes sense, that she or he is *not* listening.
- Stop and talk over what has just happened. What did person B do and how did person A feel about it?
- Reverse the situation for two minutes: B now talks and A shows in any way that she or he is *not* listening.

Talk over what you have just experienced; what really got in the way? The opportunity to exaggerate poor listening behaviour often throws into relief the bad habits that are so easy to develop. By looking at the flip side, you can highlight what matters for you to listen.

Now spend the same short periods of time with some proper attention through looking and listening.

- Person B takes the first turn to talk, on the same topic as before, and person A listens. A says nothing but focuses on listening and showing that she or he is listening carefully.
- At the end of two minutes, B stops talking and A summarises as accurately as possible what has been heard: the facts and the feelings.
- Discuss the experience. If you were A, how did you show that you were listening? How did it feel for B? And how accurate was A's summary at the end of the two minutes?
- Reverse the situation – A talks, B listens.
- Then talk over what you have both experienced. What was it like to keep silent as a listener for two minutes?

Listening cannot be continuous silence because, after a short while, the person talking misses the lack of any kind of verbal feedback. See page 43 for ideas about what to say and for another activity.

Quieten your inner voice

To think about

The word 'listen' is an anagram for 'silent'. You need to still your inner voice, the one that drifts away with all your unspoken thoughts, as well as your voice that everyone else hears out loud.

Good listeners do not rush to interrupt or make their own points. There is a great difference between active listening and waiting for your turn to talk. In order to quieten your inner monologues, you have to switch your attention fully to the client. You need to put to one side and actively ignore any other thoughts. Sometimes the thoughts will be related to this exchange, but are not helpful if they crowd out your attention to the client. For instance, you cannot listen if you are busy thinking of:

- What you are going to say when it is your turn in the conversation.
- All the suggestions you might make when this client takes a pause.
- A line of possible help stimulated by just a few words or phrases that the client has used.
- Premature worries about whether you will be able to help.

Equally, you need to put to one side any concerns not related to this client:

- What else is happening in your work: meetings, paperwork or a message that you need to pass on to a colleague.
- Any personal issues, worries or domestic plans.

Internal physical blocks

It is hard to attend if you feel unwell; for instance, you have to work harder to focus with a cold or headache. If your ill health is blocking your ability to listen, then you need to take some remedial action. Sometimes, this is an apology to clients about your cough or croaky voice, or you may need to take appropriate medication. If it really is not possible to work effectively with clients, then you need to take a break or stop this kind of work for the day. If you find it very hard to attend then your difficulty will be communicated to the clients, who may form a negative view of your interest and commitment.

Handle interruptions

People do not believe that they are receiving your full attention if your focus is constantly broken. Clients should not be interrupted for you to answer the telephone or speak with a colleague. In some working circumstances a few interruptions may be unavoidable. Handle the interruption as swiftly as possible and apologise to clients.

Clients should never feel that the telephone is more important than them. Any team should also ensure that bad habits do not develop in talking between colleagues. For instance, in some settings, workers routinely interrupt clients who are talking to a colleague, or talk across or even lean across clients, often without so much as an 'excuse me'. Clients will experience this kind of behaviour at discourteous, dismissive and as evidence that clients are a low priority in your service.

Physical barriers to good listening

Large desks, glass screens and small speaking windows are blocks to communication and clients find them unwelcoming. If your service genuinely needs physical barriers, because there is a real issue of personal security, then you have to work that much harder to show attentive behaviour.

- Your open gaze, smile, if appropriate, and careful listening need to counteract the impression of the physical surroundings that clients have to be kept at a distance.
- Be close on the other side of a screen or window so that clients feel that the necessary distance is kept to a minimum.
- Ensure that clients can make themselves heard without having to lean across the counter and shout into a communication grill.

Activity

1   Keep a brief record of your experiences as a customer or client when the service has a physical barrier as above.
    - How do you feel on the customer side of the barrier?
    - In what ways does the service counteract any negative impact on communication?
2   Does your own service have some kind of physical barrier? If yes, then spend some time standing on the other side of your counter.
    - What can you see and hear? What are your first impressions?
    - Is communication clear and does the technical system work well?
    - What does it feel like to be on this side?

To think about

Read through the following excuses for not listening to clients.

- What kind of outlook is indicated by the statements?
- What is wrong with this attitude?
- What could be the first steps to tackling such a negative outlook?
- Which comments are most familiar from your own service?

1   'We're the experts. We know what's best for clients. What's the point in listening to them? They come here for us to tell them what to do.'
2   'I've heard it all before. In 30 seconds, I know what kind of problem we've got this time.'
3   'I don't have the time to listen to clients. It's all very well if you've got masses of time on your hands but I've far too many other things to do.'
4   'I'm not supposed to talk with clients, I'm not trained. I just write down their name and their problem and pass them on.'
5   'What's the point, you never see most of them again? You never get to know anybody, so what's the point in listening?
6   'You have to keep clients in line. If you listen to their complaints, they think they can wheedle anything out of you.'
7   'I can't listen to clients going on in their own way. I have to ask them all these questions; I have forms to fill in.'
8   'I'd listen if they were pleasant to me. But clients come in here with their "I want this" and "What are you going to do about that?" '
9   'What is there to listen to? We get kids who just sit there. I'm lucky to get one word and a grunt out of most of them.'
10 'Why should I listen to clients? Nobody listens to me! We get treated like dirt in this organisation.'

Listening on the telephone

With the exception of making eye contact, all the ideas discussed so far are equally important in listening to clients on the telephone. However, telephone exchanges lose the visual element, so you need to concentrate very carefully on what people say and how they say it. See Chapter 5 for a full discussion of helping over the telephone.

2.3 Awareness of body language

Ways to communicate non-verbally

Well over half the meaning of any face-to-face communication is provided by the non-verbal messages, also called body language. You will be affected by the non-verbal communication of other people, even if you are not conscious of what you have noticed. Equally, other people are aware of your body language. So it is just as important to increase awareness of how you behave as to be aware of the sense you make of how others react non-verbally. Your objective is for clear communication, to give and receive messages with as little distortion as possible. So your body language needs to match your words and you need to be very aware of your clients.

Unspoken messages are sent through different parts of the body:

- The face and facial expression.
- Eye contact.
- Body movements and gestures.
- The distance between two people talking.
- The use of touch.

Match and mismatch

Especially in a helping situation, your body language should match the positive message of your words. If there is a mismatch, then people usually believe the non-verbal message, although they may not easily be able to explain the source of their conviction. For example:

- A reception desk worker can say, 'How may I help you?', but the words are accompanied by a wooden expression and the worker continues to turn the pages of a newspaper. Clients are unlikely to believe that the worker really wants to help.
- From the other perspective, a client who has recently been bereaved says to you, 'I'm fine; I'm coping.' You doubt the client's words because of her sad expression and the way in which she twists the folds of her skirt.

Workers in helping services are responsible for ensuring that what they say and how they say it are in accord. The first example arises when someone has been told to use a form of words, but has not been prepared to take a positive approach to clients as individuals. The reception worker has little respect for clients and this outlook leaks through the body language.

It is not the responsibility of clients to ensure that their non-verbal communication matches their spoken words. It is your responsibility to be alert to this information so that you can understand and support clients. You have to decide how far and in what way you raise any mismatch with a client. In the second example, it would never be helpful to challenge the client with, 'You can't fool me! You're obviously not fine!' Depending on the circumstances in which you are offering help, you could approach the mismatch in several different ways:

- If you have an on-going relationship with the client, then it could be appropriate to say gently, 'Are you sure? You look rather down to me', or, 'You didn't look as if you felt fine, do you?' Do not make comments inviting a client to talk, unless you have time to listen immediately.
- If you are only having a short exchange with the client, you might say something that keeps a slight emotional distance but raises possibilities. For example, 'That's good. But you know there's always someone here to talk if you want', or, 'Yes, I know you can cope, but this is probably a hard time for you.'
- If you are in the position of easing the client on to spend time with another member of your team, you could alert your colleague to your observation with, 'Mrs Watson tells me she's "fine". But she looks very sad and under stress to me.'

Awareness of your own body language

You cannot stop communicating non-verbally and you certainly should not try. However, an awareness of your own body language can mean that you use this form of communication productively – much like choosing better words to say. You can also work on any personal quirks that you realise may be unhelpful because they give the wrong messages.

Facial expression

The muscles in the face are used, more or less consciously, to produce smiles, frowns, or puzzled or doubtful expressions. Your face can look more or less welcoming, open or closed. A smile is a typical welcome. An immovable, fixed expression seems uninviting and lacking emotion. On the other hand, marked, frequent changes in facial expression can be distracting for clients, who focus more on the messages passing across your face than on telling you what they wish to say. You need to aim for a calm and alert expression that is not wooden and adjusts appropriately to what clients say to you.

Eye contact

The way in which you look at someone and how you hold or break a gaze add meaning to what you say.

- Looking directly at someone suggests that you are listening and are open to what they say.

- An unsteady gaze, looking away frequently or looking at some point in the middle distance all tend to suggest that your attention is elsewhere and you are distracted.
- A steady, unwavering gaze is experienced as a stare ('eyeballing') and is felt to be intimidating, challenging or aggressive.
- Friendly and inviting eye contact in a helping situation tends to be regularly looking at the other person, holding the gaze for a while and breaking the gaze, usually by looking down briefly.
- Be sensitive to how much the client looks at you. If clients seem uneasy, you might reduce the extent that you make eye contact. However, it is usual for listeners to hold more eye contact than talkers.

Body movements

Your whole body communicates messages. If you sit or stand upright facing the client, then you will look attentive. On the other hand, a slumped posture or turning away from the client tends to communicate inattention or not caring. An upright position can be taken too far, of course. A rigid, bolt upright position may seem unwelcoming or perhaps provoke negative images of critical school teachers ready to pass judgement.

Your hands and arms create gestures that add meaning to your words. Gestures can be expansive and cover a lot of space or be more contained. Hand and finger gestures often convey quite specific messages that vary considerably between cultures. As a helper, it is usually best to keep your gestures simple and non-expansive. Especially avoid finger pointing and wagging, which is usually taken as a criticism and especially patronising when done to adults.

Distance and touch

Non-verbal messages are also sent through the distance maintained between one person and another. Individuals may vary in their preferred personal space and less distance is often acceptable, and welcomed, between people who know each other well. The physical surroundings in which you work may place some limits on possible distance between you and clients. It is worth trying to re-duce unhelpful barriers, such as large tables, in order to be able to speak at a comfortable communication distance. When you are seated and with no barriers, a distance of about two metres is about right for most people. Let clients create more distance if they wish.

Use of touch is another aspect of distance and of closing the gap between two people. Physical contact can be a strong message of affection, support or calming. But it involves a movement into the personal space of another person and should be used with great care in a helping situation, especially if you do not know the client well. There will be occasions when a touch, hand squeeze or an arm round someone's shoulders will be appropriate but apart from the handshake of greeting, such times are likely to be with clients whom you have got to know, or those in obvious distress. You may also need to consider how best to deal with situations in which a client prefers to sit more closely or to use touch more than you would prefer.

Learning about your own body language

You have several sources of useful information:

- How clients react to you, either what they say or their body language.
- Feedback from your colleagues who see you in action.
- The opportunities of video feedback, perhaps on a course or workshop. You may feel uncomfortable about being on video but it is worth overcoming your resistance as it provides a unique chance to see yourself as others see you.

You can learn about your body language in such a way that you could make improvements. Perhaps:

- Until a colleague tells you, you were unaware that you hold a steady gaze, but that it is directed slightly to the side of the person with whom you are talking.
- What feels to you like a 'serious listening expression' appears more like a frown of disapproval to others. In a group discussion, two clients have commented, 'Is something the matter?', or, 'Don't you agree with me then?'
- You wondered if you smiled too much and should be more sober-looking, but a client says to you, 'I love your smile; it makes my day.'
- Until you watched yourself on video, you had no idea you so often fiddled with your hair.

Feedback within communication

You need a positive working atmosphere within a team so that any useful work observations, not just about body language, can be shared in a constructive way. Unless colleagues trust one another, it will not be possible for the give-and-take of feedback to be of benefit. Helpful comments between colleagues are more likely to be:

- A blend, over time, of encouragement as well as constructive criticism. Find the time to tell a colleague how well you think she handles interruptions or manages to include children in a conversation with a parent and child. If you are on the receiving end of such a compliment, then accept it graciously.
- Specific examples rather than vague generalisations. People have a chance to do something about an observation like, 'I think you need to find a way to keep looking at clients as you fill in their form', rather than, 'You make clients think you're more interested in the paperwork than them.'
- Descriptions rather than labels – a colleague needs to understand what you have observed rather than just feel praised or criticised in a general way. It is more possible to react thoughtfully to an observation like, 'You don't smile a lot when you're with clients', rather than, 'You're cold.' Specific feedback also enables you to do something, to change the behaviour of which you were unaware.
- Given in response to a request rather than imposed.
- Phrased so that the other person has a chance to consider rather than feel a defence is required straightaway. Often this means offering a suggestion of how the behaviour could be improved or developed.

- Made in circumstances when the other person does not feel exposed. The comments are better shared in a private conversation between colleagues or in supervision rather than in public.

If you are given feedback then your responsibility is to listen and to ensure that you understand by asking for an example or further explanation, not by arguing with your colleague. Reflect on the feedback you receive and consider changes you could make to improve your practice.

Making sense of the body language of other people

What you notice about a person's body language and appearance will add to the meaning you take from the words you hear. In some cases body language will emphasise and support clients' words but, in other circumstances, their body language may modify the words or give a very different message.

Cautious interpretation

You need to be aware of what you notice in clients' body language and be open-minded over what it means. For instance, a client who sits with firmly crossed arms is showing a closed body posture. This behaviour may mean that he:

- Doubts that you will be helpful.
- Wishes to defend himself non-verbally and not allow you through.
- Is angry with you or something else that has just happened.
- Is cold, since the room is chilly and he has no jacket.

A client who looks steadily at you may be:

- Genuinely interested in what you are offering.
- Trying to unnerve you by staring.
- One of those rare people who can hold an unblinking gaze and do not realise its impact on others.
- Reacting to feedback from a friend who has suggested that the client's usual pattern of looking away gives the impression of shiftiness.

The better you know someone, the more reliably you can interpret the meaning of his or her body language. Otherwise, there are no absolute rules, so caution is advisable. A good rule of thumb is to verify your interpretation, either by asking the client when appropriate or through continued observation. For instance, a client who firmly crosses her arms may feel any of the emotions described earlier. However, if she crosses her arms every time you try to discuss her partner's serious ill health, you could read the movement as a likely self-protective gesture, indicative of her concern and anxiety with this topic.

Social and cultural trends

Body language is not inborn; children learn patterns of non-verbal as well as verbal communication. The social rules and accepted variations are often only obvious when they are broken. For instance, learning-disabled young people or adults sometimes continue to use body language that is more associated with the behaviour of younger children. Autistic children, young people and adults are insensitive to non-verbal clues, for instance, about stopping talking or a give-and-take exchange with another person.

Further evidence that gestures and body movements are learned comes from the differences observed between males and females from a relatively young age. Within any culture, girls and boys learn some different ways to behave, either through observation of adults or specific instruction. For instance, within British culture you will notice that:

- Females generally take up less space than males. Boys and men often sit with legs apart or stretched out, perhaps with arms spread as well. On the other hand, females are more likely to sit with knees together, taking up less space than a male of the same size.
- Girls and women tend to touch their face far more than boys or men. Females put a hand to their mouth or cheek whereas males make this gesture far less often.

Differences between cultures, and sometimes within one culture's social or class groups, can be seen in:

- The expansiveness of arm and hand gestures.
- The meaning of gestures using the hand, fingers or thumb, which can be seriously different between cultures. An acceptable gesture within one culture may be very rude in another, or only appropriate for use with children and so discourteous used to an adult.
- The use of touch to emphasise a point or to require attention. Some cultures use touch a great deal whereas others regard being touched, especially by relative strangers, as an invasion of personal space.
- Varying traditions of how close it is normal to stand to another person. Again, when people of different cultures meet, person A may feel slighted because person B keeps moving away, while B feels that A is imposing.
- The extent of eye contact. In some cultures, holding another person's gaze is regarded as discourteous. When cultures meet, polite behaviour in one culture may be seen as the reverse in another.

There are many group and individual variations within any culture, so it is risky to set rules about the body language of people from specific cultural backgrounds. You need to be conscious of potential differences without holding firm expectations.

2.4 Using verbal communication well

The words

Spoken language is formed of many words and phrases and the sentences into which they combine. You have choices about using simple or more complex words and the length of your phrases and sentences. Everybody has an accent, although many people remain convinced that their speech is normal; other people are the ones with an accent. Even when the form of language is not so different as to be called a dialect, you will find many local variations in words and phrases from a shared language. You will not notice these differences until you talk with someone from a different geographical area to your own.

Verbal communication also gains meaning from how you speak:

- The tone of your voice, which can convey additional or even different messages from your words.
- The rhythm of how you speak and your use of pauses. Some people speak in short or single sentences, others will say several sentences before a break. The speed of speech varies and some people regularly speak faster than others.
- Spoken language varies in volume and some people habitually speak more loudly or softer than others.

You can modify any of these aspects of your speech. Everyone has developed a style in which they speak and you may be more or less conscious of your own. Personal styles can vary according to the situation in which you find yourself: the people with whom you are speaking, the formality of a situation or even your mood. It is useful to become aware of how you use your speech, so that you can adjust what you say and how you say it to improve communication.

Some appropriate ways to modify your language and delivery for clients could be to:

- Speak in simple words and phrases and in short sentences with a client with whom you do not share a fluent language.
- Simplify your language when speaking with children.
- Speak more quietly with a client who seems very ill at ease.
- Check more frequently that clients have understood or agree if their body language suggests to you that they are puzzled or resistant.
- Talk clearly and face to face with a client who has a hearing disability.

On the other hand, it would be inappropriate to:

- Raise your voice because a client is shouting. (See also page 237.)
- Talk loudly to a client who has a hearing disability. Raising your voice well beyond normal volume distorts communication rather than making it any clearer. Shouting makes it harder for someone to lip-read or to hear through the distortions entering supportive hearing equipment.
- Talk very slowly to a client with whom you do not share a fluent language, or to a child. Excessively slow delivery comes across as patronising or superior.

Activity

Experiment with saying a short phrase like, 'How may I help you?' or 'What is your problem?' in different ways, to communicate:

- A genuine wish to help this client.
- The message that you are short of time and this had better not take too long.

- An expectation that this client is going to be awkward or difficult.
- The sense of unease that you will not be able to help this client.

Now try these variations just with the word 'Yes' and any body language that seems appropriate to the message:

- Try saying the word as a welcome, with a questioning tone.
- Experiment with snapping out the word to imply, but not say, 'Get on with it!' to a client.
- Say the word in a way that conveys the message that you are expecting this client to be trouble.
- Express doubt that you will be able to help this client.

You could experiment with taping your different versions. If possible, practise and experiment with a colleague. You will then be able to give each other feedback, especially on how your body language supports your words.

Use of language in helping

Good listening is not achieved through total silence. The point that 'listen' is an anagram of 'silent' is a reminder that most people have to hold back on talking in order to improve their listening. You cannot listen effectively for long amounts of time and not say anything. If you have tried the activity on page 33, you may have experienced that the talker's need for some reaction from the listener usually cuts in well before two minutes. If you say nothing at all, the likely consequences are that:

- The person talking begins to doubt that you are listening. The social traditions of a communication exchange are that the listener says something, otherwise there is no interaction.
- The longer you stay silent, the harder and harder it becomes to interrupt the client's monologue.
- You will find your task of listening more difficult, because information will wash over you and disappear from your awareness. It is easier to listen if your verbal contributions are relevant to what the client is saying.

An effective helper, in even the shortest exchanges, is working for a positive balance between saying too much and saying too little. If you speak up after you have heard only a few sentences with anything other than a brief summary or request for clarification, then clients will have one of two reactions. Either they will think you want them to be quiet and listen to you or else they are likely to tell you, 'Be quiet and listen to me.' If you say nothing and clients talk on and on, then their reaction is likely to be a questioning 'Are you listening to me?'

Your use of communication skills within helping is different from having a conversation with a friend or a discussion in a team meeting. The combination of skills that support helping is sometimes called reflective or active listening and includes:

- Simple and brief words or sounds to show that you are listening.
- Reflecting back (paraphrasing) what a client has said.
- Use of short and accurate summaries of what you have heard.
- An open-ended use of questions.

These skills covered here are appropriate to short and medium-length exchanges with clients. You will find more in Chapters 7 and 8 about using reflective listening with counselling skills. Most early conversations with clients will be at the facts-and-information level of communication. This kind of exchange works best when you follow a series of questions with paraphrases or summaries until a summary covers the main issues of the whole conversation. Questions start open-ended and can become more focused when you genuinely understand what the client seeks. The diagram below sums up the process.

Questioning Techniques

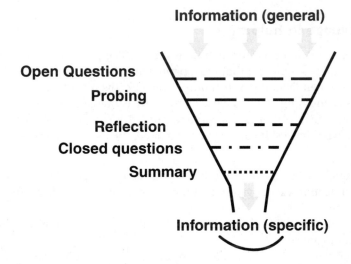

Information (general)

Open Questions
Probing
Reflection
Closed questions
Summary

Information (specific)

Encouraging sounds and words

There are a range of simple words and sounds that can show a client that you are listening, often supported in face-to-face communication with appropriate nods and smiles. Possibilities include:

- Encouraging sounds such as 'aha' or 'mmm'.
- Words like 'yes', 'right' or 'okay'.
- Short phrases such as 'I see', 'I hear' or 'I know'.

Of course, any of these suggestions could be overused or made inappropriate if they do not match what the client is saying. Perhaps you have listened into a conversation, on a train or as you wait in a queue, and the person listening has repeatedly said 'I know' or 'right'. As an impartial observer, you have probably sensed that such constant repetition creates the feel that the person is not listening and the words become a ritual or cliché through overuse. If any word or phrase is overused by a listener, the result can seem patronising or as an impatient implication to 'hurry up'. Be sensitive to the client and adjust your simple responses accordingly.

Paraphrasing and summarising

Another way to contribute effectively is to reflect back what the client has said or shown. Sometimes it makes sense to repeat the actual words, but usually you will rephrase using your own words. This paraphrasing or summarising supports the communication in two ways:

- It signals to clients that you have heard the points they just made.
- The brief summary helps you to register what you have heard and gives the client an opportunity to clarify any misunderstandings on your part and keep you both on the same track.
- Your focus on giving the client an accurate paraphrase or summary also helps you to avoid a focus on points you are tempted to make, but which may not be relevant to the issue.

Some examples of useful summarising could be:

- 'You'd like a work placement in something to do with the theatre.'
- 'You're really upset at the way you've been treated.'
- 'So, you've got two children at school and you'd like to know about after-school clubs around here.'
- 'You've had the tests and you're waiting for the results.'
- 'You sent your application in on the 5th and you haven't heard anything yet.'
- 'You've spoken three times with your neighbours about the loud music and they're not willing to turn it down.'

Occasionally, when you summarise, the client may react with, 'Yes, I've just told you that.' In that case, you can reply with, 'I appreciate that. I'm checking that I've understood you properly.' Or you can begin your summary with, 'I'd like to check that I'm clear about what you've told me.' It is often valuable to summarise at the end of a conversation so that a client feels confident that you have understood their main concerns or enquiry. You can link your summary to an explanation of what can happen next.

Like any potentially positive contribution in a helpful exchange, paraphrasing or summarising will be counterproductive if that is all you do. Questions can also be used in a positive way.

Open-ended questions

The whole point about questions is that they should be asked only to help you to understand and respond more helpfully to the client. Questions should not be used just to satisfy your own curiosity. Generally speaking, open-ended questions are more useful than closed, especially at the beginning of an exchange:

- Open-ended questions are those which seek an answer of more than one word and encourage clients to share information with you in their own way. Closed questions are those which only invite replies of one word, often 'Yes' or 'No'.
- Open-ended questions tend to start with words like 'who', 'what', when' or 'how'. They are phrased in a way that opens the doors of communication rather than shuts them. Closed questions tend to direct a conversation and check facts. The most open-ended questions will be at the start of the exchange, for instance, 'How can I help?', or, 'What are you concerned about?'

You need to use questions with care because:

- Questions starting with 'why' tend to put clients on the spot, with the implication that they should justify themselves. 'Why' questions often provoke a reply that starts with 'because' and do not encourage clients to explore the issue.
- Some closed or leading questions may imply to clients that you want or advise them to take a particular direction. For example, 'So if I could get you this childminder, you'd accept her?' Clients who lack confidence may feel uneasy about questioning you or saying, 'That's not what I was after.'
- Overuse of questions, especially closed ones, shifts the balance of the conversation into one where you ask the questions and the client gives you answers. The consequence can be that a client goes quieter and just waits for your next questions.

Less helpful closed questions can be reworded, for example:

- 'Do you want a work placement in lighting?' (closed question) becomes 'What parts of working in the theatre interest you?' (open question).
- 'Do you want a childminder from next week?' (closed) becomes 'What practical details do we need to discuss about your child's care with a minder?' (open).
- 'Do you want a home help for your father?' (closed) becomes 'What kinds of help would you like for your father?' (open).

You can reword 'why?' questions to encourage clients, for instance:

- 'Why are you upset about your noisy neighbours?' becomes 'What problems is the noise creating for you?'
- 'Why does Patty have these temper tantrums?' can become 'What do you think happens before Patty has her tantrums?' or 'What do you think Patty throws her tantrums for?'
- 'Why do you think . . . ?' becomes 'What makes you think that . . . ?' or 'What information made you reach that conclusion?'

Often it makes sense in working with a client to flag up the shift from listening actively to your asking some questions. You might say:

- 'Can I ask you about . . . ?'
- 'It would help me to know about . . .'.
- 'Do you mind if I check the details on . . . ?'

Towards the end of a short helping conversation you might use closed questions to check final details for the client and ensure there is no misunderstanding. By now it will be appropriate to ask questions such as:

- 'When would you like your child to start at the pre-school?'
- 'So the two most important issues about your father's day centre are closeness to home and the costs of the care?'

A range of languages

You may work in an area where everyone, or almost everyone, is a first-language English speaker. However, many towns and cities have districts in which different languages, dialects and accents can be heard. If you do not share a language to the same level of fluency with the client with whom you are communicating, then it can be harder to offer a good service.

To think about

If you speak more than one language yourself, you will know that working to understand what has been said and replying takes that much longer in your second or third language.

You may also have experienced that you can have a good working vocabulary for some topics of conversation but dry up when you try to express yourself on another topic. Perhaps you sound fluent when you are buying in shops or joining in everyday conversation but struggle for the words to explain the symptoms of a sick child or your utter frustration about cockroaches in your kitchen.

If you and the client share fluency to some level in a language, then you may be able to work reasonably well if you:

- Keep your language simple. Express yourself in short phrases and sentences.
- Take pauses to let your words sink in for the client.
- Use pauses and invitations like, 'Are you clear?', or, 'Shall I say anything again?', to encourage clients to ask questions or have you repeat anything they wish.

There are other practical options to consider, depending on the nature of the service:

- A service dealing with clients speaking a range of languages should seek more bilingual staff or volunteers.
- Staff can be given the opportunity to learn key phrases and some basic level of fluency in one or more local languages.
- Haringey Council in London have developed the Language Indicator Prompt System (LIPS), a written set of key prompts in 22 languages. The system is designed to support the first contact staff in public services such as Housing departments or Social Services. (LIPS is available from One Stop Shops, 40 Cumberland Road, London N22 4SG. Tel: 0208 862 3914.)

- Encourage clients to bring a friend who can interpret. If necessary, adjust your physical setting so that it is easy to sit and talk with more than one person. Include the client in your gaze and do not just speak and look at the interpreter.
- Check whether you have a local interpretation service and how you book their services. However, be aware that you cannot conduct a confidential longer-term helping relationship through an interpreter. You need the relevant fluent language.
- Have some supporting written material in key local languages. A local authority translation and interpretation service should help you but check on any fees.

A positive approach

You and your colleagues should think about and talk about clients with respect. It is possible that your own team has a positive outlook, but that new members or volunteers in your service make thoughtless remarks.

A client should never be described as having 'poor English'; this comment is derogatory and overlooks the alternative perspective that you have 'poor Spanish' or 'non-existent Hindi'. It is more positive and accurate to say, 'Luigi's home language is Italian and he has some English', or, 'Rashida can communicate in three languages but she is least confident in English.' Clients speaking in a language you do not understand should never be described as 'gabbling' or some similar offensive term. You and your colleagues presumably do not think of your conversations as 'gabble'.

Three-way communication

Sometimes you cannot easily speak directly to the client. For example:

- A child or young person is accompanied by a parent who does most of the talking.
- Adult clients who lack confidence have a companion who speaks on their behalf.
- Clients need the support of an interpreter because they do not speak English with confidence and you do not speak their home language.
- Clients have learning disabilities which affect communication and understanding.
- Clients have disabilities that affect their hearing, their speech or both.

If you are involved in three-way communication, you need to make contact with the person who is the client. Sometimes, you may be uncertain who actually is the client or the situation makes more sense if you see both people as your clients. You need to relate to parents and their child or teenager or to an adult and his or her elderly parent. At root, make sure that you include everyone in the discussion, paying at least as much attention to the client as to those who ease the communication. Several options are available:

- Use eye contact to include the person who is silent or talking considerably less.
- Ensure that you do not just look at the person who is speaking for a client.
- Definitely avoid talking about the child, young person or elderly parent as if she or he were not present. Find out their name and use it. Quieter clients may not talk but are listening. It feels demeaning to be discussed along the lines of, 'She wants to know about . . .', or, 'He can't cope with . . .'.
- Invite the quieter client to join the conversation. You might ask directly, 'What would you like to tell me?', 'What do you think about . . . ?', or, 'Your mother tells me that . . . how do you see it?'
- You may judge that the younger or less confident client could join the conversation if the more confident person would make that space. You may need to suggest courteously, 'I'd like to hear from your son now. Gerry, what bothers you about this situation?' If the parent, or other outspoken co-client, interrupts, you may need to insist, still politely, with, 'Mrs Baker, I'd like to concentrate on Gerry for the moment', or, 'I know you've told me about the . . . Mr Laurence, but I need to understand what your father thinks is most important.'
- Undoubtedly, third-party conversations are often less straightforward, since the others present (friends, members of the family and even professional interpreters) are not always accurate transmitters; sometimes they add meaning, interpretations and opinions which have to be (additionally) addressed by the helper.

2.5 Responding to clients' feelings

Feelings are an upper level of communication (see page 26) and as such need to be acknowledged sensitively – with care. Feelings are communicated both through words and non-verbally. Within helping services, an awareness of clients' feelings or their possible feelings is important because:

- If you ignore clients' feelings, you are losing information and you could be less helpful than possible.
- Problems and concerns are rarely all logical and cannot always be resolved through giving information. If you ignore the emotional content of clients' communication, then you give the message that they should not have feelings, or should not have expressed them to you.
- Clients sometimes have strong feelings about the situation or how they have been treated by a service. Such feelings do not go away by being ignored; they tend to increase and be expressed in ways that are less easy to manage within a helping service.
- Feelings are powerful and drive everyone's behaviour. It is unwise to act as if emotions do not exist.

Awareness of feelings

In short encounters with clients, your alertness to feelings will be at a basic level. You are not offering a service in which clients have time to express and explore deep feelings. However, your service will be of a poor quality if you insist on ignoring the fact that clients are people with feelings, perhaps treating them as 'cases'. For example:

- Clients appreciate a warm welcome that acknowledges them as valued individuals who have arrived to use your service or picked up the telephone to call.
- Even with short exchanges, it can useful to register that an individual client looks puzzled or uneasy. When you register these feelings, you can make adjustments to what you do. It might be as simple as offering, 'Would you like me to explain that part again?', or, 'You look uncertain, what can I do to help?'
- You may need to give some space to how a client feels about a recent health diagnosis and not focus entirely on medical options. The disease or condition can be medically treated but the whole illness needs emotional care.
- A client may have difficulty listening to all the logical possibilities for help with an elderly parent, if you avoid dealing with the clear message that she or he feels guilty about seeking outside help in the first place.

Some clients may be comfortable expressing their feelings directly, to say, 'I'm not happy about this', or, 'You're not taking my worries seriously', whereas other clients may never use 'I', saying 'you' or 'one' instead. Perhaps they say, 'It makes you feel unwanted', 'Anybody would be worried, wouldn't they?', or, 'I can take it but it really upset my child.' Sometimes feelings are expressed through denial, for example, 'I'm not really hurt by what he said', or, 'It's not exactly that I'm angry.' You need to be alert for feelings that are expressed in a way that would not be your own style.

You need also to allow for the fact that clients often have competing feelings. For instance:

- Parents who settle their young children into a care or play facility want their child to be happy and not be distressed at the parting. Yet, they would also like some sign that their child will miss them. Parents may also be coming to terms with the mixed emotions of pleasure that their child is growing and becoming more independent and yet feeling nostalgic for times past.
- A young person coming for careers advice may be excited about the prospects of a new course or job, but also be wary about the unknown or wonder if she or he will cope with a new situation.

A positive response to clients' feelings

In relatively short conversations it would not be appropriate for you to encourage clients to express their feelings in depth. However, clients may express strong feelings anyway and there are many opportunities between the two extremes of backing away from any acknowledgement and offering considerable time for clients to explore emotions. Many helping services are somewhere in between.

You can use the skills of reflective listening (see page 43) to recognise a client's expressed feelings and that they matter. Using these skills will show a client that you have heard and acknowledge what they have said. Your contribution to the conversation can be simple but consider the kind of comments that are helpful.

An example

A client comes to talk with you about local possibilities in care for elderly people. You have shown her some leaflets and begun to discuss a few possibilities. The client goes silent and then says, 'It's all very difficult. I should be the one looking after my father.'

You can acknowledge her feelings by reflecting back with comments like:

- 'You feel you ought to do it all yourself.'
- 'It feels difficult to come here and talk about getting outside help.'
- 'It's not always straightforward, I understand. You have feelings of responsibility about your father.'
- 'You have doubts about asking for some extra help.'

This kind of reply communicates to the client that you have heard her and recognise that her feelings are involved; it is not just a logical decision. In contrast you will deny her feelings with comments like:

- 'Come on now. You can't do everything yourself.'
- 'Don't think like that. He'll be fine in the day centre.'
- 'That's a silly thing to think. Women always take on too much.'
- 'Well, if you're so upset about it, you ought to talk to our counsellor.'
- 'Perhaps you should read one of our booklets.'

Later in the conversation it might be appropriate to reassure the client that her father could well have an enjoyable day at the centre or to suggest that she is not being selfish to want some help. Perhaps she would appreciate a chance to read the booklet or talk with someone else. However, if you come in prematurely with such comments, the client's feelings have been bypassed. You will lose credibility and trust by giving the message that you believe the client's feelings are irrelevant or should not have been expressed to you.

Activity

Imagine that you are speaking with a man who has undiagnosed prostate problems. He has been advised to go into hospital for an exploratory operation and you are explaining the practical details to him. He says to you, 'I think I understand what's going to happen. I suppose it'll be alright. But you hear such awful stories.'

Consider some possible responses below. How might the different comments affect this man, what might he feel? Which comments would be more appropriate:

- 'You sound concerned about this procedure.'
- 'Well, if you're so worried, I'll go through it all again one more time.'

- 'Perhaps it would help to tell me some of these stories.'
- 'You men, you're such hypochondriacs.'
- 'You don't want to listen to stories. People like to frighten you.'
- 'I'll get you another leaflet. We've got one on common worries about prostate problems.'
- 'You shouldn't think like that. What'll happen if you don't go into hospital?'
- 'It's alright to be wary. Are there particular questions you would like to ask me?'
- 'If you've got a problem with the operation, perhaps you'd better talk again with your GP.'

Be aware of your own reaction

You also need to be aware of how you react to dealing with the emotional side of clients.

- How comfortable are you when clients express feelings? Are you concerned that, if you acknowledge any feelings at all, then the emotional floodgates will open? This consequence is unlikely; in most cases clients will express the feelings relevant to what you are discussing and no more.
- Do you gloss over clients' feelings because you do not want to hear anything that might distress you? You will not be helpful if you approach work in a highly self-protective way. See page 113 for a discussion of an appropriate blend of caring and detachment.
- Does it depend on the kind of client or the subject matter? Perhaps you feel uneasy if the client is a different sex to you or noticeably older? Such feelings belong to you and are your responsibility to handle. If an older client feels able to express feelings to you, then it is for you to feel complimented that he or she feels able to communicate with you. Give the client your full attention. The support and supervision system in any helping service should provide opportunities for you to talk about the kinds of clients with whom you feel less confident or more uneasy.
- How far are your reservations based on doubts about what to say, or a belief that there will be just one right comment to offer? There is rarely a single ideal contribution to make, but some are better than others.
- Do you tend to jump ahead of the client and make too much of feelings you hear or notice – for instance, that expressed doubts mean that clients are backing out or have changed their mind?
- On the other hand, if you are comfortable with listening to feelings from clients, you may need to be cautious that you do not encourage clients to speak at greater depth or for longer than you can genuinely handle in your helping situation.

To think about

Your own personal experience will shape your reactions and is part of your learning to be a more effective helper. Like everyone else, you will have learned within your childhood about how to express feelings, or not to, and that some emotions are perhaps more appropriate to one sex than the other. Reflect one by one on the questions given above and help yourself towards a greater awareness of how you personally react to the expression of different feelings and by different clients.

▪ ⊻ 3 First contact and short exchanges

3.1 Clients' first impressions

Potential clients of your service will build up an impression of the whole organisation from what they have heard or read before their first visit, their perceptions of the first people they meet and how the physical setting strikes them.

The first contact

All organisations should value the first-contact members of the team. Unfortunately, the importance of initial-contact staff is often badly underestimated and there is no second chance to make a good first impression. First impressions are strong and shape how clients are likely to behave towards members of your organisation they meet later. A positive first impression helps clients to feel more open to your service because they feel valued. Of course, a positive first impression will not carry on if, after the first contact, clients feel poorly treated or dismissed by other staff within a service.

Negative reactions are more individual, so an offhand receptionist may provoke some clients into a more aggressive approach than others. Other clients may feel cowed and then be wary and unforthcoming. When potential clients are uncertain about using your service, an unwelcoming setting or first contact may be all that is needed to make some people back away from your service.

Some organisations may have receptionists whose main task is to greet clients and make a first-stage identification on what or who is wanted. Other organisations work in such a way that all team members at some point operate as the first contact. Sometimes first contact may be over the telephone. Other services operate in a situation where the very first contact person is not from your organisation, for instance, there is a general reception to your building.

Activity

Over the next few weeks, collect personal examples of how you are treated by the first person in a range of organisations that you contact, either face to face or over the telephone. They may not be offering advice or information; some may be commercial organisations.

- How are you greeted?
- Does the other person volunteer their name?

- If you need to be passed on, are you allowed to complete your question or explanation or are you cut off in mid-sentence?
- How do you feel about your treatment? How does it affect your view of the organisation and your expectations of other people in it?
- What can you learn to improve your own service?

Courtesy and attention

The first contact from your service must always show courtesy:

- Clients should be greeted promptly when they arrive.
- If there really has to be a slight delay, because you are on the telephone or dealing with another client, then indicate by a friendly gesture and a few words that you will not be long. Clients feel awkward and increasingly irritated if they are left, obviously waiting for your attention, and it is not forthcoming.

Give the client your full attention, shown through a smile, eye contact and a few words of greeting. Your team may agree on a choice of greeting, perhaps that the first contact says 'Good morning' or the equivalent for the time of day and follows with 'How may I help you?' and some variations along that theme.

- Clients should continue to be given your attention until the conversation is complete. If some interruption is genuinely unavoidable, then you should apologise. You should not simply ignore the client in order to pick up the telephone or turn to a colleague.

To think about

Frequently, people stop talking to an individual in front of them in order to answer a ringing telephone. This switchover is often done without any acknowledgement of the interruption or an apology. The clear and negative message is that, no matter who is on the end of the telephone, she or he is more important than the individual in front of you.

- Be alert for your experiences of being abandoned for a telephone call.
- How do you feel when this happens?
- If the interruption is really necessary, what ways of handling it make you feel more valued?
- What lessons can you draw for your own service?

Initial greeting

Some services and organisations have established a regular greeting that is given to all clients, but this approach has definite drawbacks, especially if the greeting extends beyond a very short phrase. Standard greetings of several sentences, given to every caller, are likely to sound like a formula. If clients hear other people in the setting receiving exactly the same opening comments, they feel that the words are less genuine and ritualised. The same feelings tend to be provoked if clients telephone more than once and hear an identical opening greeting. Clients do not feel treated as individuals. First-contact workers, who are less than careful, also tend to get lazy and bored by the repetitions. So they start to deliver the phrases in the same rhythm and tone each time and they become clichés. The impression given to callers can then be that the worker is being almost patronising, or making fun of the caller.

Any team in a helping service needs to discuss how clients are greeted and if there are particular words or a message that should be part of every greeting. In face-to-face communication, or over the telephone, you need something that falls between the two extremes of ''Ello!' and 'Good morning and welcome to the free information and support line of the Kempton Advice Bureau for parents and carers on 0226 783401 this is Angela speaking how may I help you'. Your tone of voice and the level of sincerity that this implies carry more importance in the end than the precise words. Valuing each caller as a special individual is critical to avoid slipping into ritualised and rote phrases carrying no warmth.

Appearances

Clients' first impressions are also formed from how you appear and dress as a first-contact person, or any other member of the team. Suitable dress for work is a useful discussion to have within your own team, since a single dress code will not apply across all the helping services.

A good rule of thumb is that you show respect for clients by dressing smartly yet appropriately for your kind of work. Suits or very tailored clothing for men or women may give a visual message that is too formal. On the other hand, sloppy clothing can look as if you are ready to slouch around your own home rather than attend to clients. A smart casual style is often the best compromise; it looks as if you have taken care but are not overdressed.

Value the first-contact person

It can be hard to offer a quality service to clients if you do not yourself feel valued within the service. The task of some first-contact workers is made more difficult by being poorly appreciated by the rest of the team.

There are several ways that a helping service can show that the first-contact person is valued:

- Consider what the first-contact people are called. Do they have a job title and in what way does it affirm their importance to the service?
- Ensure that the front person is part of the team, involved in team meetings and with his or her experience clearly valued.
- Nobody in the team should push the front person into inappropriate gatekeeping or dishonesty, for instance, saying someone is out of the office when she or he is in.
- Look at how the front person's job is defined. What is the job description on paper and is this how the tasks work out in practice? What are his or her assumed priorities: to help clients, to pass them on as fast as possible, to head off inappropriate inquiries, to prevent exploitation of the service, to protect the 'more important' members of the team?

- Offer help and support to your first-contact staff. Talk with them and listen to what they have learned about clients and how the service works.
- Look at the possibilities for relevant training.

The physical setting

Clients' first impressions are also shaped by what they see and hear as they enter and walk through your building.

- Is your service easy to find: are there notices, arrows and places where clients can easily check for directions? Do clients regularly get lost?
- Is the outside of your building welcoming or unwelcoming? What are the hallways and corridors like? How may clients feel before they even reach you?
- How straightforward is it for clients in wheelchairs or with limited mobility? For clients with young children and buggies? For clients with visual disabilities or clients with limited literacy or fluency in a language other than English?
- If clients have children with them, are the surroundings safe and interesting?

What happens when clients reach your reception area?

- Are the waiting areas comfortable and spacious for the types and numbers of clients that your service usually experiences?
- Do clients have to wait? If so, for how long? How do you explain about waiting and any system of queuing or priorities for how clients are seen?
- How easy is access to the first-contact person? Can you see each other, can you hear without shouting, having to repeat yourself or leaning forward uncomfortably? Is there some level of privacy even to the first contact?
- Is the furniture comfortable and arranged to bring people together rather than form barriers between clients and workers?

Activity

Try walking into your own place of work with fresh eyes, as if you were a new client:

- Is it clear to you where you should go to reach the service?
- How many gatekeepers do you have to pass from the entrance to the building to where the service is located?
- Is there anybody to ask if you are lost or uncertain?
- What strikes you about the setting: decor, posters and other displays, information or warning notices?
- How are clients likely to experience the setting if they have young children with them? How easy is it for clients with physical or visual disabilities?

Issues of security

Personal security may be a real concern for your service. Grills, safety glass, locked internal doors saying 'Staff only' and other such measures may achieve a level of personal security for workers but can give very negative messages to clients. Staff may say, with genuine conviction, that such measures are necessary because of the verbal and physical aggression from a minority of clients in this service. Unfortunately, few services who are concerned about the safety of their staff seem to have considered how the majority of their clients feel.

For example, in our local health centre, there are two windows through which you talk with a receptionist. Each window and the adjacent notice board have an A3-sized notice that states, 'Any patient who is aggressive or abusive to members of staff will be removed from the doctor's list. If necessary we will telephone the police.' There is no additional 'Welcome' notice or 'Thank you to our patients who are courteous'. Nothing in fact that could balance the message that this medical practice expects trouble. Most of the staff working at the practice are friendly and courteous, but the three identical notices undermine this impression. And, as you wait, you have time to count such notices!

Any setting has to achieve a balance between welcome to clients, the safety of service providers and the provision of confidentiality to clients talking with workers. However, the impact on clients is especially bad when poor treatment of clients is combined with physical surroundings and notices suggesting that all clients are a potential threat. Certainly, some settings, coupled with the behaviour of the front-line staff, almost invite clients to become awkward and argumentative.

To think about

There is a good parallel in the substantial measures taken by stores against shoplifters. Theft is undoubtedly an issue for shops. However, little consideration seems to be given to the impact of security guards, video surveillance and anti-theft devices upon the many customers who are not thieves. Everyone is treated as a potential criminal.

3.2 Positive short exchanges

A positive working relationship can be developed with clients even if you only have brief, one-off exchanges, rather than undertaking more extended work.

Be realistic

It is essential that short contacts are seen positively and that you look at your work from what you can do ('half-full bottle') and not from what you cannot ('half-empty'). It is obviously unrealistic to hope to get to know clients very well in a short time. An appropriate goal is that clients should emerge from every short exchange with something extra, that your contribution should make a small difference. That difference may be in terms of:

- Clients feeling welcome here, with every right to seek advice or help.
- Empathy for the client's tiring and frustrating search for help so far.
- A friendly face and a listening ear to guide clients to what may be of help.
- A specific referral to someone who will directly be able to help.
- Useful direct information or a positive lead to someone or somewhere else.

Find out what clients want

Positive short exchanges with clients use all the communication skills discussed in Chapter 2. Effective use of attention, questions and reflective listening will enable you to treat clients as individuals, avoiding assumptions about what clients want, need or already know. Even in a short exchange, your aim is to keep the conversation relatively open and exploratory, to avoid foreclosing on the client's expression of needs and concerns. Swift conclusions on your part can only be based on assumptions about this client or this 'type' of client or in pushing clients towards the range of services that your organisation has to offer.

The information about your service needs to be clear, through conversation and any supporting written material. The possibilities and options need to be discussed with a client in such a way that he or she can make an informed decision about what this means. If your service can meet this client's needs, then explain how and in what way and move on to the practicalities of how the client can take advantage of information, advice or help.

Perhaps you can meet part of what the client wants, but not all. You can still approach the situation positively by explaining:

- What you can offer, if the client wishes to take up on it.
- What you understand the client is seeking that is not covered in your service. However, the client may find help from another (named) organisation, helpline or individual.
- That you can refer the client directly to another person or organisation. (See page 87.)

Be personal

Use your name

It is hard to offer a personal helping service if you do not use your name.

- If the first face-to-face contact is very short, then it may not make sense to introduce yourself to a client personally. You can have your name easy for them to see on a name badge or nameplate.
- Society is generally less formal now than in previous decades, so it is most likely that you would give your personal name, with or without your surname.
- If your service works partly or wholly over the telephone, then consider whether the first-contact person, and subsequent workers with the client, offer a name. It could be standard practice that anyone who is on telephone duty gives not only the name of the organisation but also his or her own name.
- Sometimes it will make sense to offer or to repeat your name at the end of a short exchange, for instance, 'My name is Nneka. Please ask for me if you have any other questions.'
- Be prepared to say your own name more than once for clients who find it unfamiliar.

Use the client's name

In many circumstances, you will need to find out and use the client's name. Some practical issues arise about formal or more informal ways of addressing clients:

- Your organisation may be informal, but you should respect a client's expressed wish to be known more formally, as Mr or Mrs, if that is their preference. Some clients may introduce themselves as 'Miss Brewster', which suggests they might prefer a more formal mode of address. You should follow the client's lead.
- Some social and cultural groups may find an unchecked use of the personal name as discourteous. Additionally, some retired people within the older generation in Britain have lived and worked at a time when first names were not usually exchanged, except between friends. If you use their personal name without asking, older clients may feel that you are being presumptuous.
- If someone gives their name as 'Carol Brewster' or 'Miss Carol Brewster', you can ask, 'May I call you Carol?', or start by calling the client 'Miss Brewster' and wait to be invited to use her first name. It is unlikely to be felt as courteous to the client if you ask a leading closed question such as, 'It's fine to call you Carol, isn't it?'
- There is an essential inequality in a service that addresses the clients by their first name, but the workers more formally. For instance, medical services have a rarely questioned tradition of calling patients by their first name, but doctors as 'Dr Yousuf' or consultants as 'Mr O'Donnell'. As a client, it is hard not to feel that such a practice puts you in an inferior position as a patient.
- Be very cautious about calling clients 'dear' or 'my dear'. Some clients do not mind these terms and may even address you in this way. However, other clients will find it patronising, especially if females are called 'dear' and male clients addressed by their proper names.

To think about

There are different possible ways of asking for a client's name. Which of the following options might be better under different circumstances or in your own service? Are there any options that would be discourteous with any client group?

- 'My name is Ben and you are . . . ?'
- 'Name?'
- 'Could I ask your name, please?'
- 'And who might you be?'
- 'I'd like to check your name now.'
- 'And you are?'
- 'Have I got your name?'
- 'Do you have a name?'
- 'What's the name please?'
- 'How about telling me who you are?'
- 'Who are you?'
- 'What was your name again?'

Use of the client's name adds a personal touch, so long as it is not repeated a great deal, because this can create a sense of personal intrusion and be overfamiliar. Names also should not be used to emphasise a criticism of the client, for instance, 'Now, Gaby, you started this problem, didn't you?' Nor should names be repeated in a patronising way, for instance, 'Daniel, Daniel, I don't think you're listening to what I'm telling you.'

Uncertainty about names

When names are less familiar to you, ask rather than assume. You may have to ask clients how to pronounce their name and spell it. Ask courteously. This is far better than to continue saying the client's name wrongly, a pattern which will annoy people. Clients' names should never be described as 'odd' or 'difficult'. View the situation as one in which you find the name unusual or are having difficulties with pronunciation or spelling.

In work with families, bear in mind that every member of the family does not necessarily share the same surname. Partners may not be married, married women may not have chosen to change their surname, children may take either parent's surname and stepfamilies may have several names. If in doubt, ask, 'Do you all share the same surname?', or, 'May I ask, is Malcolm's surname Carpenter as well?'

The Western naming system of first name followed by more optional personal names and finally by a surname is not a universal system by any means. If you are in doubt, ask the client, 'Can I check please? Is this your personal name?', or, 'I'm not sure which is your family name.' The box below gives some examples.

Some examples of naming systems

- Traditionally in Britain women have taken their husband's surname on marriage. In contrast, several mainland European countries have the tradition of making a double-barrelled family name from the two surnames.
- Chinese and Vietnamese tradition is to have a family name first, then a generation name, followed by the individual's personal name.
- Sikh and Muslim families do not traditionally have a surname, nor do some African ethnic groups. However, families sometimes take on a chosen surname to make life easier within Britain.
- Muslim males have a religious name, which often but not always comes before the personal or calling name. The family name is last.
- In Britain the use of the term 'Christian name' for people's personal name is the consequence of a cultural tradition of christening babies that arose from religious practice in some parts of the Christian faith. In a multifaith society it is more accurate to refer to 'personal' names.

Use of written material

All clients will not be equally confident in reading or writing. Dyslexic clients need longer to handle written material and may appreciate some help. Clients who are not dyslexic may still be uneasy with written material. A proportion of people emerge from their education with a limited grasp of reading and writing and a serious lack of confidence when trying to use their skills.

It would be unwise to approach all clients with the expectation that they will have difficulties with reading. However, you should be alert to signs that a client is not happy about completing paperwork. Young people may feel more confident to say, 'I'm dyslexic. It'll take me time to read this.' Older clients may have experienced schooling at a time when literacy difficulties were more often blamed on the child and adults can still be ashamed of their difficulties. You can offer help in a sensitive way:

- 'Would you like me to go through the form with you?' is a more positive question than 'Do you know how to fill in the form?'
- 'Shall I read it out to you?' could be the reply to a strategy of 'I haven't got my glasses', sometimes used by adults with reading difficulties. Of course, a short-sighted person may actually have forgotten his or her spectacles.
- It will sometimes be possible to offer, 'You're welcome to take the form [or leaflet] away with you.' This response may be appropriate when a client says, 'My wife does all the paperwork in our family.' This comment may be true, but again is a strategy used by some adults who have trouble with reading and writing.

Endings

You need a proper closure even to a short exchange. Clients should never be left standing at a window or sitting looking at you, because they are not aware that as far as you are concerned the exchange is complete. You and the client need to finish at the same time and you can help this process:

- As the conversation moves to what feels like a close, you might ask, 'Is there anything else I can help you with?', or, 'Have we covered all you would like to know about . . . ?'
- Your closing words might be, 'Thanks for coming to see us', or, 'Please call again if we can help.'
- If you have not been able directly to help the client, you might say, 'I hope that Sergio at the Careers Advice Office [your suggested and named organisation or individual] will be able to give you more information', or, 'I think you'll find the telephone helpline [named] will have some practical suggestions about how to help your child.'
- Leave clients with the option to take up your suggestions or not; it is their choice. So avoid the pressure of, 'You will call Sergio, won't you', or, 'Don't forget to call the helpline.'
- It is wise to avoid standard ending phrases as much as standard greetings. They are unlikely to sound genuine.

- If it feels appropriate, then say, 'Thank you for coming in', or, 'I'm glad you were able to drop by.' Say 'Goodbye', 'See you again' or 'All the best with . . .' as appropriate.

3.3 Dealing with mistakes and complaints

All helping services need clear guidelines on how everyone should deal with common problems or difficulties.

Take preventative action

Positive effort within a service can avoid complaints that need never have arisen or can prevent some developing from a minor irritation into something more serious:

- Be clear about what your service or organisation offers and, just as important, what it does not. At least some problems arise because callers have been given the wrong impression. The problem might be as simple as the belief that your publications are free when they are not.
- Ensure that commitments to a caller or personal visitor that 'someone will get back to you' are honoured. Your first-contact person should make a note and ensure that the request is passed on properly.
- If you have the opportunity, deal with problems early rather than letting them grow. Many people who are dissatisfied are still willing to accept an explanation. Dismissive or discourteous treatment pushes the most tolerant client towards serious complaint.
- Brief and train the whole team to understand the importance of courtesy and good communication skills with clients.

Courteous communication

Listen

The best approach to difficult situations with clients is to hear what they have to say:

- Attend fully to clients and listen to what they want to tell you. Show courtesy and respect.
- Avoid redirecting them immediately, especially if they obviously want to talk with you. Clients may need to clarify their problem.
- Respect their right to tell you as much or as little as they want. Use open-ended questions to help you to understand the nature of the problem. You might ask, 'What happened?', 'Please tell me how things went wrong', or just, 'Tell me about it.'
- Make sure that you understand the nature of the problem from the client's point of view. You certainly do not have to agree with the complaint itself and it is unhelpful to start to justify the actions of your organisation.
- If you need to pass the client on to someone else, summarise the problem for your colleague, so that the client does not have to repeat everything.

Acknowledge feelings

Many clients, who want you to acknowledge that something has gone wrong, are not angry. They may be frustrated, puzzled or disappointed in a service that they had trusted. Clients may be ready to give you the benefit of the doubt, anxious about raising the issue or confident that you can resolve the problem once you know what has gone wrong.

Your role is to listen to clients' feelings and watch the messages of their body language. Make sure that you have recognised the expressed feelings. It is not your role to agree or disagree with what clients feel or the strength of the feelings. You can show empathy with clients' feelings by comments like:

- 'I appreciate that you want this mistake put right.'
- 'I do understand that cancelled appointments disrupt your arrangements.'
- 'I can see that this has made life very difficult for you.'
- 'I realise that you are very fed up about this whole business.'
- 'I understand how disappointed you are.'
- 'I can hear that you feel strongly about . . .'.

Be cautious about using words to label clients' feelings that they have not used themselves. It is better to reflect back the same or very similar words and phrases. For example, a client who has said, 'I'm very concerned about . . .' is unlikely to appreciate being told that she or he is 'cross' or 'upset'.

Even relatively calm clients, who are ready to listen to you, will become irritated if their feelings are ignored. They will think you are rude if you use dismissive phrases like, 'You don't really mean that', 'You're only saying that because you're upset', or the patronising, 'Don't you think you're making too much of all this?' Even if clients are agitated, you should avoid blunt demands that clients 'should calm down' or, 'Don't raise your voice to me.' Remain calm yourself and keep your voice steady and low. Summarise the client's feelings to show that you have heard. (See also page 138.)

Take appropriate responsibility and action

Make sure that you get a clear sense of what the client would like to have happen now. Clients are not particularly interested in your rules and system, your problems with the computer or other organisations who have let you down. Clients are interested in their concerns and problems and this is a very reasonable perspective for them to take. They want to know what you are going to do for them, not what other people have failed to do for you:

- Give clients information that is appropriate to how you will now help. They want to hear, 'I appreciate that you want your name spelled correctly on any letters. I'll follow this up with the person responsible', rather than, 'It's on the computer, it's all so complicated and they only put in corrections once a month.'
- Explain what you can do, or what you can now do through consulting someone else. Do not make promises, for yourself, or on behalf of colleagues, that may not be kept. Offer something that can be done and not a list of what you cannot do.

- If the person wants to take a complaint further, then explain their options and give the relevant written material for your organisation.
- Make a written note of the complaint, if appropriate. All services and organisations should monitor complaints or problems since patterns may show you how to improve the service.

It is wise to avoid routine and formula responses to clients at any stage, whether in face-to-face communication or over the telephone. Like any communication, an exchange dealing with a problem or complaint needs a closure, but clients will not feel personally treated if they realise that everyone is given an identical last sentence. Much like greetings (see page 55), you need a number of different ways, appropriate to this client, in which to bring the exchange to an end. Depending on the circumstance, you might say:

- 'I'm glad you told us about . . .'.
- 'We'd much rather know when something has gone wrong.'
- 'Thanks for letting me put this right.'
- 'I'll get back to you before the end of the week with an answer on . . .'.
- 'I will speak to you again on Friday about . . .'.
- 'Again, I would like to say sorry about . . .'.

Activity

Think about a recent experience when you have been dissatisfied with service of any kind.

- In what ways was your complaint handled well or handled poorly?
- What did you want as a result of someone hearing your complaint?
- How could your treatment have been improved and what lessons can you take for your own service?

Individual differences between clients

People complain in different ways and they have learned these behaviours:

- Some clients will complain quietly, especially if they realise that you are ready to listen. However, even clients who prefer to be courteous will have a breaking point if they are treated rudely.
- Some clients start at a loud and confrontational level. They believe that aggression is the best approach, or may have no idea how to complain in any other way. They may turn their complaint into a personal attack on you but you should not retaliate with personal remarks in return.
- On the other hand, some clients may be unduly apologetic. They may understate their concern, say they do not want to make a fuss or create any trouble. However, what they have to say may be very important to your service or part of it, as well as to themselves. Unless you listen and follow up, you may miss a serious issue or alternatively leave such clients with a problem that worsens.
- Occasionally, clients continually change their story or seem to mislead. You can deal with this situation by comments like, 'Mr Jones, I heard you say . . .

and then I heard you say . . . Which is correct, please?' Avoid the challenge of saying 'You're lying.'

- You are a representative of your service, so it is inappropriate to push the complaint away with 'I didn't do this' or 'Why are you blaming me?' You are not accepting personal responsibility for what happened; you accept responsibility on behalf of your organisation to deal with the problem now.
- Focus on the facts of the complaint and acknowledge the underlying message. You might ask questions like, 'What leads you to say that?', or, 'What exactly went wrong?'

Activity

- Select a number of complaints or problems that arise within your service and consider the best and worst ways of handling them.
- Practise some common scenarios with a partner and listen to constructive feedback on how you behave and sound.
- How might you improve how you react to complaints – both as an individual and the service as a whole?

A system for complaints

Clients will not always want to make a formal complaint. Most people with a grievance want someone to listen to them and to have their concerns treated with seriousness, not belittled or dismissed. Sometimes people want an apology, which, if appropriate, should be given with genuineness. On some occasions, there will be a solution to the problem. Often people want to be reassured that the same problem will not happen again. If their concern is handled with courtesy and the client feels appropriate action will be taken, the complaint may end at that point.

Services should have different levels of dealing with complaints. However, clients should never be pushed into making a more formal complaint than they wish. For example, clients who want to explain what happened and to have the courtesy of your attention will feel ill-used if their explanations are cut off with, 'You have to put all this in writing.' On the other hand, nobody should be dissuaded from taking their complaint to a higher level when they feel sufficiently strongly about their experience.

Activity

Find out about the general complaints procedures of your service. It should be clear to you and to the clients of your organisation:

- How to get help, if they are dissatisfied with the initial advice, information or decision.
- How to express their dissatisfaction, including how to make a formal complaint.

☑ **4** Sharing information and offering advice

4.1 Information services for clients

The scope of your information service
Possibilities

Providing information may either be the major part of what your organisation offers or just one aspect of a broader service. Helping services can provide information through a number of different channels. Personal callers may be able to:

- Consult with a member of staff.
- Read your information resources in books, articles, leaflets and fact sheets.
- Access the information you have stored in files and databases on the computer.

Clients may also be able to:

- Ask for written material to be sent through the post.
- Ask their questions or request written material by email.
- Seek information over the telephone, perhaps through a dedicated information helpline.
- Consult your service's web site on the Internet.

Quality and appropriateness

Any service needs to ensure the quality of their information:

- Be clear about the nature and boundaries of your service. This understanding will help to shape what kind of material you need available and to identify the gaps in your current information base. You will need to find material to close that gap or you may consider writing some original material (see page 75).
- Be clear about what your clients want and need. Without making restrictive assumptions about your client base, you should be able to pinpoint key features to ensure that information is useful to clients, and that they can and will use it.
- For instance, you may judge accurately that many of the young people who drop in to your service are not enthusiastic readers. So, you will need short fact sheets, lots of graphics and posters with lively informative pictures. Consider a CD-ROM and video displays as a source of information.

You need to ensure the accuracy of any information:

- Make sure that any of the available material is suitable and accurate, including material from outside your service. If it is sitting on your display shelf, or on your mail order list, then clients will feel that you are endorsing the publication – and you are.
- Make sure that at least one person, preferably two, reads any leaflet or book that could go on your shelves, reading list or mail order. Even if books or pamphlets are given to your service, check them before they go on display. You want to be sure both of the accuracy of any information and that it carries a supportive message to your clients.

Updating information

Your range of material needs to be checked on a regular basis to ensure that it is still accurate:

- Information on local or national organisations and services needs to be updated on a regular basis. Organisations change their address and telephone number or add an email address. Contact names change, as can the name of the organisation itself. New useful contacts will develop.
- Fact sheets, information and advice packs should always be dated, so that clients can see how recently the information has been prepared.
- Leaflets or information sheets may have new versions, especially on topics where research and the practical application of new ideas is in a state of change. Handbooks may be revised and you should have the latest edition.
- Resist the temptation to keep old material unless you are confident it is accurate and still used by clients.

The regular updates may be the particular task of one member of the team, but some might also be appropriate for volunteer workers or young people on work experience to complete.

Is the information useful?

Another important way of updating your information base is to ask your clients about its usefulness. This exercise can be part of a more general monitoring of your organisation's work (see page 7). You may be in a position to ask clients directly about the usefulness of the information you have offered or to find out if another recommended service has been of value and in what ways. It is important to:

- Ask more than just a few clients. With reactions from a very small proportion of your client base, you may get views that are biased in the positive or negative direction.
- Explain your reasons for asking: that your aim is to improve the service and not to check up on particular referral agencies or encourage gratitude from your clients.

Activity

- Find out how often and in what ways the information base of your organisation is updated.
- How do you know what is useful for clients? How does your organisation find this information?

Helping clients to access information

Personal callers need a straightforward system of access to material. A small selection might be effectively displayed on an open stand or a table. Even a limited array of leaflets or booklets will benefit from some thought to how you present it to clients:

- Someone may need to tidy the display from time to time.
- It may be useful to put the copies of the different leaflets or sheets into containers so they do not become muddled or torn.
- Consider notices that invite clients with, 'Please take a free leaflet', or, 'Information on careers – please help yourself'.

If you have more than a small range of resources, you need a logical system of organising the material and labelling the different sections to support clients as they browse or look for something in particular. You may have:

- Labelled sections or headings.
- An alphabetical system within sections.
- Logical collections of leaflets or booklets, so that similar material is placed together.
- Clear labels on boxes or files.
- Visual images or pictures that will support a written label. Relevant pictures or graphics can help clients whose eyesight is not sharp for reading or who have limited literacy skills.

Clients need to be able to see the information and be attracted to the idea of browsing. If you have a range of information leaflets to which you refer in conversation, depending on the client's expressed needs, then you need a straightforward system for finding the one(s) you want.

A relevant explanation by a member of staff and clear notices should let clients know:

- Which material they can borrow and which can only be consulted on site.
- Whether leaflets or booklets are free or whether there is a charge and how much.
- Whether they can photocopy material, or print out or download information from the computer, and any cost or restrictions on this service.

Offering direct help to clients

A few leaflets on a table may not need much explanation. Broader information resources will benefit from a positive approach to help clients access the information. Clients should be made to feel welcome because you communicate a sense of generosity and openness with information. It has been collected precisely to be shared with clients. Avoid the idea of the information base as a precious possession to be guarded. Such an outlook can be communicated, not deliberately, by notices like, 'No food and drink in the reading area', or, 'Please do not tear pages out of the magazines', let alone, 'Clients who abuse these facilities will be banned'.

A positive approach

Clients usually welcome clear directions for where they can get help: either a clear sign for the 'help desk' or immediate help from the first member of staff they approach:

- If your service has a help desk or an information officer for personal callers, then make sure that these are easily found and available.
- If you are asked about the information resources and this is not your main responsibility, then respond with, 'I'll find out', or, 'I'll take you to someone who can help you with that.' Clients do not want to hear, 'I don't know', or, 'I'm only a volunteer.'
- Make an active approach to clients who look uncertain. You can offer, 'Would you like some help?', or, 'Can I help you find anything?' If you are uncertain what a client wants, you might start with, 'Have you used our information service before?', or, 'What sort of material are you looking for?'
- Have some written material in the main community languages and, ideally, some bilingual staff.

To think about

Draw on some of your own experiences of asking for information and help, not necessarily in information services:

- For example, how does it feel in your local supermarket or DIY warehouse if you go up to a member of staff to ask the whereabouts of an item and are told, 'It's not my section', or, 'I only work here Saturdays'?
- How does it feel in a large library or other information resource centre to wander about aimlessly, uncertain whom to ask for help?
- What kind of response do you want to your requests for basic help and direction? What would make you pleased or relieved?
- How can you help to bring your service close to the ideal?

Involve clients in the use of the information base and work to boost their confidence and feelings of competence. Your skills can be used to create a feeling of joint problem-solving with the client and not an unequal buzz of being the person with all the answers:

- Be seen to explore with clients what information will be helpful to them, rather than having set packages given out after a very short conversation.

- Ask clients what they feel could be helpful in the context of explaining what you can offer. Offer a range of options to help focus on what they need.
- Often clients will appreciate more help than, 'It's over there', or, 'All you have to do is press a few buttons.' Be ready to show clients how to use displays of pamphlets and what topics are covered in what section.

Limits to literacy

Some clients of your service will have limits to their ability to read and write. They will not necessarily be illiterate but may be what is called aliterate, with a limited ability and confidence with the written word and a low interest in exploring information in this way. See page 68 for some ideas.

Help with computer access

Even clients who are fully computer-literate will appreciate some guidance on what they can access on the computer terminal and in what way. Many clients will need practical help, patience and guidance on the first and perhaps subsequent times when they access files and databases on your computer.

Some clients will be at ease with a computer, but perhaps wary of unfamiliar systems. Some young clients may have a superficial knowledge of computers, but this experience is restricted to a few types of files and plenty of games. Some clients will not know where to start with a keyboard, mouse or screen. Although the schools are now full of computers, and some have their own network, this situation is relatively new. Most adult clients will not have encountered information technology in school. So, unless they have had reason to learn because of their work, clients may be starting from scratch. You can help all clients by clear communication and patience as they learn:

- Explain at a steady pace, but not with patronising slowness, and check on clients' understanding step by step. Be ready to repeat your words and actions.
- Show clients how to get in and around the files and then invite them to try. The combination of 'tell–show–do' is the most effective way of teaching.
- It is unhelpful to lean over someone's shoulder and press buttons yourself or to grab the mouse. Clients will not learn easily under these circumstances and it is an invasion of personal space.
- Boost a wary client's confidence with, 'Well done', 'You're getting the hang of it', or, 'You only forgot the last bit. You remembered everything else.'
- If there are several clients who want to access information through the computer, you could organise a group session.
- Some clients may find it helpful to write down the instructions. Consider making a basic notice of instructions on the location of particular files.

Sharing information in conversation

Sometimes you will make information available to clients through a conversation, either face to face or over the telephone. Good communication skills are covered in Chapter 2, but the main points are summarised here:

- Listen to what clients say and what they ask.
- Avoid assumptions about what clients need to know or are likely to ask about because of their age, gender, ethnic background, apparent social class or any other broad description of them as individuals.
- Answer clients' questions and concerns before you consider exploring what may be related questions or concerns which they have not yet expressed. Resist giving more information than clients want or need.
- Be alert to clients' feelings about asking for help, even for information. They may be concerned that you will think they are asking foolish questions or should know the answers already.
- Sometimes it will be important to explain the consequences of different options to clients: what will most likely happen if they take a particular route or what are the advantages and disadvantages of a course of action. The pros and cons can be especially important to explain with medical decisions but many life options have an element of, 'What will probably happen if . . .', or, 'Does this option effectively close down your taking this other option?'
- Be aware that an individual client may be standing in front of you, but behind what she or he says can be a network of family and friends that matter to the client and may be his or her direct responsibility.

How you share information

You can pass on information to clients in more or less helpful ways.

- Clients are more likely to listen to and be motivated to take in information that addresses the questions that they want to ask.
- If you definitely need to convey new information then it helps to flag up that the conversation is changing direction. You might say, 'If you would like to take that option, then I need to explain this', or, 'I would like to let you know that, if you do . . . , then . . .'.
- Give information to clients in manageable amounts; nobody manages well with a long stream of facts and options.
- Pause and allow the client to comment or ask questions about what you have said. Sometimes it will make sense for you to ask, 'Am I being clear in how I explain?', 'Do you see what I mean?', or, 'What questions would you like to ask me?'

Ask the client appropriate questions

Sometimes you have to ask specific questions in order to give useful information, to guide the client towards the appropriate source of information or to an alternative service:

- You might need to ask, 'How old is your mother now?', 'How is the school trying to help with your son's dyslexia?', or, 'What kind of child care are you looking for?'
- Ask open-ended questions that invite the client to comment. For example, 'How do you feel about that?', 'Does that sound like a possibility?', or, 'How do you think this service might suit your elderly mother?'

- Sometimes clients seek information or advice on behalf of someone else or in order to help them to support a family member or friend. You may have to ask questions to draw out information about another person who is not present in the conversation. Although this information is second-hand, you could still be in a better position to help. You might ask, 'How does your mother feel about attending a day care centre?', or, 'What does your son feel are the main problems that dyslexia creates for him?'

Clients in crisis or distress

You may work within a service where you cannot simply pass on relevant information and leave clients to absorb the impact. For example:

- Health professionals have had to learn a great deal about the inappropriateness of announcing diagnoses to individuals and then leaving, whether this information is about individuals themselves, their children or other people about whom they care deeply.
- Educational services sometimes pass on information about children's learning or behaviour problems without any sense that this communication is more than just information. The emotional impact can be high and has to be recognised by responsible professionals.
- In the 1990s many organisations undertook substantial redundancy exercises, or 'downsizing', with great variety in the consideration and extent of the information and advice services associated with the event. The term 'survivors', used to describe those employees left in the organisation, highlights the power and emotional impact of downsizing.

Clients who are under stress or in shock are not in a receptive state to take in and understand large amounts of information, especially if that information tends to add to their stress and confusion. If you work in an organisation where clients may be under personal stress, then your communication skills need to be fine-tuned to clients' immediate feelings and their ability to hear and understand. Some possibilities are:

- Keeping information in small amounts, so that clients have time to take in the facts and ask questions if they wish.
- Not trying to press information and understanding beyond the point where clients can cope. Offer a chance for them to return in the near future. You can explain with, 'In this situation, people often think of questions to ask later on. Please call me if you would like', or, 'I would be happy to talk it through with you again, or to answer any questions'.
- Being sensitive to clients and their dignity. They may wish to show their distress in private. But do not use their discomfort as an excuse to leave, or bustle about producing tea or glasses of water. You need to attend well to the client and be ready to ask, if it seems likely, 'Would you rather be alone for a while?', or, 'Would you and your partner like some time together and then we can talk some more?'
- Showing clients, even those you do not know very well, a calm presence. You can be supportive without claiming to know more about their feelings than is

possible. You might say with consideration, 'I appreciate this may be hard to take in', or, 'I do understand that news like this can be a shock.' Adjust what you say to the situation, the client(s) and the information that you have given.

- Avoiding set phrases of sympathy or condolence. If you say almost exactly the same words to all clients, the phrase will soon sound like a cliché, empty of genuine feeling.
- Being aware that clients may not share important information with you, if they are still coming to terms with bad news or have been unable to accept a diagnosis of disability or serious illness for them or somebody about whom they care a great deal.

When information is very unwelcome or a shock, clients may grasp at one bit of what has been said. The possibilities for misunderstanding then multiply. For instance, a surgeon who lacks confidence in dealing with 'patients' as real people with feelings may stress that 'the operation was a success'. This apparently positive message may hide the more important communication that, 'I have removed the cancer in your breast, but I am sorry to say that it has moved into your lymphatic system.' Sometimes, information must include an honest admission of ignorance. One of us was told the case of the parents of a blind child informed by a consultant, that, 'There is nothing physically wrong with your son's eyes.' They took this to mean that the child's sight would improve with time. In fact, the specialist meant that he could find nothing damaged in the physical apparatus of the eyes. It was a confused way of admitting, 'I don't know why your son is blind.'

4.2 Writing your own material

Newsletters, flyers or posters are part of the public image of your organisation and also an important way to inform potential clients or anyone who refers clients. It is worth taking time and care, so that the end result gives an accurate and positive image of your service. Some resources will be written and published by other organisations or individuals. However, you may need to write original material of your own.

Planning a publication

You need to plan in detail, with the help of colleagues, the aim and content of any publication. If you have sole responsibility for the writing then make sure that you consult with colleagues and ask for feedback on your drafts.

The basic information

What do you want to say in this leaflet, fact sheet or poster?

- What are the main messages you want to include? What do you want readers of the leaflet or someone who looks at your poster to take away in their mind? Unless you are clear about your five or six main points, then you will not draft them clearly.

a

**Helping Young
People cope with
Divorce or
Separation**

RELATEEN
A Project of Basingstoke Relate
Chute House, Church Street, Basingstoke, Hants, RG21 7QT

b

RNIB Helpline
0345-66 99 99

Information, support and advice for
anyone with a serious sight problem.

We can:

● put you in touch with specialist
  advice services

● send you free information
  and leaflets

● give you details of support groups
  and services in your area

**If you or someone you know has a
serious sight problem, RNIB can help.**

Call Monday to Friday 9.00am - 5.00pm.
Calls charged at local rates.

All calls treated in confidence.

Royal National Institute for the Blind   R N I B

c

- You can think about the content in terms of what must go into this publication and what you and your colleagues would like to go in if there is space.

Your readers

Whom do you want to notice and read your publication?

- Are you clear about the groups of people with whom you wish to make contact through the written medium?
- Is this a leaflet for clients who have already made contact with your organisation, one that needs to reach potential clients, or both?
- What are the implications for the level of language in the publication, the kind of examples or appropriate illustrations?
- What do you want your readers to notice? What would you like them to believe or feel about your service?

Any practical limitations

You need to know the budget for this publication. Financial limits will affect whether you can use colour printing, how many pages, the quality of paper, illustrations or how many copies can be made.

Although any organisation has to operate within the limits of its budget, it is worth noting that the general public has expectations about the quality and readability of any written material. Especially now that good quality print can be produced from a personal computer, clients are unlikely to be impressed with badly photocopied information sheets or leaflets that are full of spelling mistakes. All materials affect the public's view of your service.

The content

Clear messages

Your leaflets should describe the service you offer in everyday language. Information booklets or fact sheets should be written clearly and simply.

- Most areas of expertise have some shared professional language. The words and phrases used regularly in discussion may seem ordinary to you and your colleagues. However, not all of these are used between people who do not share your background.
- Material for clients should be straightforward to read. It often helps to imagine that you are talking with clients and be guided by spoken language more than a more formal written style.
- Watch out for clichés and buzz words. The general public is familiar with organisational claims that 'We care' or 'We listen to you' and has become cynical. Avoid generalities and be specific about what your service offers.
- Use headings and bullet points to break up text and guide readers through different parts of the content. Keep sentences and paragraphs relatively short, so that the information or explanations are clear.

Choices

Your budget may limit more expensive ideas that you would like to implement but still aim for the best quality affordable.

- There will be choices about the quality of paper. Choose one that is not too thin and consider the colour and texture.
- Can you produce something in-house with word processing or desk top publishing software or will you need a commercial printer?
- Will colour printing be an advantage?
- If you have a budget for illustrations, then choose appropriate images that will support your messages. Any illustration should add to your publication and not be used just to break up text. Some illustrations will need a caption.
- Photographs or line drawings should be consistent with the image of your organisation, as well as sometimes being a means to reach out to new client groups. For instance, perhaps your service is more heavily used by particular age groups or ethnic groups. Without being misleading, your illustrations could send the message, 'We're here for you too.'

Be careful about the match between content and illustrations:

- Amusing cartoons can be suitable for a leaflet about healthy eating but are inappropriate for a booklet about coping with bereavement.
- Clip art that comes with popular software such as Microsoft Office may be easy to access but some images are seen so often that they risk becoming visual clichés.
- Eye-catching images on the cover of a leaflet may grab clients' attention but will confuse the message if the images are inconsistent with the content.

Draft and redraft

Thorough planning at an early stage will ensure that your first draft covers the points that must go into the publication and subsequent drafts can focus on style and other features. It is a truism that you cannot improve a first draft until it is actually written. Somebody has to put pen to paper or fingers to the keyboard. However, it is very unlikely that a first draft will go forward unchanged. Good leaflets and booklets typically have several drafts before everyone judges that the message is clear and accurate. The first writer may work on future drafts but other opinions should also be invited.

Feedback from colleagues can be helpful so long as it is specific and constructive. A comment like 'This leaflet is confused' is less helpful than 'I can't understand this section' or 'There seem to be two possible meanings to this sentence.' The criticism of 'Needs more information' or 'Not very user-friendly' is far less use than 'We need something on opening times' or 'I think our clients will be confused by words like "agencies" or "quality assurance".'

Feedback from clients

It is worth asking for the opinions of some of your clients at the planning and drafting stage. Having experience of using your service, clients are well-placed to offer informed comments from their perspective.

- On a leaflet about your service, clients might suggest, 'You really ought to explain the difference between your drop-in advice sessions and the appointments part', or, 'Perhaps you could have some older women in the illustrations. I nearly didn't come because I thought that you only saw teenagers and young women.'
- On a booklet about activities to support young children's play and learning, a client may suggest, 'You keep going on and on about how this is "fun" with your child. That's true enough, but I think you should admit to some of the difficulties. What if you're tired, what if you've got older children who want you? Be realistic.'

If they have the time and are willing to make comments, clients can give you useful insights about use of language in a booklet and sections which are muddled from a client's viewpoint, even though they seem clear to you.

Final checks

A useful check on a final draft is to read it out loud, either to yourself or in a group of colleagues. If you read silently, it is possible to miss oddities of language. Once you say the words aloud, you hear the slightly odd phrase, pick up any repeated words or phrases and directly experience a very long sentence, as you struggle to make it through without taking a breath.

Ensure that any written material, however long or short, is thoroughly proof-read. Drafts on a computer can be spell-checked, but the word processing package will not tell you that your correctly spelled word does not carry your intended meaning. It may just be the difference between 'form' and 'from', but it could be the more serious difference between 'public' and 'pubic'. Proof-reading is also necessary to pick up any factual inaccuracies. For instance, your computer will not tell you that the opening times for your service are wrong. Read posters very carefully and ideally have more than one person do this checking. Spelling errors make written material look sloppy and some mistakes can create real embarrassment.

Different versions

Some material may be suitable for different subgroups of clients, but you are aware that it should be expressed in different ways. With care, it is possible to tailor the same basic information and key messages for different readers. You will find a very effective example in material from the Child Accident Prevention Trust. CAPT undertook a study into the emotional after-effects of accidents to children. The project team wrote up their findings in four different practical booklets: for children under 8 years, for children and young people over 8 years, advice for parents and carers and a set of guidelines for professionals. Contact CAPT at 18–20 Farringdon Lane, London EC1R 3HA. Tel: 0207 608 3828. Fax: 0207 608 3674. Email: safe@capt.demon.co.uk.

Different languages

Ideally, any written material would be produced in the languages spoken and written within the population of your potential clients. However, this task requires thought and planning as it is not simply a matter of translation. It is unwise to distribute leaflets or posters about your service in a number of different languages unless you are able to offer these languages within your service. If you offer telephone help or face-to-face counselling, make sure that you do not imply this service is available in any more languages than you can genuinely offer within your team. If your service offers further written information, then it should be readily available in the languages into which any general leaflet has been translated.

Review and reprints

The costs of commercial printing mean that it would be unwise to change these written materials frequently. When your organisation is running low on leaflets or posters is a sensible time to review whether the written content needs changing. Material developed on your in-house computer can be revised and printed on a more regular basis.

Activity

1 Look with a fresh eye at any written material that is produced by your own organisation.
   ● Is it really clear to people outside your area of work? Ask for the reactions of friends or family.
   ● Helpful leaflets are concise whereas long and wordy material tends not to be read in its entirety. Is your material about the right length?
2 Send off for some free material or information leaflets from several organisations that are in a different area of helping to your own.
   ● How clear is the material to you? Are there areas which you find confusing?
   ● What lessons could be learned by your own organisation?

4.3 Electronic communications

Many helping organisations now consider electronic communications within their service. There are several possibilities:

● An email address, as well as a telephone and fax number, for handling questions and requests for information.
● On-line Internet discussion groups relevant to topics covered by the service. This option is more of a possibility if your service has a very clear focus of concern.
● A web site dedicated to the concern of your service.

Using computer technology in these ways is a reality for some potential users of your service. However, it is easy to overlook the fact that many people still have no access to a computer, at home or at work. Many home computers are old systems or do not have an Internet link. Although your organisation might consider these possibilities, communication and information search via computer is certainly not taking over from personal contact by telephone or face to face. Electronic communication is an addition and not a replacement.

Use of email

Your organisation may already deal with enquiries by post, so offering an email address may seem a natural addition to the service. However, you should only add this option to your Information service with a clear understanding of the practical details involved.

Increased pressure to respond?

Your service does not want to raise expectations beyond your ability to reply:

- If your organisation is funded only to offer a service to a particular group of people or in a limited geographical area, then make this clear in your publicity information.
- You may not know whether an email address will bring in a significantly increased number of queries. You could contact an organisation similar to your own which has offered email, and ask how their enquiries increased.
- In some ways, email is a natural extension to seeking information or advice by letter. However, people who use email on a regular basis tend to expect a prompt reply, faster than they would expect a reply through conventional post. They may work in organisations where it is usual for email to be checked and a reply sent within a day. Unless your service has the staff to answer all emails promptly, you should let clients know the likely delay in your publicity material.
- Alternatively, you can use an email facility with auto-reply. Use a wording that thanks senders for their mail and indicates when they can expect a reply.

Confidentiality

Many points from page 10 about confidentiality also apply to email but additional practical points arise.

- Many users regard email as part of a confidential system, rather like a private conversation. On the contrary, email can be fairly public. If enquirers email from their place of work, colleagues may be able to access their mail, perhaps not with any intention to pry.
- Email service providers sometimes store past emails, although not in a very obvious file, and not on your computer. The sender may assume wrongly that the email has been completely deleted.
- Some helping organisations offer information and advice on highly personal issues and senders may need confidentiality. Then you can suggest that

enquirers email you with their name and address for further contact, but do not recount personal details and experiences within the email itself.

- Emails can be tagged with levels of urgency or confidentiality. However, this facility helps to inform the recipient but does not offer greater security.
- Emails that fall outside the scope of your own service should never simply be passed on. Check with clients for permission to redirect the mail or suggest an alternative contact or service directly to them.
- As well as conventional email, it is possible to use a system that removes the emailer's address. The communication between enquirer and service passes through a third party on the Internet. The Samaritans, for instance, offer the option of ordinary email or an anonymous system.
- Services need to develop a system for who deals with emails. Access should be carefully considered and can be restricted by use of passwords to establish different access levels for computers within a network.
- Make sure that you have a regularly updated virus checker on your organisation's computers that operates automatically on start-up. Viruses can be transmitted from infected discs and from electronic transfer. So, viruses cannot pass between computers just with email, but they can be imported with files attached to the email.

Using the internet

Some organisations are wary of using the Internet because of the threat of hackers. Unauthorised entry in computer systems and files is an issue, but the risks can be overstated. Steps taken within your organisation about confidentiality, for instance passwords, can help to protect against intrusion. You can also consult your Internet Service Provider about the measures they can offer. It is possible to become too concerned about hackers. After all ordinary telephone lines are not completely secure and apparently private face-to-face conversations are sometimes overheard.

The world wide web

A web site is a permanent location on the Internet where people can go to read information about a given topic. Web sites can be accessible to anyone who has an Internet link, either of their own or through buying time on a computer, for instance, in a public library. Some helping organisations have started to use this facility on the Internet to promote their service. You may reach an increased number of interested callers without having to take on more people to answer telephones or post out fact sheets.

The first page of a web site is called the home page. This page gives information about your organisation: what you do and how to contact you by email, address or telephone. The pages following the home page can be used to give further information about your organisation, extracts from any of your publications, updates on issues that affect clients of your service and links to other web sites. This information should meet the same standards as any other service that you offer:

- A web site needs to be updated on a very regular basis and it is good practice to show the date when you last updated the site. An old web site will give a poor impression of your service. So, it needs to be clear who, in your organisation, is responsible for the web site. This person is called the Site Editor.
- Internet information can be downloaded and printed out. In the process, users may change what is written, so it is useful to include a disclaimer on the site that the organisation cannot guarantee the accuracy of information that has been downloaded.
- Make sure that your professional indemnity insurance covers the Internet. You are providing a service of information and possibly advice, or implied advice.

Web sites can be made more or less difficult for visually disabled users. For instance, moving images or flashing graphics can be hard for Internet users with visual disabilities. The Royal National Institute for the Blind has a web site that explains how to design an accessible site. Contact the RNIB on http://www.rnib.org.uk.

Discussion groups

The Internet offers a great variety of on-line groups and some helping organisations have set up discussion or news groups. Some groups are set up primarily for professionals within a field to communicate but many are for service users to exchange information and ideas. Some operate like a self-help support group in virtual space. If a group is established under your service's name, you may wish to organise it with a moderator, which vets contributions before they reach the discussion site. This system can block misleading information entering the group. If your discussion group allows free access, it will be important to post a notice to the effect that your organisation is not responsible for the accuracy of all the information or ideas exchanged.

An internet search

You can use the facilities to search out information in the same way as you consult books, journals and individuals. You may be able to extend your knowledge base and track down new ideas that become part of your service. Do not simply trust information from the Internet; double-check as you would for any other source of data.

Further information

Use of the Internet is likely to grow for helping services. Some organisations, whose main form of help is over the telephone, have already developed services on the Internet. For further information and some very practical suggestions, consult *The Internet guidelines for helplines* (1998) from the Telephone Helplines Association, 51 Grays Inn Road, London WC1X 8LT.

4.4 From information to advice

The boundary between information and advice

It is not always easy to draw the line between a service that offers only information and one that also gives advice. Some helping organisations offer a service in which information is made available and clients are helped to access that information but clients are left to use the information as they wish. Some services judged it would be irresponsible to offer clients only information with no further guidance. Two examples are:

- The careers guidance service for young people takes the approach that clients will need some active help on how to use the substantial resources on further education, training and careers options.
- Some helping organisations concerned with health issues have also developed an advice service. For instance, organisations for clients who are HIV-positive or who have developed Aids take the approach that clients need active guidance on their options and what these will mean.

The policy decision to move towards advice rather than information services should not be left to individual workers. A whole service or organisation needs a clear and agreed framework for how all its team should operate. When the philosophy of a service leads to some kinds of advice and precludes other options, the organisation must state this bias honestly and publicly. For instance, a support service for young women uncertain about their pregnancy should not imply that all options will be considered, if the avowed aim of the service is to persuade clients to continue the pregnancy rather than consider abortion.

Responsible advice

In practice there is often a shifting balance between giving information and giving advice. You need to be clear where you are in a helping relationship with clients and alert them when you are moving beyond information to advice. You might say:

- 'If you take that route, I'd like to explain what comes next.'
- 'The usual consequences of taking that option are . . .'.
- 'This alternative is unlikely to be possible, unless you also . . .'.
- 'This possibility won't go easily with what you said earlier about . . . Would you like to talk that through a bit?'
- 'If you want to consider that . . . it almost certainly means that you'd have to . . .'.
- 'Sometimes people don't fully realise what . . . means. Can I explain please.'

In none of these possibilities are you necessarily directing a client in one direction or another. You are not saying to clients 'you should' or 'you ought not to' in terms of what they finally decide to do. You are advising them how to think further, to consider more broadly the likely consequences of their actions. For example:

- A parent may be very disappointed that her child has not been accepted by her first choice of school. You can share the information that the parent can make an appeal and how this is done. As well as giving the parent relevant forms or contact addresses, you might also explain that parents who have made successful appeals have spent some time thinking through their case and writing a persuasive argument. Your contribution to the conversation is close to advice in that you alert a parent, who believes the process is simple, to what is really involved in an educational appeal.
- Responsible health information often needs to be blended with advice, so that clients can make informed decisions. You might offer a client, with a serious and possibly terminal health condition, the available information about possible treatments. However, you must also balance this with honest information about the likely impact, short-term and long-term, of these alternatives, from the best knowledge of you and your service. The client may need to be alerted to the possibility that experimental treatments have unpleasant side-effects. Clients who continue to think in terms of possible cure may need advice that helps them to consider the quality of their remaining months.
- A school or sixth form college careers officer can share information with students about the gap year between A levels and taking up a university place. The officer might explain how applications work with a gap year and that the majority of departments are now favourable to the idea. However, advice would also be appropriate so that students understand that their required personal statement on the UCAS application should give positive reasons for postponing university entry. Young people studying Maths and Physics should also be advised that these departments do not look positively on students who want a gap year, because apparently students in these subjects are seen to 'go off the boil'.

Activity

- Note down some examples from your own service that illustrate the difference between giving information and giving advice to clients.
- In what ways do you take care about responsible advice and leaving the choice or decision up to clients?

Clients make a final choice

The final decision must rest with the client. Helping services are not in the business of telling clients what to do. It has to remain the clients' choice as they have to live with the consequences of their decisions. Clients' friends and family can be considerably less inhibited about telling and directing; they do not share your obligation to be impartial. Understandably some clients will push you to tell them what to do and to go several steps beyond advice. You may be pressured with, 'Do you think I should . . . ?', 'What do you think I ought to do?', or, 'Come on! What would you do in my position?' There are several positive approaches to this kind of pressure. For instance:

- 'I appreciate that this cannot be a simple decision. You are weighing up . . . against . . .'.
- 'Perhaps you need to consider what matters most to you . . . the chance to . . . or the possibility that . . .'.
- 'I may be able to help if we go through your options together. Shall we do that?'
- Some clients appreciate the logical approach of 'Let's take each possibility in turn and see what's on the plus and the minus side for each one.'
- Some clients respond better to comments like, 'What feels like the better option to you?'
- Sometimes it is helpful to explain, 'My role isn't to tell you what to do, but I will help you all I can to think through your decision.'

Inexperienced helpers can be tempted to offer clients quick solutions, but responsible advice involves listening or showing respect for what clients have tried already. Telling clients what they should do is rarely helpful. For example, parents of wakeful children are often on the receiving of blunt 'do this' prescriptions. Specialist sleep clinics, rather like clinics for enuresis (older children's inability to become toilet-trained) often offer the first time that anyone has really listened to the parents and worked towards advice that is realistic and respectful.

Advice by letter

Before the telephone, people often sought advice from friends and relatives through letters. There is also a tradition of problem pages in newspapers and magazines stretching back to Victorian times. Many helping organisations respond to requests for information through the post but a few, for instance, Cruse in its work with bereaved clients, offer a facility for exchange of letters. Asking for and receiving advice by letter can be especially appropriate:

- For clients living in sparsely populated parts of the country, where there is no realistic way to offer face-to-face conversations.
- When clients prefer the medium of a letter. They can start, write and complete a letter at times convenient to them. They can think about what they write, without the sense of having to reply instantly that even a sensitive telephone conversation can create. A letter can be put to one side for a while, but clients might feel that they will not easily reestablish telephone contact.
- For clients with hearing loss or who are deaf who may prefer to write or fax. Not all services have a text telephone facility.

Email is a natural extension of advice by letter and, with the cautions expressed earlier (see page 81), could well develop into the modern version of information and advice through written communication.

Activity

Make a collection of problem pages from a range of newspapers and magazines. Do the answers:

- Seem to address the main issues expressed by the writer?
- Make some assumptions that are not expressed in the letter?
- Acknowledge the feelings that emerge through the letter?
- Seem to miss, or misunderstand, the feelings expressed?
- Use the letter to make a point relevant to the problem page but possibly not to the writer of the letter?

The difference between advice and persuasion

There is a fine line between information-giving and advice and there is also a boundary between offering advice and trying to persuade a client. There is a place for your own views, but these have to be shared carefully and, in many instances, your personal opinion will not be appropriate to share.

For example, a local authority drop-in or telephone service for parents might offer information on the different kinds of child care available locally. Informative leaflets and the chance to talk with an advice worker could help parents to understand the different options and to consider how they can find a good childminder or nursery. However, it is not within the role of the advice worker to challenge whether the parent should be seeking child care at all, or to attempt to persuade a mother to stay at home on the grounds that the worker thinks the child is too young to be left. People who fail to recognise the boundary between advice and persuasion sometimes speak of 'counselling clients out of a decision'. However, such an approach is a dishonest way to cover up a persuasive exercise with a client, which can rapidly approach bullying.

Activity

- Consider how far you have a clear boundary in your service between advice and persuasion.
- Discuss the issues and risks with a colleague.

4.5 Referrals

Responsible referral

You may be able to offer a wide range of helping services within your organisation but the possibilities will not be endless. Good practice is to know the boundaries to your service as well as any limits set by your resources and budget. Clients may approach you on an issue that is not within your area or expertise and then a referral is a positive option:

- Listen carefully to clients so that you can make a useful referral.
- Explain your reasons for suggesting the referral, by linking what clients have said to what you know this other person, group or organisation offers.
- Referrals should be made positively, to benefit the client, rather than in the context of 'We can't do that' or 'I don't know anything about . . .'.

Informed consent

You should never refer someone on without their knowledge and their informed consent. It does not matter how much you believe the client might benefit from the referral, service or product. See also the comments about email on page 81 and holding a database on clients on page 17.

Clients have the right to choose whether they want to take up on a referral. Sometimes, previous experience may lead clients to be very wary or to reject potentially useful help. If you listen, you will then be able to understand the source of clients' current resistance. You can reassure clients if their experience was not typical and it may help to say honestly that you feel they saw indifferent or bad practice.

Automatic referral – an example

Victim Support operates an automatic referral system with the police, who pass on names and addresses of people who have experienced crimes like theft, physical assault and arson. Victims of these crimes are not asked by the police if they wish their details to be given to the local Victim Support. However, in the case of sexual assault, domestic violence and loss of family through manslaughter or murder, victims are asked for their consent and there is no automatic referral.

In their code of practice, Victim Support justify the lack of informed consent for some crimes on the grounds that the police would not necessarily tell potential clients, or hand out leaflets, and automatic referral ensures a more constant state of referrals. We still believe that informed consent to referral is an essential part of any helping service, is crucial to respect for clients and their right to personal privacy and even more important when individuals have already experienced the intrusion of a crime.

Internal referrals

An appropriate option can be to refer clients to a colleague in your own organisation. The first-contact person in your organisation may have the responsibility to listen to clients so an appropriate suggestion can be made for how a client moves on within your organisation. The first contact should make this role clear to clients.

Obviously, in order to make sensible internal referrals, you need to know your own organisation: who offers what kind of expertise, their title or how they are described and their availability face to face or over the telephone. A referral should always be offered with confidence. For example, 'My colleague Zainab will be the best person to help you on that issue', rather than, 'It's no good asking me, that's not my area.' The best person to help may not be available at the time and, again, this situation should be communicated to clients in a positive way. There is a great difference on the receiving end to hearing, 'Sam is our continence specialist' followed by 'he's in every Wednesday from 9 to 5', in contrast with, 'There's nobody here now.'

External referrals

It is good practice to make sure that any organisation does cover the concerns or information enquiries that you believe they do. You could call them yourself and explain how you anticipate referring clients to them on the basis of suggestion, rather than formal referral. It is also worthwhile checking from time to time that the organisation continues to cover the same concern or information and that their contact address and telephone number remain the same. Find out and update regularly the range of local organisations and groups that offer a service to defined groups of clients. Some national organisations have a network of local branches and it will be useful for you to know whether there is one in your vicinity.

Informal suggestion

You may know a number of organisations that are appropriate for questions or concerns that are frequently put to you, but which are outside the scope of your service. Clients are helped by the approach of, 'We don't cover that issue but I think that [named organisation] would be able to help you.' Sometimes you may be able to suggest more than one potentially helpful contact.

Referral directories

Sometimes, you may use referral directories and databases to help clients to find an organisation that appears to be well-suited to their needs. Explain that you are not making a personal recommendation but that from your knowledge the organisation looks appropriate. Make sure that you know the kind of entries and how they are organised within a directory. Clients will not expect you to have total recall of a large directory, but they will be less confident in your help if you seem to have no idea how to find a type of entry.

Monitoring your referrals

Responsibility needs to be taken within your organisation to ensure that any referrals are based on reliable information, in the same way that your information sources are updated (see page 69).

- Does an organisation or self-help group still exist at the same address and telephone, fax or email?
- If you are referring to an individual, does this person still undertake the same kind of work and can she or he take more referrals?
- Is the service free, or is it still free? If fees are involved, then what kind of cost is likely?

It is valuable to gain feedback on how your clients are received at the referral agency.

- Sometimes you will be in a position to meet clients again and can ask, in a general way, about the helpfulness (or not) of the referral. Ensure that clients believe that you genuinely want to know. Some social or cultural groups, including some older age groups within British culture, have an approach of 'mustn't complain' and may not volunteer that they have been poorly treated by the referral agency or individual.
- If you are unlikely to see the client again, then consider asking some of your client group if you (or a colleague) could contact them later to hear their views.
- You could offer a short feedback sheet, easy for clients to complete and send back to you. Stress that you are not checking up on the clients themselves, perhaps by saying, 'We often suggest that people in your position make contact with this organisation and we have no way of knowing whether it is useful.'

Ways of making contact

Referrals are made in different ways. Your approach will almost certainly be part of your service's overall way of working, not a matter of personal decision. For instance:

- You may give the information to clients who choose whether to make contact themselves.
- Alternatively, you may offer to make the first contact on behalf of clients. Clients who lack confidence may want your help with the referral. Some clients with disabilities affecting communication may appreciate your making the first contact. It is also possible that the other person or organisation works in such a way that they prefer you to contact them on behalf of a client.

Be sure that your client has made an informed choice for you to start a referral; there must be no sense of pressure. Clients should be able to say 'No thank you' just as easily as 'Yes, go ahead' to your offer of, 'Would you like me to contact . . . ?', or, 'Would you like to talk with . . . ?' Clients have the right to make their own decisions, and not necessarily to explain those choices to you. However, in a friendly working relationship, clients will usually do so.

Referrals should not be rushed. Give clients a chance to think matters over if they want. Reassure them that they can sit and look over the material about another organisation or look through the directory in a relaxed way. You can also offer clients the choice to come back and talk with you at another time. Assertive help through pressured referrals will never be genuinely helpful. This approach can develop either dependency or resistance in clients who are told, 'You really should . . .', 'You'll be sorry if you don't . . .', or the equally disrespectful, 'Well, do you want help or not!'

Discuss with clients the information that you will pass over to the referral agency if you make the contact.

If you contact the referral agency by letter, it is good practice to give clients a copy. If you speak over the telephone, tell clients what you have said and communicate the reply of the referral agency.

Easing the handover

Sometimes you will support clients in their move to the suggested referral:

- Young people or adults who lack confidence may appreciate some basic help at the 'what do I say to them?' level. You are not rehearsing entire conversations, but uneasy young people may be reassured to know that they simply go to a reception desk and say, 'I'm Maggie Pearson and I've got a 10 o'clock appointment with Jan.' They may be uncertain about how much they should say and to whom.
- Manage clients' expectations of what is likely to happen if they call a telephone helpline or try a local self-help group. Some clients have very little idea or have worrying and unrealistic ideas which you can correct.
- There should be a gradual and more explicit handover when you have spent some time with a client, offering your counselling skills. It may be that new problems have emerged that are not within your area or that a client has taken a long time to disclose what is troubling him or her (see page 171).

▼ 5 Help over the telephone

5.1 Telephone helping services

Permanent helplines

In numbers of client contacts made each year, telephone help and counselling lines undertake more work than any other type of counselling agency. The *Telephone Helplines Directory* (see page 107) runs to over 200 pages in an A4 format. Some organisations offer their help mainly through a telephone helpline. For example:

- The Samaritans pioneered the service of help over the telephone. Their aim is to have helpers available 24 hours a day to befriend callers who feel they have nobody else to whom they can turn for understanding and acceptance with any problem.
- Childline offers a 24-hour service for children and young people in danger or distress. Callers are offered support, advice or counselling and children can be helped with a referral to other helping agencies.
- The London Lesbian and Gay Switchboard offers a 24-hour nationwide service for lesbians and gay men seeking advice, information or counselling.
- Message Home Helpline offers a national service to people, especially young people, who have left home suddenly and wish to send a message to their families. The helpline also offers advice and can support callers in finding a place of safety.

Some organisations offer telephone contact with clients as part of a choice of services. For instance:

- Help the Aged runs SeniorLine, a national advice and information service, and they also publish advice leaflets, lobby government on issues that affect older people and provide support services through projects or in partnership with local groups.
- The Children's Legal Centre has an advice line for anyone to ask about legal issues affecting children and young people. The centre also produces pamphlets, information sheets and a newsletter *Childright*.
- The Women's Nationwide Cancer Control Campaign (WNCCC) focuses on the detection and prevention of cancers in women. The telephone helpline gives information and advice about breast and cervical screening procedures. The

organisation also provides pamphlets and information tapes, screening services and conferences.

Temporary helplines

Some telephone services are a time-limited response to a specific situation. Serious health concerns have sometimes arisen from irregularities in local screening such as cervical smears. A temporary helpline is then established so that people can call for specific information and advice if they think they may be within the affected group. You may be familiar with information helplines set up in the event of a serious motorway traffic accident or air crash and provided after a television news report. Helplines are regularly offered for a short period of time after a relevant television documentary or when serious problems have been raised through a fictional programme. (There is more about this kind of line on page 97.)

Boundaries to the service

Services offering a telephone helpline need to be very clear, as in any helping service, about what is being offered and what is not. The telephone help may focus mainly on information, although there may also be an element of advice. Some lines are set up to offer support through listening and attention. Many helplines offer a service to specific groups of people defined by a similar experience, or by the social or ethnic group that they all share. You need to have a clear understanding of the boundaries of your service. For example:

- BLISS (Baby Life Support Systems) is a charity established for the families of sick, newborn or premature babies. The Parent Support Helpline supports

parents or other carers affected by the birth of a baby with special care needs. Callers can be put in touch with support groups but are not given medical advice.

- The Muslim Women's Helpline offers an information and counselling service specific to women and girls in the Muslim community on family, marriage, emotional problems and other personal issues.
- There are many rape and sexual abuse helplines. Some, like the London Rape Crisis Centre, offer a nationwide coverage to all callers. However, some have a local remit and limit their service to female callers, or to males.
- The Advisory Centre for Education runs a helpline for adults with concerns about children and young people in the state school system. Their general helpline deals with a wide range of questions, but the specific school exclusions helpline is dedicated to that single topic.

Helping over the telephone

Conversations over the telephone focus on talking and listening but, with current technology, there is no visual element. A great deal of information is gained and transmitted through the medium of body language (see page 36) so telephone communication can be at a potential disadvantage. Your full attention is necessary to ensure that you listen carefully to what callers say and how they say it, and are not distracted by the appeals of what you may be looking at as you talk.

Some helplines offer reliable information and straight answers to callers' questions. All the skills of listening are required to ensure that callers are heard properly and their questions are taken seriously. However, straightforward answers are possible, including suggestions for someone else whom the caller could contact. The messages that could be gained from the caller's body language are far less important under these circumstances, since emotional issues are not to the forefront.

For example, the Science Line deals with a very wide range of questions from the general public about any matters of science. The aim of the helpline is to promote the approachable and friendly face of science, when many non-scientists feel intimated by the subject. So it is important that the science information officers who answer the helpline take the questions seriously, as well as giving clear and accurate answers. Some callers are children with questions that can sound odd or amusing, but which matter to them. Adults and young people will genuinely want to know the answer to their questions, but it may be equally valuable that they feel respected by the scientists who provide answers.

Easy access

The great advantage of telephone helping services is that they are available simply at the end of the line. Apart from the cost of the call, which is not always borne by the caller, limitations to this easy access are twofold: the times when the helpline is available and the pressure of the number of callers trying to make contact. Callers who have access to their own telephone can just pick up and dial when they want to ask questions or talk. Some callers may need to build up the confidence to call or to be in the right mood. Callers may not want to wait for an appointment to see someone to talk, although some may move to that point after a supportive telephone call.

Welcome anonymity

The loss of visual information in telephone communication can be an advantage when callers prefer to talk in relative anonymity. They might not want to take up the offer of more personal counselling, even if this is available. Callers may be more comfortable not being seen and able to respond to a sympathetic voice on the end of the telephone line. The helper may be imagined in a way that the caller wants and needs to envisage: perhaps as a friend, an older sibling, or a parent or grandparent figure.

Control of the call

A further advantage of telephone helplines, when callers are uncertain or experiencing mixed emotions, is that callers are in control of the conversation. The telephone call can remain a very brief exchange, if callers want, or because they have changed their mind about talking. They can hang up. It is a very different situation from having arranged a counselling appointment which the client wishes to leave after a very short period of time.

Intimacy of the telephone

Telephones are so much a part of everyday life that talking on a helpline can feel very personal to callers:

- It is a one-to-one conversation in which they have the full attention of the helper.
- Speaking directly into the telephone, with the sense of the helper's ear just at the other end of the line, can give a feeling of closeness.
- The visual privacy offered by a telephone conversation may make the exchange seem more personal and with less distractions from the surroundings.
- Callers are likely to place the call from a place where they feel comfortable, or at least their preferred location for calling. They do not have to become accustomed to new surroundings which they visit for advice or counselling. A sense of familiarity and the ease of being in your own home surroundings can be crucial for some callers.

Relative cost of service

Telephone communication may the best way of making contact for the service offered by many organisations. However, another issue has to be the higher real costs of offering a face-to-face counselling service. Some organisations offer this personal time and attention to a small proportion of clients but it would be prohibitive in terms of time, space and cost to try to offer the service to everyone.

Text telephones

People with severe hearing disabilities need a text telephone (Minicom) to communicate with your service. This system includes a telephone, keyboard and screen. It is possible to have the text option built into the same telephone number used for speaking calls. Callers type in their messages which they can check on their screen and the receiver sends back replies. The system takes no longer than the speed of typing and so is closer to immediate two-way, interactive communication than either faxing or email. There are simple codes of communication that avoid interrupting each other, for example, callers show that they have finished this part of the message by typing in 'ga' (go ahead). The end of the conversation from the caller's perspective is signalled by 'sk' (stop keying) but you can add a reply if you have not finished. The complete end of the exchange is signalled by 'bi bi' (good bye) and 'sk' (stop keying).

5.2 Good practice for telephone helplines

Access and availability

Some callers may have limited opportunity to contact your telephone service, especially if they want to make the call when they are alone at home or are using a public call box to ensure privacy. Few telephone helplines can offer 24-hour, 7-day-a-week availability, so most organisations have to decide how much time they can realistically offer. Good practice is to ensure that:

- The availability of the helpline is given in any information about your service.
- Details are also communicated clearly on a friendly answering message in operation when the helpline is closed. It is potentially distressing for callers with a pressing concern to fail to get any answer or to hear an unwelcoming message.
- If the regular volume of callers significantly outweighs your resources, then any written material or queuing message should encourage callers to keep trying.

Publicity and increase in potential callers

You need to think about the limits of your helpline coverage if your organisation is offered publicity. It might be an entry in a local free magazine or else you may be invited to join a local radio phone-in or a television programme. It can be very tempting to feel that free publicity should not be refused. Yet, it is wiser to make a considered judgement about how your organisation will become involved.

Helplines and television programmes have become such a developing area that the topic was discussed by Maxine Rosenfield in an article in *Exchange*, the newsletter of the Telephone Helplines Association (No. 4, February 1998). Some practical suggestions included:

- Helplines operating at Broadcasting Support Services after documentaries or soap operas covering serious illness can experience 400–500 telephone calls in the three hours following the programme. Even twenty live lines do not necessarily enable all callers to make contact.
- It is unwise to encourage a level of calls to your helpline that will overwhelm your ability to answer. Potential callers may develop a negative view of your organisation and communicate the criticism to others.
- An alternative is to have your address given after a programme and then you respond to written queries. Be prepared to cope with a substantial number of letters, which should be handled promptly.
- Another possibility is to work alongside the producers of a programme, offering information and advice, on the clear understanding that your organisation will be mentioned in the credits but not the helpline number.
- There are rules for broadcasters about the quality of support services offered as part of a programme. It is worth obtaining a copy of the *BBC Producers' Guidelines* from BBC bookshops.

Calls deserve your full attention

Pay attention

While you are on your organisation's helpline, you should not attempt to do anything else at the same time, whether this is to check your diary, write notes irrelevant to the call or allow your mind to wander. The caller will not be able to see you scribble or wave across the room to a colleague, but the inattention will almost certainly sound in your voice or through your missing something that the caller says.

You will be far more able to concentrate if you remove distractions:

- Organise comfortable seating arrangements with everything you need close to hand.
- Helplines should offer privacy and even callers who ask factual questions can be distracted by background noise from your end. Callers who want to discuss something very personal will feel increasingly uneasy if they sense that other people can listen to the call.
- In large organisations several workers may be on the helpline at the same time. You will need headsets for privacy and convenience, and ideally separate cubicles or work stations.
- In small organisations the helpline room may double as a resource room or similar. You need a team agreement about silence, or avoiding the room when the helpline is operational.
- Small, specialised helplines sometimes depend on volunteers working from home. You must be sure that volunteers only take calls at agreed times when they are not torn between the needs of callers and domestic responsibilities. It is also crucial that other members of the household respect the privacy of callers. Young children, who cannot be expected to understand, should be in bed so that they cannot pick up the telephone.

Starting a call

Callers to a telephone helpline should be welcomed through an initial greeting. Your organisation should have some suggestions for what is said: the name of the organisation, your own name and an invitation for the caller to start (see also page 55). You can use phrases such as, 'What can I do to help you?', or, 'How may we help?' You would usually avoid questions like 'What is your problem?' or 'What are you worried about?', even if callers usually want to discuss something that is worrying them.

Reflective listening

Support and advice over the telephone use all the skills that are discussed in Chapter 2. When the helpline service requires the use of counselling skills, you will work through the progression described in Chapters 7 and 8. Some main points are given here.

- Callers cannot see your face, so you have to demonstrate that you are listening by the way in which you audibly respond to what is said. This may mean using more expression in your voice than when face to face.
- The caller will begin to doubt your attention if you make no sounds at all. Use simple verbal encouragement to enable a caller to continue. You might use words and sounds like 'okay', 'yes' or 'uh-uh'. These have to replace the combination of sounds, nods or encouraging looks and smiles of face-to-face communication. Avoid overdoing the non-specific verbal encouragement, any more than you would when able to see the client.
- Callers often want somebody to listen to their perspective and hear their story without rushing to give advice. They want someone to listen because non-judgemental attention is precisely what their family, friends or other professionals have been unable to give.
- The skills of reflecting back and summarising (see page 44) will help you understand what the caller wants to communicate. These skills also show callers that you are concerned and interested in what they want to tell you or ask.
- Some callers may have very strong feelings that they want to express.

Dealing with silences

You need to tolerate silences, as you would in a face-to-face conversation, but not allow them to go on too long. It will be a considered judgement as to what is 'too long'. Be ready with some non-specific comments to encourage the caller back into conversation. Depending on the conversation so far, you might say:

- 'What's going through your mind?'
- 'What are you thinking about now?'
- 'You were telling me about . . .'.

Telephone conversations that start with silences will often be with a caller who is finding it hard to get started. It is important to give more than one invitation for a caller to speak and to offer encouragement patiently. If the silence continues, then it is not going to be a good use of the helpline for you to hang on indefinitely. You can end the call with a comment like, 'Please call back when you feel more able to talk.'

Sometimes a silent call will be an inappropriate caller. You should have team discussions in your service about how to deal with such callers (see also page 105) but, in general, the same pattern of an invitation to talk, followed by an active closure, will be more useful than expressing frustration or anger.

Children and young people

Offering telephone support to children and young people draws on the same range of skills. Children can be experienced users of the telephone, but this may be the first time they have called someone whom they do not know personally. They may lack confidence in how to start such a conversation or be uneasy about how they will be treated.

- When you use respectful communication skills, the younger callers will be reassured, just as with wary adult callers.
- Young callers may be unused to being asked for their own perspective, ideas or feelings, but your genuineness will encourage them.
- They should be treated with the same courtesy as adults. For instance, young people should not be addressed by terms like 'dear', when these would not be considered polite for adult callers.
- You may appropriately adjust your language to talk with young callers but do not attempt to make major changes towards what you perceive to be 'teenage-speak'. You will not sound genuine and there is a high chance you will get any street slang wrong, because it changes quickly and differs between social and ethnic groups.

Opening up a call

Your task is to find out what callers want or need, without making them feel that you want them to hurry. You need to keep a conversation open, so that it does not rush more quickly to some end point that makes sense to you but not necessarily to the caller. You should be guided by the caller because helpline calls are a telephone conversation in which you have no direct investment in where the conversation goes.

- You can use open-ended questions (see page 45) which are non-directive and encourage callers to say more.
- Sometimes it makes sense to open up the call in an active way. You can flag up the shift in the conversation with permission-asking questions like, 'Can I ask you about . . .?', or, 'Do you mind if I ask you a question about . . .?'
- Good use of questions will not feel intrusive to callers and some specific queries may be necessary if possible advice depends on the caller's exact experience.
- Open-ended questions and asking permission communicate respect and show callers that you want to address their personal situation.

ChildLine
Speak to someone who cares
CALL FREE
0800 1111
Or write FREEPOST 1111 London N1 0BR

Information

Some helplines specifically offer information but advice lines will often give information too.

- The helpline needs to operate close to any information resources that you might need. You need to be able to reach or stretch across easily.
- If you regularly suggest that callers make contact with other, specific organisations, then have those details close to hand.
- If you need to stop to find something out for a caller, do not just go silent. Tell the caller what you are doing. For example, 'I'm just going to check that for you. Could you hold on a moment', or, 'The programme's just loading, bear with me for a moment.' If finding out takes longer than you expect, then reassure the caller with a comment like, 'I'm sorry to keep you. I'm going through the directory now.'
- Avoid putting the caller on hold with taped music. People frequently experience this technique with commercial organisations and usually find it impersonal – if not irritating.

Activity

Even one or two minutes can feel like a long time if you are left on hold for a telephone call. Start a record of your experiences of being put on hold by commercial organisations.

- Use a stopwatch, or an accurate watch with a seconds facility, to time how long you wait to talk with a real voice or to have a real person come back to talk with you.
- How much time actually passes before you start thinking, 'Where are they?' How long before you feel nobody is bothering with your call?
- How do you feel about taped music or recurring automatic messages?

Sometimes you will not be able to help directly yourself. Positive approaches could include:

- 'I would like to check the answer to your question with my colleague.' Ask to put the caller briefly on hold, offer to call the person back or arrange for him or her to call you.
- 'Now that goes outside my area of expertise. But my colleague Michael is experienced with . . .'.
- 'I would be pleased to put you through to our specialist in . . .'.
- 'I think that [named organisation] would be able to guide you on . . .'.
- 'Your GP [or some other specific kind of person] would be the best place for you to start with that kind of query.'

Such suggestions combine honesty about the limits to your knowledge and experience with a practical suggestion. You are then opening doors for the caller rather than closing them.

Respond to callers' feelings

It is not unusual for callers to start with a request for information. But then what they say may indicate that their feelings, perhaps overwhelming anxiety, are more crucial than a logical question-and-answer exploration. Alternatively, a caller may start with general worries and be pleased and reassured to pass on to solid information. The communications hierarchy in Chapter 2 may help you to move the conversation between levels.

You should neither push callers to talk about their feelings, nor insist that the caller is probably experiencing a particular emotion. Always be guided by callers in how far they want to go in talking about their feelings. You do need to remain aware that telephone conversations can be especially sensitive and hence it is particularly important to avoid leaving a caller feeling raw. Callers may be alone at home, without support or possibly using a small period of time to call, knowing that soon they have to appear strong for someone else.

It is possible to check out feelings with callers in a way that gives them a choice. You might ask, 'How are you doing with this?', when the issue could well generate strong feelings or anxiety. You cannot see the caller, so you have to be alert to the following clues:

- What callers say, including their use of words.
- Their tone and the level of energy, or lack of it, in their conversation.
- The pace of their speech.
- Their pauses and silences.

Such clues help you to respond sensitively and flexibly and you offer callers a further choice with, 'You sounded worried when you said . . . do you want to talk about that?'

Sometimes you need to gauge to what extent the worries are central to the caller's concern. You may even be able to ask directly, 'How important is this to you on a scale of 1 to 10?', to get your perceptions aligned, or offer your own rating for checking. Hopefully you will be able to explore the possible source of strong anxiety. Perhaps a caller to your health line has previous experiences of ill health or distressing medical investigations. Callers may have a friend or relative with the disease that they fear. Alternatively, the caller may have all-purpose fears about his or her health or a particular condition.

After you have listened carefully, you can offer specific comments such as:

- 'What makes you think that your son may have a drink problem?'
- 'What do you think of the possibility that you might be depressed?'
- 'Have you considered that your parent's health problems could be affected by how little he seems to be eating?'
- 'You sound very concerned about the downside of going in to speak with your child's teacher. I wonder if you have thought about what may happen if you don't say anything.'

You will also have a sound basis to make suggestions about how a caller might proceed next, perhaps with respectful comments like:

- 'Have you thought about asking for help with . . .?'
- 'If you want help on . . . then you could . . .'.
- 'You probably need to see your GP first, but the sort of person you need is a . . .'.
- 'The kind of person who covers this area is called a . . . [named professional such as a clinical psychologist, speech therapist, urologist and so on].'
- 'There is help with . . . from [name of organisation].'

You can offer more information if callers wish but it is crucial that they retain their own choice about taking action now or later, or doing nothing.

The end of a call

Length of time taken by calls

Helplines that combine information, advice and support may receive calls that vary considerably in length. For instance:

- Some callers are clear about what they want to know. They ask their questions and you can answer fully in a matter of minutes.
- Some callers need more time to recount an experience or the details of what has led up to their current confusion or uncertainty. You can help callers feel heard, perhaps for the first time in a distressing or confusing sequence of events. You will support callers as they move to a clearer idea of what they want to know or how they can move their situation forward. Such calls will definitely be more than a few minutes, but callers can experience real progress within 20–30 minutes.
- Some callers have difficulty in expressing their concerns or communicate a number of interlocking events or anxieties. Such calls can last for a considerable amount of time and you will need to consider bringing them sensitively to an end at some point.

Helpline teams need to discuss and agree some working time-limits for calls. Limits may not be an issue if you work on a helpline that is mainly information, but support helplines deal with calls that can become very long. Some organisations have a working limit of about 50–60 minutes for the longest calls. The limit is usually held for two main reasons:

1 The most experienced helpline worker cannot hold concentration indefinitely and 50–60 minutes is the point at which anyone needs a break.
2 A helpline aims to offer a service to a wide range of callers. Opportunities will be restricted if callers are allowed to talk for a very long time.

Helpline workers sometimes feel uneasy about closing a conversation with a caller who appears to want to continue. However, apart from the two practical reasons given already for time-limits, it is useful to remember that:

- Even 20–30 minutes of uninterrupted attention will be a luxury for many callers. Most people in their daily lives do not have someone else who really listens to what they want to say.

- You will have offered the respect of taking callers' concerns seriously, without pushing advice and judgement.
- Within 50–60 minutes a skilled helpline worker can often support callers in moving from feeling miserable and unable to see any possibilities. You can help them to a point where they are more able to gain some perspective on the problem and a practical focus.

Unless you genuinely have a very good sense of time passing, it is useful to have a watch or clock in your sight so you know accurately how long the call has continued.

Closing a call

Some helplines experience short calls which have a natural close once the caller's questions are answered. Other helplines deal with many callers whose issues and worries do not have a natural end point. The close of a call may happen in different ways:

- Callers themselves end the call by indicating that their question has been answered.
- Callers may end the call by just hanging up.
- You sense that the call is finishing and help it to close by asking, 'Does that answer your question?', or, 'Can I help you with any other query?' Avoid standard finishing phrases as discussed before.

Be aware when you are initiating a close and use your skills to ease the caller towards the end of the conversation.

- You may use phrases like: 'Our conversation must draw to a close now . . .'. 'Is there anything else you would like to say/ask?' or 'I can't deal with that now but . . .' (and offer some option).
- You can affirm that the other person is welcome to call back at another time or day.
- Some callers may need to be orientated to the present and back to very simple actions. You might ask, 'What are you going to do today?', or suggest to the caller, 'Make yourself a cup of tea and call us back if you want'. You could encourage a shift in a caller's emotional state by returning to something positive that she or he raised earlier in the conversation.
- Callers may apologise for talking so long and it can be appropriate to reassure them with, 'You were very welcome to talk', or, 'I was glad to listen.'

Realistic expectations

It is important that helpline workers develop realistic expectations for the work. You need a positive outlook both for your own well-being and in order to be of value to the callers.

- You will sometimes share useful information. Callers may now know what steps to take to tackle a problem or perhaps that they have legal rights to exercise when they had believed they had none.

- The main benefit of your time to callers is that they now feel that somebody cares and will listen.
- However, you will not solve people's problems or make everything fine in complex or long-running difficulties. Some callers appreciate help in how to cope with a situation which they know cannot be changed. They want support in expressing their feelings and learning to live with the circumstances more easily.
- You open some doors and reassure callers that they are not making a fuss about nothing. You may make a difference today, at the time of this call.

Helpline workers, especially those taking callers who express strong feelings or recount distressing events, have to accept that they will most likely never know what happens to the callers. Opportunities for team discussion and supervision are important for dealing with these issues.

Inappropriate calls

Any organisation, just like individuals on their home telephone numbers, can be targeted by inappropriate calls of different types. Some services and groups, by the nature of the topic they cover, attract more than their fair share of offensive or obscene callers. The name of your organisation may, for instance, attract racists or callers who have especially offensive attitudes towards your client group, perhaps because they are women or you address the needs of lesbians and gay men.

Repeat callers

Callers who want help that your organisation does not offer need to be told courteously the boundaries of your service. They may be given, several times, a suggestion of a more appropriate service to call. Your team needs some agreement about the point when helpline workers say firmly, 'Please do not call us again. We cannot help you.'

Return callers who repeat what they have said on previous occasions can be given some latitude, depending on the nature of your helpline. Disorientated callers may be unaware of their repetitions and depressed callers may continue to circle around the same issues as part of their emotional despair. However, it will not be helpful to the caller, and will be wearing for you, if the conversation endlessly revisits the same stories. Summarising the issues, to show that you have listened and understood, is the first step to preventing repetition. However, you may need to interject with courtesy through comments like, 'Sally, I remember what you've told me about your neighbour. Now let's see where we can go with this', or, 'Dennis, I recall the details about your benefit situation. You remember we talked about . . . now what happened over that?'

Hoax and offensive calls

Hoax calls can be hard to identify, since genuine callers sometimes recount unusual or unlikely events. Some may have difficulty in shaping what they want to say and initially sound incoherent or slightly bizarre. Of course, some callers who think they are being funny are recognisable quickly. Depending on the circumstances, you might say sharply, 'The helpline is not set up for this', or you can just hang up the phone.

Some genuine callers habitually use considerably more swear words or sexually related language than you would choose yourself. It is their style and a real concern lies underneath. The content of the conversation, as well as the exact words used, will soon indicate whether the caller's intention is obscene. This intention is not always immediately obvious because obscene callers may engage you in a sequence of conversation that circles slowly towards the intended focus.

As soon as it becomes clear that the caller wishes to offend, shock or distress with no legitimate concern, then you should terminate the call. There is little or no value in trying to remonstrate with such callers. Indicating that you are distressed by the content of what they say will only encourage some of them. Your options are to hang up or place the receiver down for a short while before hanging up. The second option may induce confusion in the caller who is left wondering how long he or she has been talking into thin air.

There is no point in continuing a call once it becomes clear that the caller's sole intention is to gain personal sexual satisfaction. Not only are they taking up valuable time but also the sexually orientated callers can spend their money on the commercial sex lines.

Persistent offensive, threatening or obscene calls may need further action. Even frequent nuisance calls from silent callers can be seriously wearing for the team. Talk through possible options with your telephone supply company, who should have someone who deals with the problem. If the calls have very disturbing content or include threats to the organisation or its workers, then you should consult the police.

Positive attitudes for helpline workers

The basic training should prepare people for work on the helpline but should also select out individuals who are not suitable. The qualities necessary for a good helpline worker contribute to the central goal of helping the caller, whatever their information, advice or support needs. Helpline workers need:

- An outlook on callers that is respectful of their concerns and leads to listening to callers, not telling or pushing unrequested advice. As in face-to-face counselling, helpline workers need to hear what the caller is saying rather than rush to shape the conversation in a direction that makes sense to the worker.
- Warmth expressed through their words, their respectful listening and the replies they give. Purely informational helplines still need workers who show a human interest in their callers and their questions or confusions.
- Patience in helping a caller to express a request for information or advice and in listening in order to understand a problem. Callers will not be helped, and vulnerable callers could be undermined, by workers who take a cold, over-intellectual approach or who refuse to accept that an issue concerning the caller is a genuine problem.

The more a helpline is likely to have callers with emotional issues, the more helpline workers must have an empathetic approach, a willingness to tune into the feelings of the caller and to respect those feelings.

Workers will not be appropriate if they want to make judgements, offer solutions prematurely, dismiss expressed feelings or are unable to deal with the expression of strong emotions from callers. Some helplines deal with callers in extreme crisis and workers cannot be helpful if they frequently become overwhelmed with the experiences and emotions they hear.

Workers with very strong philosophical or religious beliefs will not be appropriate if those beliefs cause them to direct callers or to judge them negatively. If your helpline has a religious orientation, then this must be absolutely clear in any publicity, including any entries in directories.

Further resources

- The Telephone Helplines Association was established to meet concerns about the quality of helpline services. The organisation offers support to members, a newsletter, *Exchange*, and a range of publications. Contact them at 61 Gray's Inn Road, London WC1X 8LT. Tel: 0207 242 0555. Fax: 0207 242 0699. Email: 101342.3246@compuserve.com.
- *Telephone helplines: guidelines for good practice* (1993, 2nd edition) from the Telephone Helplines Association.
- Maxine Rosenfield, *Counselling by telephone* (Sage, 1996).
- Pete Sanders, *An incomplete guide to using counselling skills on the telephone* (PCCS Books, 1996). PCCS can be contacted at 48 Seymour Grove, Old Trafford, Manchester M16 0LN. Tel: 0161 8779877. Fax: 0161 8779878.
- *The Telephone Helplines Directory 1998* (2nd edition). Available from Resource Information Service, The Basement, 38 Great Pulteney Street, London W1R 3DE.

⚃ 6 Helping other people: a positive framework

6.1 Background knowledge for counselling skills

Counselling and the humanistic tradition

During the 1950s Carl Rogers developed the humanistic tradition as an alternative to the perceived limitations of psychodynamic and behavioural approaches influential at the time. Psychodynamic therapy (developed originally by Sigmund Freud) mainly took the view that everyone was unhealthy psychologically. The resultant process seemed to offer an expensive, lengthy discovery of personal insight but little action. On the other hand, the behavioural approach (developed originally from animal studies by B. F. Skinner and John Watson) was seen as potentially cold towards clients, who were treated as behavioural symptoms, rather than as individuals with feelings and thoughts.

It is important to realise that since the 1950s both the psychodynamic and behavioural traditions have diversified beyond recognition. However, at that time Rogers' humanistic approach was optimistic and seemed to be more respectful of clients as people. Rogers emphasised essential core conditions of helping: that the helper had to offer empathy, warmth (also called unconditional positive regard) and genuineness (sometimes called authenticity). The approach was described as person-centred because the aim was to support clients in becoming the person they aspired to be. This process was also called self-actualisation.

Naturally, criticisms were soon voiced about the humanistic approach. Two main concerns were that:

- An undiluted person-centred approach may fail to go anywhere. It can create a cul-de-sac of being and not doing.
- The tradition can avoid ethical issues; for instance, what if the person whom the client wishes to become is grossly selfish and damages others?

A further concern emerging from the first two was that, like any tradition, the person-centred approach is a child of its time and place. It emerged from California in the 1950s and 1960s, which was largely an affluent and optimistic setting within the American culture of individualism. Without adjustment, the approach does not transfer to cultures and communities who believe that appropriate limits need to be placed on individual wants and personal development. Self-actualisation as a goal does not make much sense to clients who face serious practical problems and realistic limits to what they can do with their lives.

A more practical focus was offered by Gerard Egan, who has been extremely influential in the field of counselling. Egan developed a staged approach which charted the possible movement in a helping relationship whilst staying true to the core conditions of empathy, warmth and genuineness. Egan's approach is directed towards helping clients to set and achieve goals in agreed areas of their life. His book *The skilled helper*, first published in 1975, has continued through revised editions. The most recent at the time of writing is the fifth edition, *The skilled helper: a problem management approach to helping* (Brooks Cole, 1994).

Therapy or counselling

There is an unresolved discussion about the differences, if any, between psychotherapy and counselling. Some writers try to make a very clear distinction, but there are no consistent differences, especially given the great variety of help practised under the two umbrella terms.

A distinction was that therapy was a long-term process, whereas counselling was always short-term. This no longer holds now that some forms of therapy are intentionally time-limited. Some counsellors help clients in serious distress, so it is inaccurate to claim that this approach is limited to basic coping skills or temporary problems. Undoubtedly, some therapists focus strongly on events earlier in clients' lives, especially in childhood, and on bringing so-called unconscious thoughts to the surface. However, effective counsellors may also help clients to acknowledge and resolve the impact of past experiences on their current behaviour and ways of facing problems.

Counselling or using counselling skills

On page ix we explained that this book was addressed to readers who will use the skills of counselling but were unlikely to be a full-time counsellor. Your clients will benefit from your counselling skills but will not be likely to regard you as their counsellor. The same professional and ethical issues apply whether you use the skills within your job or are specifically employed as a counsellor. The relevant professional organisation is called deliberately 'The British Association for Counselling' and not just 'for counsellors' and the BAC codes of practice are broadly applicable.

6.2 Essentials in counselling

All the points made on page 4 about myths in helping are equally relevant when you use counselling skills. Some more specific issues are raised in this section.

Helping is centred on the individual

An essential perspective is that clients are people, not problems. Individual clients may view the 'same' life experience in very different ways, and will show personal reactions and perspectives. One person's problem may be another individual's opportunity; one person's minor irritation may be another's serious problem, and vice versa. Take the example of being made redundant:

- Louisa is devastated. She has worked hard for her position and invested time and considerable energy into her work. She cannot see how she can use her qualifications and skills in any other job that she would want to do.
- Kashif is angry. His firm kept him on long enough so that he made the rest of his department redundant and then, a week later, he received his notice of redundancy. He believes he could get another, similar job but cannot see how he will ever trust any senior management again.
- Erin is cautiously optimistic. She knew redundancy was a possibility and she had been thinking about a possible change in her line of work. She wants a chance to talk through practicalities and boost her confidence.
- Jack is delighted. He wanted to be made redundant and had just bided his time for the best conditions. He has plans to set up his own business with the redundancy money and cannot wait to get started.

Activity

On the basis of your own experience and that of people you know, note the different possible reactions to the following life events:
- An offer of promotion at work.
- A long-term next-door neighbour moves away.
- A teenage daughter leaves home to go to college.
- A couple break up after a ten-year relationship.
- A young woman finds out she is pregnant.
- The family pet dies.
- The company lottery pool wins a considerable amount.
- Any other examples you would like to imagine.

Individual life experience

People's experience will affect how they see themselves as potential clients of a service that encourages them to talk about problems.

- In a number of cultures, including the British, women seem to find it easier to ask for help, whereas boys and men have usually been socialised towards appearing strong, not showing softer feelings and in many cases not talking much about problems. Boys and men can be enabled to talk through problems and share feelings but helpers, for instance in youth services, need to consider carefully how to make the experience safe and acceptable to clients.
- Talking may not be seen as potentially useful by clients who have limited experience of working through different options verbally. Talking about feelings may be especially resisted and this wariness should be respected. Clients may feel that airing their feelings is self-indulgent, 'navel-gazing' or even potentially dangerous, 'because who knows what might come out'.
- People from communities with a strong sense of cultural and religious identity can be doubtful about seeking external help. They may have explicit pressure

to keep any problems within the family or immediate local community, supported by clichés like, 'We don't wash our dirty linen in public.' Some helping organisations respond to this preference by establishing a service that draws on skills within the relevant community.

- The social position of some potential clients may make them reluctant to ask for help. For instance, people within the helping professions may feel 'I'm someone who gives help to other people; I should be able to cope.' Specialist telephone helplines have been established in recognition of the stress for professions like doctors, dentists or religious leaders.

Priorities in facing problems

Clients' experience may lead them towards a different order of priorities than you. Helpful interventions have to walk a delicate balance between respecting the client's view of what is most important and encouraging alternative perspectives, especially when clients' priorities put them or someone else at risk.

Case studies

1 Lisa did not like being hit, but her past experience and childhood told her that men hitting women was a normal part of life and did not count as a real problem unless the domestic violence became excessive. Although Michaela at the community centre was very concerned about the violence, Lisa's perspective was that other family problems, especially her son's bed-wetting, were a much higher priority at the moment. Lisa could see absolutely no way to change the violent situation, but hoped for some help with her children's behaviour. Michaela recognised that if Lisa developed trust in her, it might later be possible to offer support for the domestic violence. However, Lisa was likely to back away if Michaela insisted on tackling the violence as a priority when Lisa clearly stated that she wanted help with her child.

Comments

- In your service, what kinds of different priorities emerge between the perspective of clients and the helpers? How do you handle these?
- Reflect on personal experiences, with public services or commercial organisations, when your priority was different from that of the person trying to help you. What happened if your priorities were overlooked?

2 Different kinds of help can be more supportive at the different stages of a long-term problem. Thomas developed terminal cancer and he and his wife Olivia knew that he had no more than about a year to live. They were offered support from the local hospice and from the community health visitor. During the remission months when Thomas's health seemed back to normal, he and Olivia most welcomed the visits of the hospice worker who listened and encouraged them in plans to make the most of the time remaining. At that point they found the community health

visitor much less useful. Her conversation was mostly of people who had died from cancer and she was negative about Thomas's wish to seek a second opinion on his prognosis. However, in the last months, when his symptoms returned and worsened, the community health visitor became the most helpful as her practical ability to respond to symptoms was now appropriate.

Comments

- Helpers whose background encourages them to do something can feel at a loss if supportive conversation is required more than action. In what way is this distinction an issue in your service?
- If your service offers different kinds of help, how do you ensure that clients are asked what would be most helpful and when?

Social and cultural traditions

Clients bring assumptions grounded in the social and cultural background of their childhood and current life. If you do not share this background, then you have to listen very carefully to understand perspectives that you do not share and that may be very different to your own.

In recent decades, Western culture has developed a new tradition of criticising social targets that were previously above criticism. Open complaint is more usual about family, older people, or professionals like the police, teachers or doctors. However, for many people, particular targets remain off-limits. A client may not feel anything like relief if she is encouraged to unload feelings of anger about her parents. She may feel a painful sense of guilt and disloyalty. Emotional conflict may arise for any client, but it is likely to be especially sharp for clients from communities in which family loyalty and commitment are highly valued.

The Western view of growing up is that young people break their ties to the family and set up their own life. Maturity is defined through independence, which means leaving home, establishing new loyalties and a separate life from parents. However, this view is alien to many other cultures. In African, Asian and Far Eastern cultures, maturity is seen as the growing ability to take on adult responsibilities and to become part of a family network of interdependence. Couples from two different cultures may face serious misunderstandings. What to one partner is a mature loyalty to the family, which may involve financial contributions, is to the other partner an inability to become independent and show loyalty to the new relationship or young family.

Clients own their problem

However much help you can offer, remember that clients own their personal problem, family dilemma or difficult career choice. In the end, it is their decision how to view the issues and what, if anything, to do. Clients live with the consequences of decisions or their reluctance to make a decision. The counsellor's role is to help the client to solve his or her problem, not to solve it for the client.

If you work with individuals or families who have serious problems, then it is possible to feel a heavy sense of responsibility to relieve the pressure. The cliché 'A problem shared is a problem halved' can be misleading in these circumstances. If you take someone else's problem entirely upon yourself, the result will be two people weighed down. Some of the stress in the helping professions is caused by difficulties in finding a balance between caring and objectivity – between compassion and detachment.

A clear view of 'Whose problem is this?' should not lead to lack of support for clients, or a cold 'You get on with it' approach. The perspective on ownership is important to ensure that clients feel enabled, that what you offer has helped the client to feel more competent and confident to do something constructive. In brief, ownership of the problem is faced through:

- Your positive outlook communicated to clients.
- Encouragement to help clients to take problems one step at a time.
- Encouragement to focus on what can be changed or managed.
- Resisting explicit demands from clients to sort out their problems for them.
- Regular supervision and support within your team when clients' problems weigh you down and you find it hard to maintain an appropriate distance.

A positive relationship with clients

Caring detachment

Counselling skills should be offered in a way that creates mutual trust and respect, so that clients feel safe to disclose and explore their concerns. Clients need to feel that what they are saying matters to you and that you are genuinely concerned for their welfare, that you care about them and their lives. However, your caring has to be tempered with a level of detachment because this approach enables you to be a better helper by providing an alternative, perhaps more objective, view of the reality of the client.

You cannot help if you feel overwhelmed by the complexity of clients' problems. The last thing that distressed or confused clients need is any sense that their supposed helper is now distressed as well. You need to be able to stand back from what clients tell you and to consider other perspectives and possibilities. You need to be able to support clients as they move on from their current position and you will find this hard to manage if you become a part of the problem by being over-absorbed in clients' current concerns.

A safe balance between caring and detachment can be especially difficult in helping services where helpers share common experiences with clients or when helpers have strong beliefs. For example:

- Men who have been separated from their children through custody disputes can be a great support to fathers who contact them. But clients have to be approached as individuals and a situation avoided in which any automatic assumptions are made about where responsibility or blame lies.
- When a client describes a problematic work situation in which he or she differs from the other people involved by ethnic group identity (or sex), an

impartial helper does not quickly assume that the situation is obviously shaped by racism (or sexism). Social or cultural groups who regularly experience inequalities in society include individuals who are badly behaved or selfish and share responsibility for a negative situation.

Warmth

Your words and body language should communicate a welcome to clients and an invitation to talk with you. Warmth can continue to be expressed even when you encourage clients to work hard on their problem and consider perspectives that are not easy for them.

Respect

It is not possible to help other people unless you feel respect for them. You may not agree with clients' decisions, but you need to respect their right to make them and to run their own lives in the way that best makes sense to them. You need to find respect for the efforts that clients have made, for the issues that they have faced and for their choice to seek help.

Genuineness

An effective helper behaves in an open way, without hidden agendas or desires to manipulate clients in any way. Helpers should be honest and never pretend to agree or understand. Genuineness is most easily seen through a convergence – or match – between what you say and do as a helper.

Genuineness, sometimes called being authentic with clients, is not possible if counselling skills are diverted to an unspoken objective of the helper. The term 'counselling' is sometimes used inappropriately to cover behaviour that is designed to persuade. You may have heard phrases like, 'Counsel Priyash out of taking this course. It's not suitable for him but he won't listen to me', or, 'Somebody's got to counsel Caitlin out of taking her complaint further.' In either of these examples, somebody may well need to have a conversation with the individual but counselling skills should not be used for persuasion.

Emotional needs of helpers

Wanting to help other people is a natural and legitimate motivation for anyone within a helping service. There can be a great deal of pleasure in seeing clients become more confident and able to face a situation effectively. Work that gives personal satisfaction will also meet your emotional needs in some ways, but that is not the main objective in offering counselling skills to clients:

- Helpers are there for their clients. At no point should the balance move so that clients are shifted towards meeting your emotional needs.
- Unaware or irresponsible helpers may want to feel indispensable to clients, make friends or be tempted to rework problems in their own lives through the choices they suggest to clients.

- Clients are often appreciative and express thanks for help. But it is not their responsibility to ensure that you feel needed or affirmed in your practice.
- Clients are certainly not there to support a helper's perspective on life, philosophical beliefs or to prove a pet theory.
- Workers or volunteers in a helping role need other sources of emotional satisfaction in their lives besides time with clients. You need a personal life which provides a respite, opportunities for you to receive as well as give and, frankly, to help you avoid the risk of delusions of grandeur.

6.3 Personal styles in helping

Everyone brings some personal biases to their helping and it is essential to become aware of your own inclinations. Personal bias in style will affect how you learn your counselling skills and to an extent what you will need to unlearn. Self-awareness remains important because your own tendencies will creep into your work, particularly when you feel at an impasse with clients.

Before anyone learns counselling skills, she or he will have some ideas about how best to help and what to say. You will have learned from what you have observed when other people have tried to help, as well as your own experience of what is genuinely helpful or not. Look at the following general descriptions and honestly consider which approaches are closer to your own style. The word 'client' is not used here because we describe ways of helping that are common before people have learned counselling skills.

Seeking more information

One tendency in talking with someone seeking help is to probe for further information. You might ask questions like, 'How often does this happen?', and, 'What did you say next?' Or you might direct the other person towards, 'Tell me some more about your family', or, 'Why do you think taking a year off will make things better?'

Questions and invitations for more information have a place in helping others when you use counselling skills (see page 139). However, people who have a strong bias towards questioning run a number of risks:

- You shift a potentially helpful conversation to a narrow channel of communication: one person takes the role of asking the questions and the other person of answering.
- You cannot know what will be useful questions until you have listened carefully to another person's concern; you can only guess.
- Without this understanding, your questions can feel intrusive to the other person. She or he may go quiet, answer your questions but not find them useful or challenge you with, 'Why do you want to know all this?'
- You may ask questions because you are personally interested in the answer or have decided that the topic you wish to probe is important. The focus is on your curiosity or personal judgements rather than the view of the other person.

Are you someone who is comfortable with a questioning style? Maybe other parts of your work role require the ability to find out information within a limited time period. You may need consciously to hold back on questions and concentrate on listening to counsel more effectively. Trust that the information will come because most people will tell you what they need to say when given the space. You will soon learn enough about the perspective of the other person to ask useful questions.

Making an interpretation

Some people's first inclination for helping is to offer an explanation or interpretation of what is happening, how someone is feeling, or why he or she is acting in a particular way. You might offer comments very early in a conversation like, 'Don't you think this is all linked up with being a middle child?', 'Sounds like the male menopause to me', or, 'If you're honest, don't you mean it's you that wants your son to go to college nearby?'

Are you keen to shape up another person's problem or concern in a way that makes sense to you? Perhaps you find it useful to look for possible explanations in your own personal life and perhaps you are genuinely insightful, but there are risks in interpretation as an early approach:

- Without listening and working to understand someone else, you will not have a sound basis for any tentative links or suggestions.
- With support, other people will often come to their own views of what is happening underneath the obvious and their insight will be stronger for having reached it themselves.
- Swift explanations and interpretations run the risk of being wrong and annoying the other person.
- On the other hand, your insights may be uncomfortably close to the truth and the other person is not yet ready to hear that perspective.
- The drawback of pushing an interpretation is that you are implicitly trying to teach, without clarifying whether the other person needs or wishes to learn.

Supportive

Some people's first inclination is to support and reassure when faced with confusion or distress. If this is your inclination, you may offer comments like, 'I'm sure it will all work out', 'Your child's behaviour is perfectly normal for his age. It's just a phase', or, 'Everyone goes through this, there's nothing serious to worry about.' Supportive comments are sometimes meant to affirm the other person, for instance, 'I'd be angry too in your position', or, 'I think we could all do with showing our feelings more.'

People who have a strong inclination to offer general reassurance often genuinely wish to help and may be affected themselves by the distress or worries of others. There is a place for support and reassurance, but only within the context of hearing about what concerns another person:

- You cannot offer an optimistic outlook without some grasp of the situation. There may be real cause for concern.
- Uninformed reassurance can very easily be experienced as patronising. The other person is distressed or confused and you appear to be saying that there is no sound basis for their feelings.
- It is usually better to acknowledge someone's feelings and explore them in ways helpful to the other person, rather than stopping with the message that you agree with their feeling this way.
- You may be correct that the other person's experience falls within the normal range of children's or adults' behaviour in a similar situation. However, that other person still wants some help on how to deal with the situation personally.
- You best show support by giving time and attention. Your helpful presence demonstrates support and earns the right to help.

Evaluative

Some potential helpers want to shape up a problem or issue in an evaluative way, by making a judgement about right and wrong, or 'ought' and 'should'. Evaluative comments may direct the other person in a different direction with, 'Isn't it about time you looked at this from your partner's point of view?', or, 'You can't keep on trying to be a big success like your elder brother.' Some evaluative judgements are about how the other person experiences the situation, for instance with, 'Don't you think you're making too much of this', 'You don't really mean that', or even, 'When are you going to tell me what the real problem is?'

You will have opinions about people to whom you offer help, but evaluative comments are rarely, if ever, helpful.

- Such comments usually come across as if you are playing the expert and the moral authority. The other person may well feel that you are reprimanding them and being patronising, and perhaps you are.
- Denial of people's feelings will close down a potentially helpful conversation because it is disrespectful.
- It is not your business in using counselling skills to tell other people what they should do or how they should feel. If you have listened and worked to understand, then you will earn the right to suggest alternative perspectives to another person.

Telling

Telling is really a combination of interpretation and evaluation. Some people feel a great pressure to offer solutions to problems, to have something to suggest that the other person does. It can feel very satisfying to hand out quick advice, but this approach is not usually helpful. Examples of the telling approach are, 'You need to get out more. Try a local evening class', 'Stop breastfeeding your baby, then she'll stop waking you up in the night', or even, 'You're just going to have to learn to live with this.' One telling approach is to focus on the personal experience of the supposed helper, to the exclusion of the concern raised by the first individual. An example would be, 'I know exactly what you mean. When my mother died . . . Let me tell you . . .'.

Many television programmes, radio phone-ins and some of the magazine problem pages take the approach that helping is the same as telling people what to do, and telling them quickly. You may be lucky with your suggestions but the risks are high:

- Experienced helpers recognise that they have no way of knowing what might be useful until they have listened properly to the other person.
- Telling often proposes that people do something they have already tried and that failed to work. The helper loses credibility for not exploring the issue fully first.
- There is a strong possibility that keen tellers create dependence in others. If your idea is both new and it works, then the expectation is that you will produce an easy answer next time. It does not help the other person to be able to solve his or her own problems next time.
- If the advice does not work, you will have little understanding of why and may well be blamed with, 'You told me that would work. Well, it didn't! It made things worse!' Without deeper understanding and exploration the commitment of people seeking help to the solution proposed is likely to be low, and hence they are unlikely to put the effort required to make even the best solution work.
- There will be times when you have no idea what to suggest and, if you are not in the habit of listening, then you will feel bad about saying, 'I don't know what to tell you to do.'
- There are rarely neat solutions or even a way to remove a problem completely. For some people, help comes through finding ways to live with a situation that they cannot change, or learning how to prevent past experience from distorting their approach to the present. The positive focus is on the other person's learning to live with particular circumstances and not on your telling them they will 'have to learn'.
- Sharing your own experience prematurely may be offered with sympathy but you cannot know if it will be helpful to the other person and certainly not whether you really do 'know exactly how you feel'. The recounting of an important part of your life will push away the other person's experience unless it is directly relevant to their needs.

Part of helping other people is working with them to the point where they feel able to consider options in what to do about a problem or concern. Counselling skills will enable you to help them to reach that point and to gain personal satisfaction in what they have learned and managed, not what you have told them to do.

Understanding

The initial approach of experienced helpers is most often to attempt to understand what the other person is saying and to show that they are working to grasp that perspective. Until people have experienced ideas and practice in counselling skills, this approach is less common than the others described in this section. Some people are more natural listeners, but many have one or more of the tendencies to shape up and drive a conversation faster than is genuinely helpful.

Activity

Read through the three examples one at a time. Consider each of the possible responses that the potential helper has made.

- What do you think the response has contributed to the exchange?
- How might it lead the conversation?
- Is it helpful? If so, in what way?
- Which response(s) would you be more likely to offer? Be honest with yourself – what is your first inclination?

Discuss one or two examples with a colleague and exchange ideas. You will find comments on this activity on page 121.

Example one

Simon is talking with you about his home situation and says, 'It's getting beyond a joke at home, my mother lives with us and she and my wife just can't get on. My mother says she's trying to help out, with the children and cooking – that sort of thing. But my wife thinks she's being criticised and I suppose Mum has always been keener to tell people what they're doing wrong than to praise. Now I dread going home at night; I'm pleased if I have to work late. But then I don't see much of my wife and the boys have gone to bed. When my father died, I felt we had to ask Mum to live with us, but my wife said it would cause trouble. It's not her family's way.'

1 'Can you tell me more about the arguments between your mother and your wife?'
2 'You're torn between your loyalty to your mother and your feelings for your wife and sons.'
3 'It sounds as if you're in the middle of some sort of culture clash. You and your wife's families have different traditions.'
4 'Perhaps you should consider sheltered accommodation for your mother.'
5 'You can't expect your wife to do everything. It is your mother after all, not hers.'
6 'I'm afraid daughters and mothers-in-law often don't get on. It's very normal you know: two women – one kitchen.'

Example two

Yan-Ling is talking with you about her career: 'I don't know what to do for the best. I've done well in publishing and I've found it very interesting up until recently. I've got a good salary, but I feel I'm not going to go much further. No, that's not really true. It's that I'm fed up with all the new qualifications in the area I cover and next year they're going to change them all again. I keep thinking is this all there is to my life? I always wanted to develop my photography and I didn't have the courage. I can see some openings and a friend is interested in starting a business. But, I'm not sure.'

1 'You sound a very sensible individual to me. I think you'll sort out what you really want, if you put your mind to it.'
2 'What's happening with the new qualifications next year? I hadn't heard anything about yet another lot of changes.'
3 'It sounds like a tough decision. Do you stay in a job that doesn't interest so much any more? Or do you take the risk of starting out in something new?'
4 'In the current economic climate I'd have thought you'd be grateful to have a regular job and a good salary.'
5 'It's obvious that you're the kind of person who always goes for the safe option, but then regrets what could have been. You lack the courage of your own convictions.'
6 'I suggest we draw up a list together. I find it helps to put all the pluses of an important life change on one side and the negatives on the other. Then we can talk about each one in turn.'

Example three

You have been asked to speak with ten-year-old Clement because several of the primary school staff say he is surly and aggressive. Clement has said very little in the conversation, then towards the end of your time he bursts out with, 'It's not fair! The teachers say "this is a telling school". They keep on about "don't hit them back, it only makes things worse". But I've tried to tell Miss a million times and she just says, "Don't tell tales". And I tried to tell the helpers in the playground and they said, "You're a big boy. Sort it out for yourself". I have to hit Harry and his gang; they won't leave me alone.'

1 'I'm afraid your teachers are right. However badly you feel, hitting people never solves anything.'
2 'I think you're especially stuck because you're a boy. We adults haven't been very good at helping boys to talk about things.'
3 'You need some other options. I can help you with ways to deal with these boys without hitting. We call it assertiveness.'
4 'Life does seem very unfair when you're young. I was young once, you know. It does get better, trust me.'
5 'You feel you've got no choice. You've tried to "tell" like the teachers say and that didn't help. So, you can't see how else to defend yourself.'
6 'This Harry and his gang, are they white boys? Because you know the school has an anti-racist policy.'

Different personal styles – activity from page 119

The responses to the examples have been kept short. Responses are often longer and combine more than one of the approaches. The types of responses given are as follows, with examples one, two and three in order.

Understanding: 2 3 5
Interpretative: 3 5 2
Seeking more information: 1 2 6
Evaluative: 5 4 1
Telling: 4 6 3
Supportive: 6 1 4

6.4 Setting the scene to use counselling skills

Stages in the process of helping

A staged model creates a framework for helping that grows with the relationship between client and helper. Egan returned to a three-stage model after working for some years with four stages. Richard Nelson-Jones explains helping through five stages. We use a four-stage model because we have found that this framework works best for the public services and businesses with whom we have been involved in practical application of the skills.

The staged model places counselling skills in a framework that is progressive, and focuses on problem-solving in which the helper and the client together work towards what the client can do. The process of helping is one of sharing expertise, building trust and a joint commitment to the way of working on the issues and to the end result of change for the client. Consequently, helping can only happen if helpers value clients for themselves as individuals and accept clients' rights to make decisions for themselves. The model assumes that helping will be a relatively short-term intervention with a client: a series of sessions stretching over weeks or at most a few months, certainly not years.

When you use counselling skills within a staged framework, you are far more likely to be guided by what you have learned by listening to the client. There is a sense of growth in each individual helping relationship, however brief. The four stages are as follows:

- Stage One: understanding the client's perspective, the problems as she or he views them and the current situation for the client.
- Stage Two: exploring alternative perspectives with the client, working in greater depth on a problem and establishing how the client would like his or her situation to change.
- Stage Three: exploring with the client the different possible ways of achieving his or her preferred goals and making definite plans for action.
- Stage Four: the client puts plans into action, evaluates to what extent the goals have been achieved and revises plans if appropriate.

The Counselling Model

Task goals	Understanding your client's perspective	Stimulating the client to greater understanding	Designing change programme	Changing, supporting and measuring progress
Model	STAGE 1 Exploration / Focusing	STAGE 2 New perspectives / Goal-setting	STAGE 3 Programme census / Programme choice	STAGE 4 Implementation / Evaluation
Process goals	Earns the right to help	Uses right to help and tests commitment	Jointly commits with client to change actions	Earns right to finish, or recycle

Adapted from Egan and Cowans (1979)

The diagram of the diamonds shows how each stage has an opening-out phase of gathering information and then a closing-down phase of decision-making. The opening up and exploration in each stage sees the helper drawing out or contributing information and the closing-down phase moves to an interim decision with the client. The funnels and filters diagram on page 44 is an appropriate model for basic questioning, particularly within the context of clients' need for information. However, that model fails to stress the need for a broad exploration of a client's issues and concerns that lies at the heart of counselling. As such, the image of the four diamonds becomes a much better symbol for the process of communication developed as you use counselling skills.

Each of the stages is only successful to the extent that you have communicated effectively in earlier stages. So, contracting at the very beginning of helping and Stage One are especially important. Unless you make a psychological contract with a client, you can fail to manage expectations about what will happen and how. The skills of Stage One are crucial, because a helper who fails to see the issues through a client's eyes will not have a firm basis for any further helping.

The counselling skills build upon one another. So the skills of Stage One remain important throughout the helping process. The skills of Stage Two are more complex and can feel more challenging to the client than those of Stage One. It is important that you understand and remain aware of the helping process. Then, you will be conscious that you are moving into stronger interventions because it is justified by what and how the client is speaking with you. No new behavioural skills are required for Stages Three and Four, although a range of approaches can be used to help clients in action planning. The stages are *not* rigid. You will sometimes return to an earlier stage, for instance when a client shares a new concern or trusts you with a sensitive experience. You are aware of the stage of helpful interaction and that guides your use of skills.

The helping relationship described in this chapter and Chapters 8 and 9 assumes that you spend uninterrupted, private time with a client. Sometimes you move through the stages fairly quickly; helping is not always a long-drawn-out process. At other times you and a client may spend several sessions exploring within Stage One. It is not unusual that clients first surface a less important problem and are only prepared to talk about more worrying concerns when they feel able to trust you. A helping conversation will often have a circling quality as you return to Stage One skills if the client discloses a new concern. The staged approach is flexible and will help you to focus on the client, rather than on your initially preferred helping style. We want to stress that the stages are to guide you towards the most helpful interventions and to avoid premature comments or suggestions.

Counselling skills will be useful in the following types of work situation:

- Offering help to clients who ask for time and attention, either in face-to-face conversation or over the telephone.
- In services primarily for one set of clients, for instance children, young people or elderly people, but where you aim for partnership with parents or other carers who may ask for your time.
- Offering help and support to colleagues who ask for time to discuss a work issue that concerns them.
- In your role as a supervisor who gives time to team members to talk about their work, not necessarily serious problems.
- The examples used in Chapters 8 and 9 are all two-person conversations, but counselling skills are also relevant to working with groups (see Chapters 10 and 11).
- Application of the skills will also support you in short conversations within your work. You will be able to make the most of short periods of time, but realise that genuine helping cannot be rushed.

Reservations about a staged approach

We have talked with some potential helpers who have expressed doubts about a staged approach. Reservations include the claim that stages can be rigid and helpers are able to judge when clients need more confronting interventions at an earlier point than the model would suggest. In fact the staged model has considerable flexibility. Most doubters that we have encountered have been under unrealistic pressure over how many clients they can see in a working day. Some have also been within a professional framework that has failed to develop a tradition of respect for clients.

These two factors, unless acknowledged and addressed by the potential helpers, run a high risk of perpetuating an unhelpful service in which clients are seen as names on a list that can be sorted out promptly and pushed, if necessary, into accepting what they should do for the best. Such a service, whatever those delivering it may want to believe, is not genuinely helpful to those on the receiving end.

It is not, of course, the client's responsibility to 'keep within the stages' of the model. The value and flexibility of this staged model is to enhance the helper's awareness of what clients are saying and how they are currently comfortable to handle their problem or concern. Nor is there *any* sense of driving the helping conversation in a particular direction.

Contracts in helping

The use of agreements

Many people think of the word 'contract' in terms of legal agreements like hire purchase or buying your home. A firm, 'sign on the dotted line' kind of agreement would not be appropriate for helping others. However, you will find non-legal examples of a contract in agreements between parents and their children's school or between students and their college. Children's and family centres have long worked with contracts for families about their children's attendance and any planned work with parents. The growth in customer charters is another example of informal contracts. Such agreements tend to cover two broad areas concerning the relationship between individuals or groups of people:

- Practical issues about the service being offered and accepted: where, when, how often and similar questions.
- Bringing expectations and assumptions out into the open. An effective contract covers both sides of the relationship: 'What you can expect from us as service providers' and 'What we expect of you as users of our service.' The more personal contracts, for instance with children and young people, are more about, 'You agree to work towards these objectives', and, 'I agree to support you in these specific ways.'

Activity

Collect examples of contracts and customer charters from a range of services.
- In your opinion, how well does each example communicate about the two main areas: the practical details and clarity about expectations and assumptions for both sides?
- Compare the examples with any explicit agreement within your own service.

Contracts in helping

There has to be some flexibility in how you establish an agreement with a client. You would sensibly take different approaches with a colleague who says, 'Have you got five minutes to talk with me?', a wary, young person brought to you by his parents, a client who has asked for help in making his career change or a client who wants someone to listen to her worries about her teenage daughter. There will be no ideal form of words that you should use with everyone but you need to cover:

- Practical issues of time and place.
- Your approach to helping and the client's expectations.
- Confidentiality.

Time and place

You need to know and be clear with clients about how much time you can offer, where and when.

- Depending on the circumstances, your response might be, 'Yes, I have five minutes, but that's really all I have at the moment. Will that be enough?'
- You may work in an informal service, where clients or colleagues ask for your time without warning. You will need to learn to say, 'I'm busy right now, but I can talk with you this afternoon at 2.30.' You may prefer other words such as 'involved with', 'fully booked until' or other alternatives.
- If your service has an appointments system, then clients should know the time of their slot and how long they will have. It is a fair expectation that clients should arrive on time, but it is equally fair that they expect to see you promptly and not be left waiting.
- If you see clients more than once, then you should discuss at the first session when you will next meet or, if appropriate, how many times you will need to meet. You might suggest and the client agree that you will book in, say, three meetings at given dates and times. Alternatively, it might make sense to say that you can offer more sessions, but that the client can make a decision about taking up on that offer at the end of the first session.

Privacy

It is not appropriate to use counselling skills in the corner of a busy room or reception area, nor to depend on snatched conversations in hallways. Your time with a client should not be interrupted for anything less than a genuine emergency. So you need to ensure that you and a client are not interrupted, either by the telephone or colleagues sticking heads around the door. If you allow such interruptions, you communicate disrespect to the client – that other activities take priority over your attention to him or her.

- Use a suitable space appropriate for counselling and freed from distractions.
- If necessary, switch your telephone through to someone else or place it on answer phone mode with the shortest number of rings and the sound turned low.
- Put a 'Do not disturb' or 'Occupied' notice on the outside of the door.
- You will need to speak firmly with colleagues who act as if clients are always interruptible.

It is unethical to encourage clients to talk if you do not have the time to listen properly. It is your responsibility to create a more realistic schedule, as hard as this may be, because it is unfair to raise expectations of attention to the client that you cannot fulfil.

Expectations and assumptions

Clients will come to you with some prior expectations about the way in which you will help them. At the beginning of your first conversation you need to manage clients' expectations, to give some idea of how you will behave in the helping role.

Listening and talking with the client

Clients may expect you to tell them what to do or that you will direct them with a series of questions. Clients' assumptions about your behaviour as a helper will emerge throughout your conversation and you can deal with issues as they arise. It would be unrealistic to try to lay every assumption to rest at the beginning. However, at the outset it is useful to explain your approach in brief.

You might say something like, 'I want to understand what is happening from your point of view and then we'll talk together about what might help.' Depending on what clients have said to you or the way in which they approached you, you might say, 'Let's start with you telling me about your current issue and how you feel about it. I'll be in a better position to help you if I understand what's going on.' You may even wish to share the four-stage model with your client, so that the process is clear.

The conversation is confidential

Clients may have differing expectations about the boundaries around the conversation. Some may fear that you will repeat everything to colleagues or report back to the client's doctor, employer or whoever has made the referral. On the other hand, some clients may believe or hope that you can keep secrets, even if what they tell you means that someone else is at serious risk.

In most organisations those will be some limits to complete confidentiality these. You need to explain the situation briefly to clients before they disclose personal information (see also page 10).

Assumptions that become clear later

You cannot realistically explore all assumptions before you start to listen and talk with clients. Your contracting should not last for ages and some clients will not express their expectations at the beginning. They may feel that questioning what you are likely to do will be impolite. Alternatively, clients may wait to see how you interact with them before stopping you with, 'But I thought what would happen is . . .', or, 'When are you going to start helping me?' In some cases, clients may not be clear that they have expectations of what you will do, until you obviously are not behaving in that way.

At any point in a helpful exchange, be ready to deal with clients' assumptions and expectations, because they have become important here and now. You might remind clients of the conversation you had at the very beginning, explain how you work since clients did not understand, or maybe listen and explore, as necessary, how clients expect you to help and how they view themselves in this process. Certainly, though, it is a good idea to spend some time contracting and reaffirming expectations at the end of each stage. The coming together of the diamonds indicates a point to take stock and to ensure that helper and client are working together to a shared agenda.

Many of these points are equally applicable to contracting in group work (see Chapters 10 and 11).

Activity

1 Practise a few sentences that could set the scene when you start to talk with a client. How will you address:
- Practical issues?
- Your approach to helping?
- Confidentiality?
2 Consider how you could reply to clients' assumptions expressed in the following examples.
- 'Aren't you going to tell me what to do?'
- 'What kind of things do you want me to say?'
- 'My friend said you were good at sorting out what was the matter with children.'
- 'You're the expert, you tell me what I should do about . . .'.
- 'You've got to help me.'
- 'When are you going to give me some ideas about what to do?'
- 'I've been to people like you before. I don't know why I've bothered, you won't understand.'

Reluctant clients

It may become clear early on that some clients are not confident that you will be able to help. Clients may have been encouraged, even pushed, to talk with you. In some settings, you may find that clients are told they have to come to you, for instance, school pupils may be left in little doubt that they should keep the appointment that has been made for them. You will need to address issues with colleagues in the broader setting, if you become aware of pressure on potential clients. However, there is no need to abandon the session just because a client is less than enthusiastic.

You need to acknowledge clients' reservations as they show them and then open the door to the possibility that their time could be well spent with you. For instance:

- To a reluctant 14-year-old student, you might say, 'I hear what you say, Marsha. That Mr Arkwright told you to come, that it wasn't your choice. On the other hand, I understand there's a long-running problem with your Maths teacher. You've got 30 minutes of my time and my job is to listen to your side of it. And I don't report back to Mr Arkwright.'
- To an angry young man who has diabetes and is careless about his medication, you might say, 'I know that talking won't take your diabetes away. But talking with me, and me listening to you, might help you to deal with what you feel diabetes is doing to your life.'

You may work with clients who have first been seen by a colleague or referred by another part of your organisation. It can be useful, and sometimes crucial, to know how your part of the service is described. What do colleagues, or other people, say to anyone whom they think could benefit from your counselling skills? How do they start to shape the potential clients' expectations of you? For example:

- A counsellor available for parents of newborn infants realised that the ward staff described his work as being 'with problem families'. The medical team did not use this phrase in direct conversation with parents, but they said it within parents' hearing. The ward team meant that the counsellor helped 'families who had any kind of worries about or problems with their newborns'. However, the shorthand 'problem families' gave a negative message to parents who would have welcomed a chance to talk.
- A psychologist involved with several children's centres realised that the teams described her work in different ways. The workers in one centre highlighted parents' problems with phrases like, 'Trish is good with difficult children', or, 'You need to talk with someone when you can't cope.' Other centres gave more positive and inclusive messages like, 'We find it helps to bounce ideas off Trish and she's here for parents as well.'

Activity

Do your clients pass through even an informal referral system to reach you?

- How do your colleagues, or any other involved parties, describe your work to potential clients? What do they call you, by title or informal description?
- Take the opportunity to ask and listen to how others introduce you into the conversation.
- In what ways could a different introduction through others create a more positive start or accurate expectations for the client?

◼ ⊻ 7 Understanding and extending the perspective of clients

7.1 Stage One: using counselling skills to understand clients

Empathy

Nobody can help by jumping to conclusions, so your entire aim at this stage is to manage, as far as possible, to look through the client's eyes.

- What is the difficulty, confusion or hard choice from her point of view? How is it affecting her life; how does she see it all?
- Where does he want to start? What is he ready to talk about at the moment and what does he think is important?

Stage One counselling skills build empathy. The term 'empathy' means the state of feeling *with* someone, of being in tune with their perspective, seeing the world through their eyes.

Empathy is not the same as sympathy. If you feel sympathetic towards someone, you feel *for* them and may be sorry for them or agree that life is rough. You can feel sympathy for someone and not understand much of how he or she experiences the situation. In contrast, you can feel empathy with another individual if you have taken the time to listen and to explore with the whole objective of understanding better the feel of this person's world. Building empathy does not necessarily take hours of time. If you focus on a client, then you remove the background noise of how you would feel in this situation, what would be the main problem for you or possible ideas to suggest. Most clients will experience that they have your full attention and will talk. You will learn a great deal about this individual's perspective in a relatively short period of time.

Basic understanding

You have three aims within Stage One of using counselling skills. To:

- Understand your client's perspective.
- Show to your client that you are working to understand his or her frame of reference.
- Help clients to become more concrete about their concern or problem.

In Stage One you work to understand, and show the client that you have noticed and understood, this individual client's experiences, behaviour and feelings. You let the client know that you understand what he or she has explicitly told or shown to you. At this point, you should not try to probe into what the client is half-saying or implying. Stay with what he or she has chosen to share with you. By listening and exploring in a respectful way, you gain the understanding and earn the right to look deeper in Stage Two through skills that support advanced understanding (see page 144).

You work within basic understanding by showing the qualities of warmth, respect and genuineness that are discussed on page 114. Your careful use of the Stage One skills also communicates these qualities through:

- Attending, including listening and looking carefully.
- Being genuine – showing a match between what you say and do.
- Reflecting back and paraphrasing.
- Helping the client to be specific, to share examples of experiences or reactions.
- Summarising.
- Careful use of questions.

The following rules of thumb will guide your use of the skills:

- Attend carefully all the time to the messages communicated by word and body language by your client.
- Listen especially for the basic messages, rather than giving energy to thinking, 'I wonder what she really means by that.' Focus on changes in emphasis and energy from the client to help flag his or her key issues.
- Respond to your client fairly frequently (see page 33 about the impact of long silences from you) and keep your responses fairly brief. If you speak for too long, the balance of talking passes from the client to you and you then have to work to pass the focus back to the client.
- Be flexible and tentative so that the client has room to move: to agree, deny, explain, add more or shift the emphasis.
- Be gentle but not so much that the client remains vague, rambles or consistently avoids following through on issues or topics that she or he raised in the first place.
- Respond to the feeling communicated by words as well as the specific content, unless there is a good reason for emphasising one over the other.
- After you have responded, attend carefully to clues from the client to confirm or deny the accuracy of your response. Some clients will tell you clearly, 'That's not what I meant', or, 'No, you're not getting my point here.'
- Make a mental note of apparent stress or resistance from clients. Time will tell whether these are because your response was inaccurate or uncomfortably accurate.
- Move gradually to the exploration of what emerge as key topics or feelings for this client.

Case study: an example of poor practice

A year after Thomas's death (see the case study on page 111), Olivia was offered counselling within her health practice. Her GP was aware that Olivia had difficulty in coming to terms with her loss and continued to miss

Thomas deeply. She agreed to see the clinic counsellor, feeling that perhaps she could be helped by someone outside her family, who were very supportive but in distress themselves.

Olivia was uncertain how to talk in the counselling session and the male counsellor said very little initially, leaving Olivia uncertain about whether he understood what she was saying or somehow believed she was making a fuss about nothing. At one point he asked her, 'Why do you think you are so upset?' She replied, 'Because I loved my husband very much', and felt that the counsellor looked surprised, as if older people should not have such feelings. The counsellor started to tell Olivia that she was in particular 'phases of bereavement' and suggested that she was 'in denial' at the moment. Olivia said she was not denying her loss, 'I know my husband is dead. He died in my arms.' The counsellor went silent at that point.

Eventually, Olivia asked the counsellor if he had lost someone very close to him. She felt he simply did not understand the feelings she had expressed. His response was non-committal and Olivia decided there was no point in continuing with the session. The counsellor gave her a leaflet on bereavement and she later realised from the wording that he had been reading aloud from this leaflet to her during part of the session. The poor quality of Olivia's session not only increased her distress but it led her not to seek any further outside help because, 'If that's counselling, I don't want any more of it'.

Comments

It is crucial that any organisation that offers use of counselling skills to clients is effectively monitored so that the quality of the service is ensured.

- In what ways does your service prepare and support helpers who offer counselling skills?
- What additional training is given to enable helpers to support clients in distressing situations such as bereavement?

Attending

Careful attention uses your senses of vision and hearing (see page 30). You need to listen carefully to what the client says, trying your very best not to label or interpret what you hear. Accuracy is key. You also need to be alert to the client's body language which can convey vital messages alongside the words:

- Active listening is hard work, because all your attention is on the other person's experiences and expressed feelings. You need to quieten your internal dialogue that otherwise will distract.
- Listening, combined with the other skills of Stage One, communicates respect for the other person. It is a reliable way to prevent swift assumptions such as, 'It's this kind of problem, then.'
- As well as the actual words, also listen to how the client speaks and the feelings that emerge through tone of voice, choice of words and emphasis.

These are usually more valuable in fully understanding the client's perspective.

- Use the evidence of your eyes, noticing the client's body language and how it may change with what is said. At an early stage of talking with a client, you will make a mental note of your observations. Sometimes it may be appropriate to share them with the client but only tentatively (see page 135).
- It is just as important not to draw conclusions about body language alone as it is not to depend just on spoken words. If a client's body language suggests to you that she is tense about the issue she has raised, you file this in your mind as a possibility, not a certainty.
- You cannot just listen and look in a helping session. You will have to say something yourself as well. The other skills of Stage One will help you to make appropriate responses within the helping conversation.

Helping yourself to attend

How you sit when you speak with a client can help you to attend and also show a client that you are focusing on him or her. Ideally, remove any barriers between you, like tables, and sit at the same level. SOLER is a shorthand used to describe a good attending position. The letters stand for:

- Square: sit facing the client, square on. If your seating arrangements mean that you have to sit slightly to one side, then make sure that you turn well towards the client.
- Open: use your body language to communicate that you are open to what the client has to say. Avoid crossing your legs and arms in any way that shuts down on your body. If you do not know what to do with your hands, experiment with holding them in your lap or to one side.
- Lean forward: as you sit, lean slightly towards the client. If you lean back in your chair, you may communicate reserve, trying to create a distance between you and the client or an inappropriate laid-back outlook. If you lean too far forward, clients may feel you are invading their personal space, or placing pressure on them. Leaning well forward is the body language equivalent of 'Come on, tell me!' A useful rule of thumb is that the top of your back should not be touching your chair.
- Eye contact: looking does not mean staring, which can be disconcerting for clients. The best approach is to make regular direct eye contact with the client and to break that contact occasionally, probably by looking down.
- Relax: within an attentive posture, that avoids distracting gestures, try to relax. This suggestion can feel hard at the outset but with practice you will be able to be alert and relaxed. Like everyone, you need to become aware of your own habits, such as fiddling with your ear. You may be unaware, so remain open to feedback from colleagues or friends (see also page 39).

Listening and assumptions

It does not matter how experienced you become in using your counselling skills, you will never become a mind reader. Careful listening, combined with the other

Stage One skills, is the only safe, practical way to avoid making assumptions about what a client is about to say or the meaning that she or he places on an event. For instance:

- You know that Nathan's son was recently involved in a road traffic accident. You assume that he wants to talk with you about how Michael is coping with his injuries and the aftermath of the accident. By listening, you quickly realise that Michael is coping well. Nathan is worried about his other son, Jamie, who witnessed his younger brother's accident. Jamie has flashbacks and nightmares and tries to keep Michael safe from harm in ways that are seriously annoying to his brother.
- Tamar says that 'something awful' happened on the train today. You look expectant and she says, 'This young man offered me his seat.' You are confused about the meaning of this event and reflect back in a neutral way, 'A young man offered you his seat on the train and you felt awful.' Tamar goes on to explain that for her this was a watershed event because she felt the seat was offered to her as 'an older woman'. There have been other recent incidents that have added to Tamar's very mixed feelings about approaching her fortieth birthday.
- Yasmin says to you, 'I think a lot of my problems come from being the youngest of six children.' You hold back your expectation of what being the youngest in a big family means. In your own experience it meant being the last in line, no new clothes and very few photographs of you in the family album. Yasmin continues with, 'I look now and I can see that I was completely spoiled. There were ten years between me and my next brother. Everybody indulged me: Mum, Dad, all my older brothers and sisters. It was lovely at the time but . . .'.

To think about

As you practise your Stage One counselling skills, keep a personal note of the times when you successfully hold back on your assumptions and what the client tells you is very different from what you were expecting. Be pleased with yourself for not jumping in with your own assumption.

As with any notes about your use of counselling skills, ensure that you keep such records in a secure and confidential way.

Reflecting back and paraphrasing

One helpful pattern of response is to reflect back to the other person what you have just heard. Sometimes, but not always, you will reflect back almost the client's exact words. On other occasions you put the ideas or reactions into your own words, because continuous repetition sounds odd and is likely to irritate clients. However, you should not add your own words just in order to change a client's meaning, so that what is said makes more sense to you.

There are a number of different ways to start a paraphrase of what the other person has told you. For example:

- 'You are finding it hard/frustrating/tiring to deal with . . .'.
- 'So, what happened was that . . .'.
- 'You're pleased that . . . but you wish that . . .'.
- 'You sound very excited about the prospect of . . .'.
- 'You say you are uneasy about . . .'.
- 'You were telling me earlier about . . .' (when a topic has been left, possibly unfinished).
- 'If I've got it right, you most want that . . .'.
- 'Can I see if I understand you? You started to . . . but then . . .'.
- 'So far, you've managed to . . .'.

You can reflect back to clients what they have said about experiences, what they did in a particular situation and how they felt. When clients voice their feelings, it is appropriate to reflect them back because those emotions have been shared with you. Listen for nuances in what clients say and acknowledge mixed emotions that take clients in two directions at once, for instance:

- 'It sounds as if you've got mixed feelings about the promotion. Part of you is excited at the prospect, but you're also wary about the increased workload.'
- 'Sometimes you're half-pleased that your parents say "no" to your plans and then at other times you're annoyed about their interference.'
- 'You're fond of your cousin and you feel a strong sense of loyalty to her, but you still think she's put you in a difficult position over this secret.'

You should reflect back with some caution, especially as you are learning about the client and not delivering an instant interpretation. You should not overdo the tentative phrases or else you will sound too doubtful, but there are times to use expressions like:

- 'It seems . . .'.
- 'It looked like . . .'.
- 'I think . . .'.
- 'Perhaps . . .'.
- 'So what you seem to be feeling is . . .'.
- 'I sense you feel that . . .'.

You can also, with care, reflect back what the other person is telling you through body language combined with what the client said. You should not reflect back your observations of non-verbal communication until the client is relatively comfortable with you. Some people are unnerved by the idea that their body betrays feelings and reactions that they have chosen not to voice out loud. Examples of a careful comment could be:

- 'When you were telling me about your neighbour, you shivered. It seems that Tuesday's incident has left you very uneasy.'
- 'You looked so pleased when you told me about your media project with Jamal. You and he seem to be getting along better now.'

At Stage One in a helping relationship, you should only reflect back to clients what they have said or clearly shown you. As the conversation progresses, you may feel justified in taking a considered guess, even if the feeling words are not said by the client. You have to have a good reason, from what you have heard and seen, to step even a little further than what the client says. It is not your role in Stage One to probe under the surface of what has been said.

A note about what you say

Some courses on basic counselling skills start by telling participants to use a specific phrase as their response to clients during the course practice, usually organised with other participants as clients. The phrases told to us have included, 'What I hear you saying is . . .', and, 'How do you feel about that?' Some people with whom we have spoken had emerged with the idea that they could only ever use this single phrase in talking with clients. They said that such an approach was rigid and could never appear as genuine to clients. We agreed completely with them, but it is possible that the course tutors had not intended this result.

In teaching basic counselling skills we sometimes restrict participants to a limited choice of phrases in the early stage of learning. We have found that this temporary measure helps people to resist their own personal biases and to focus on the client. When people have learned to be still, to listen and to rein in their desire to question, interpret or be supportive, then they are ready to drop the interim restrictions on what they say.

Reflection to help clients be more specific

Unless clients are able to talk through their concerns in a fairly specific way, the discussion stays at a vague level. You have two main ways of helping clients to become more concrete about their concerns: the skills of reflecting back and questioning (see page 44).

Finding 'I'

Sometimes it is useful to restate what the client has said in more specific terms. Many people use their words, at least sometimes, to distance themselves from what is happening; their 'I' becomes lost in the words they say. You may experience some clients who frequently take this approach. For example:

- 'Anyone would be upset when . . .'.
- 'It's so annoying when he . . .'.
- 'You feel worthless when your husband does this kind of thing.'
- 'I know one shouldn't feel this way, of course, but . . .'.
- 'People shouldn't do this to you.'
- 'We're all fed up about . . .'.

You could reflect these examples back in a way to bring out the client as the 'I' in the statement. You might reflect each of these comments back to the client with slight changes, for instance:

- 'You feel upset about . . .'.
- 'You feel annoyed when he . . .'.
- 'When Greg contradicts what you've said to the children, you feel like you're worthless.'
- 'You feel angry with your mother and you believe as well that you shouldn't feel this way.'
- 'You feel sure that your supervisor should not go through your files without asking you.'
- 'You feel fed up and you believe that the rest of the team share your feelings.'

Sometimes clients describe a situation in a way that places the emphasis on other people, for instance:

- 'She should stop . . .'.
- 'They've got no business . . .'.
- 'He should understand that . . .'.
- 'They shouldn't make me feel . . .'.
- 'Don't you think it would be better if I . . . ?'

You could paraphrase these comments with:

- 'You'd like Anna to stop interrupting you in meetings.'
- 'You feel that your neighbours should not ask you to wait in for their deliveries because you're at home.'
- 'You'd rather that Damian understood that . . .', or, 'You believe it would make a difference if Damian understood that . . .'.
- 'When your parents ask if you've done your homework, you feel they're suggesting you can't keep track without being nagged.'
- 'It sounds like you believe it would be better if you . . .'.

Highlighting choice

Some clients describe situations in such a way that they appear to have no choice or are stuck between two impossible options. They may say:

- 'I can't get up on time. I've always had this problem with punctuality.'
- 'I have to keep the shared kitchen clean, it's disgusting otherwise.'
- 'You have to learn to be hard or else other people take advantage of you.'
- 'What's the point, I know it's not going to work out.'
- 'I want to lose weight but I've always eaten too much.'
- 'I'd like to stop smoking but I can't.'

You could paraphrase each example with:

- 'You find it hard to get up on time and so you're often late.'
- 'You believe that if you don't clean the kitchen, nobody else will.'
- 'You feel you have no choice but to be hard with other people.'
- 'You believe this idea can't work.'
- 'You want to lose weight and you think you eat too much.'
- 'You want to stop smoking and you find it hard', or the tougher version, 'You want to stop smoking and you choose not to stop.'

When clients use words like 'can't', 'won't', 'have to', 'ought to' or 'should', they are telling you that they feel some sense of compulsion or of having no real choice. A similar message comes when they join together two thoughts with 'but' rather than 'and'. Changing the words in your paraphrase (as in the last two examples above) highlights the nature of the issue and helps the client to see more clearly the meaning of what she or he has said. Words do not, of course, provide a resolution. Some problems are genuinely difficult to resolve. Clients may also be faced with a dilemma, in which they are torn between two equally unpleasant, or pleasant, alternatives (see page 160).

Remember what you have noticed

At Stage One in a helping conversation, you would highlight the client's approach through reflecting back only. Some clients will be more alert to your use of words than others, will listen, stop and think about what they have said and how they talk about this issue. You should not in any sense pursue clients to acknowledge what you have noticed. If clients do not react to your paraphrase, then hold this perspective in your mind, because it may be useful to return to it further in the conversation or in another session. At Stage Two, it will be appropriate to explain what you have noticed about how this client views the problem, with the encouragement to consider this perspective.

Activity

Listen in to your own use of words as you talk or think about issues and problems in your own life. Experiment with restating comments to yourself and experience how the change of words may give an alternative perspective. For instance:

- Practise making 'I' statements out of comments that distance you from an issue – even simple ones like 'It's hot today'. Become aware of the ways that you distance yourself. Do you use 'you', 'people', 'it's' or any of the other ways with words from page 136?
- When you face a situation that appears to have few alternatives, try rethinking 'I can't' into 'I don't want to' or 'I choose not to'.
- Perhaps you are someone who often says or thinks, 'He makes me feel . . .', or, 'They shouldn't . . .'. Try replacing those phrases with, 'When he . . . I feel . . .', or, 'I should . . .'.

Summarising

A good summary is brief and includes not only the facts and the words, but also the feelings that clients have expressed. For example:

- 'So, Phil regularly submits his reports at least a week late. You sound annoyed by this, Angie, like it's getting you down.'
- 'You've realised that Jamie has frequent nightmares and what sound like flashbacks about his brother's accident. You're sure that Jamie feels

responsible for the accident, although you've reassured your son many times that it wasn't his fault. And you feel confused and frustrated, because your family doctor believes that Michael is the only one who should need help, because he was the one injured.'

Put the ideas or descriptions at least partly into your own words but the language should still be primarily in the words used by the client – particularly emotional words.

It is especially important to summarise the main points if the client shifts to another topic, or when the conversation or session is coming to an end. The summary affirms that you have understood and helps the client to focus on the main points as she or he has expressed them. Summaries are also important to link several elements of the problem together, as you and the client move towards a conclusion at the end of Stage One about what the client sees as the issue.

Careful use of questions

You can help clients by encouraging them to explore the issue in more detail and to become more specific about elements of the situation. Any questions should be asked within the client's framework and not because of your particular interests or curiosity. Questions have to be used with care, since a long sequence of questions can feel like an interrogation.

The more useful questions are open-ended rather than closed (see also page 45). You invite the other person to explore and explain, rather than give you a one-word or very short answer. For instance:

- 'Would you like to say some more about how you see the possibilities in your career?'
- 'What happened then?'
- 'How did you feel about that?'
- 'Could you give me an example of that?'
- 'What decided you to do that?'
- 'You've gone quiet, would you like to tell me what you're thinking?'
- 'I understand that you're worried about your teenage daughter. Tell me a bit more about what is making you so worried.'

Clients who have been on the receiving end of a great deal of unsolicited advice from friends or family may never have been asked for their opinion of the situation. You could ask:

- 'What do you think is going on with your child's night waking?'
- 'How do you think . . . has come about?'

Clients may be quiet for a moment as they consider their own views and beliefs. Leave silence so that they can work through their response. They may also feel pleased that you have shown respect in asking for and listening to their views, and waiting for their answer.

Rephrasing 'why' questions

Questions that start with 'why' tend to be less useful because they guide clients towards a justification of their position or trying to think up a reason to satisfy you because you appear to want an explanation.

- Instead of, 'Why did you get so angry about . . . ?', you could reflect back with, 'You became very angry when . . .'. Or ask, 'What do you think made you so angry about . . . ?'
- Sometimes the words 'what for' are an improvement over 'why'. For example, instead of 'Why do you think your son locks himself in his room?', ask, 'What do you think your son locks himself in his room for?' The 'why' question more often brings responses like, 'To stop me getting in', or, 'Because he's a pain.' The 'what for' question is more likely to encourage the client to consider a new angle, and to bring responses like, 'Perhaps to get some privacy', or, 'I suppose he doesn't know what else to do when we've all got so angry.'
- Instead of 'Why do you think Alric's drinking is a problem?', you can ask, 'How does Alric's drinking affect your life?' In addition, this last example helps to keep the discussion focused on the client who is present. You can only counsel the person who is with you, not his or her absent partner, friend or colleague.

Helping clients to be more specific

Some clients will be more concrete in how they talk than others. As you listen, you may have a clear visual image of what the client has experienced and why it troubles him or her. On the other hand, some clients talk more in the abstract and you are left feeling uncertain about what she or he means in practice. It can be helpful to invite the other person to give specific examples or more description of a given event. For example:

- 'Lucy, you say that your mother interferes with how you bring up the children. Can you give me an example?'
- 'You've told me that sometimes your confidence seems to disappear when you face your boss. You used the phrase, "I feel frozen". Can you describe to me the most recent time this happened to you?' Or you might ask, 'What does "frozen" mean to you?'

Both of the above examples have placed a question after a reflection or paraphrase of what the client just said. This approach puts your question in a positive context of exploring what the client has said rather than directing with just a question.

Sometimes you will need to ask a question because you are confused. This is perfectly all right, as you need to understand in order to help. For example, perhaps the client is assuming that you know details of her or his personal life when you do not. For example:

- Lindsay, who is nominally Christian, is married to Annop, whose background is Hindu. Lindsay says to you, 'It's the time of year. I always feel down in the autumn. It's because Divali is coming up and I know Annop and I will have a row, however hard I try. I'm so relieved when it's over, but I'm sad too because

Divali should be a nice family time, more like I feel that Christmas is. It's the same each year; it's got that I call it my Divali time. But only to myself, of course. Annop only sees it his way, never mine.'

You understand that the celebration of Divali leads to rows between Lindsay and Annop but you are confused about how this happens. If Lindsay seems unlikely to explain, you will need to intervene, for example with, 'Lindsay, I haven't understood what happens around Divali time that is linked with the rows between you and Annop.' Lindsay then explains that Annop is convinced she spends much more time and attention on preparing for Christmas than she does for Divali.

Activity

Be alert to situations in which you are on the receiving end of questions from someone else:

- What kind of questions help you to explore an issue?
- What kind tend to narrow down on the conversation?
- How does it feel on the receiving end if another person asks you a whole series of directive questions?

Moving on from Stage One

Potential helpers often find Stage One the most difficult in the helping model. The emphasis is on the perspective of the client and you may doubt that you are really doing anything. You may be very tempted to fall back into your personal bias (see page 115), with the result that you will not gain a full understanding. The work you then try to do in the later stages of the model will be less effective because you only understand parts of the client's problem rather than the bigger, more complete picture.

Stage One is complete when:

- Clients have explored their situation thoroughly from how they see it or all they are prepared to discuss at the moment. If clients are starting to circle back to the same issues or information, it is very likely to be time to move on.
- You feel you have a good understanding of the client's situation and concerns.
- Your exploration with the client has led to an agreement between the two of you on the problem or the nature of the choice that the client is facing.

In every case, however, Stage One should be completed with a summary to ensure that you and your client have a shared understanding of what the problem is – and what it is not – from the client's perspective. You may even use the end of Stage One to check whether the client wishes to progress further with the issue or not as appropriate.

Your Stage One exploration with a client does not have a fixed time period. Some helpful conversations may last in total, all stages, for 10–15 minutes; others will stretch over several sessions with the same client. Often, you will move into Stage Two skills with the client within the same conversation. You recognise that the time is ready for a different kind of exploration.

Making a choice of priorities

Sometimes clients have to decide which of several possible aspects or concerns to take further. Other problems are not dismissed, but you cannot explore everything in detail at the same time. If there are several possibilities, then be guided by your client and help him or her to reach a focus for the next part of your conversation. There is no one right way to choose and you will need to guide clients in the light of your understanding of them and their current situation:

- Some clients can be most highly motivated to explore an issue that they could resolve fairly easily alone. Some clients lack confidence or are just now accepting that they could make a difference. Then their success in understanding a smaller problem will boost their confidence to do some painful thinking about more difficult issues.
- Regardless of difficulty, some clients want and need to face the most pressing problem, or the immediate crisis. They will not be able to concentrate on anything else or what they could learn for the future until they have some sense of facing up to the present. This may encourage you to work on addressing a symptom (such as finding it hard to get up in the morning), rather than the cause (worries about problems at work). Be aware of what you are doing and ready to look at deeper issues when the client is ready.
- The client's best priority is to focus on that part of the problem over which they have some control. For instance, Alastair has told you about his long-standing problems with a colleague. You may have helped Alastair to get through the perspective of, 'My colleague makes me feel mean if I say "no" to her demands for help', or, 'She should stop interrupting my work'. Alastair has begun to acknowledge that he cannot make the colleague change her behaviour but that he could look at his own reactions, feelings and contribution to the difficult situation – in other words, what Alastair can do to make the situation less difficult and more manageable.
- Clients who have several important concerns may only have given you a hint of their deeper worries. You need to respect the priority they give to an issue with which they feel able to trust you for the time being. Clients may choose to return to a more distressing or confusing issue at a later time. If they do, you will need to return to using Stage One skills to explore this issue and its relationship to your previous discussion in more depth.

You may go through a similar process of helping clients to sort out priorities at the end of Stage Two (see page 159) when you work with them to develop goals for action.

An example of Stage One exploration

Wai is an early years worker in a nursery. She is having supervision from Leela and they are discussing Wai's frustrations in her working relationship with Monica, the speech therapist who visits the nursery.

Wai: I can't put my finger on it. Monica's got good ideas. I think she's probably a good speech therapist, but the children don't enjoy her sessions.

Leela: So, you don't have worries about Monica's professional abilities?

Wai: No, I don't – well, except that she doesn't seem to be making much difference to the children! And she was all right about giving me some written suggestions in the end – although I had to remind her twice. You know, Leela, it's funny. None of the children are pleased to see her. I honestly don't think they would go to the sessions if I didn't stay as well.

Leela: You're concerned that the children aren't really happy to be with Monica? That and the fact that you can't see much progress from the sessions?

Wai: Yes. So I think, why are we bothering?

Leela: How did you feel about this week's session with Monica?

Wai: Much the same as always. The children don't warm to her. Could you have a word with her, Leela?

Leela: I'm willing to have a chat with Monica but I really need more to go on. Why don't you talk me through this week's session as you remember it? You've noticed something, so let's see if you can put your finger on it. Help me see the session through your eyes, Wai. So, how did Monica start?

Question

- What skills does Leela use in this short extract?
- Wai has a gut feel of worry but cannot put her concerns in a concrete way. How does Leela help Wai to get closer to the observations that have fed her concern?

Activity

During the next couple of weeks, make a conscious effort to use some of the Stage One skills in conversations with colleagues, friends or family.

- Focus on your attending skills, listening and looking, in everyday exchanges.
- Try reflecting back and paraphrasing rather than moving swiftly to give advice or shape up a problem for someone else.
- Ask open-ended questions rather than closed ones.
- Sometimes use a summary to check that you have understood what another person has said.

Reflect on what has happened in exchanges and what you have learned.

We would add a cautionary note from our experience of suggesting this kind of activity to a wide range of people. First, the most likely consequence of using Stage One skills is that another person will be encouraged to say more. So, please do not practise your skills unless you have the time to listen. Second, you may receive feedback that surprises you from friends or family. We were told the story of a son who stopped his father in his tracks with, 'Dad, why are you listening to me today?'

Personal experience

You may have noticed that there has been no suggestion at Stage One to share your own experiences with clients. There is no way of knowing whether a personal experience is appropriate to share until you have listened well to the client. Your unvoiced experience may support the help you offer, but the emphasis in the relationship must remain with the client.

We do not recommend sharing any personal experience in Stage One unless you really know that your experience directly parallels that of the client, in terms of situation, experience and resulting feelings. In addition, even if all of the above is true, sharing your own experience should only be done tentatively and in the spirit of summarising the client's perceptions from your personal experience. In Stage Two, it is far more likely there will be appropriate opportunities for you to share something personal (see page 151).

To think about

Can you recall times when someone else, perhaps with a wish to help, gave you a detailed account of their own experience?
- To what extent was it helpful and in what ways unhelpful?
- How did you feel if you were told, 'I know exactly how you feel', or, 'The same thing happened to me'?
- What can you learn from times when the recounting of other people's personal experiences created a block for you to talk about your own?

7.2 Stage Two: exploring alternative perspectives

Advanced understanding

The objective of Stage Two is to help the client to explore new perspectives. The opening-out phase of Stage Two is possible because you have worked hard to see the situation through the client's eyes. You remain focused on the client and certainly moving into Stage Two does not give you permission to direct clients, or to tell them how they should view the situation or what they should do. All the skills described within Stage One are equally important now, but through giving the client the time to understand their issue fully you have earned the right to use the skills differently and in a stronger way. Unless you build your basic understanding, showing respect for the client, the approaches of Stage Two can be at best unhelpful or at worst destructive to a client's well-being.

By the end of Stage One, you should have a thorough understanding of how the client sees the problem, and have checked that your perception is accurate through the summary. You will neither know nor have heard everything, but you have enough observational information to apply your counselling skills in more advanced ways. You can use reflecting back, summarising and questions in ways which are potentially more challenging to the client. Your use of skills should enable the client to think in new ways, to consider the issues from fresh angles. Stage Two is designed to make the subjective view of the client (gathered in Stage One) more objective and realistic, so that achievable goals to address the issue can be agreed.

Your overall objective is to support clients as they consider other perspectives or acknowledge the importance of experiences, feelings and thoughts of which they may be scarcely aware. You are not implying that the client is wrong, just understandably focused on his or her own point of view.

Put into words what the client implies

You are only justified in putting the implication into words on the basis of all that you have heard from your client. Perhaps you attempt to express ideas or experiences that have emerged in a confused way from the client. On the basis of all you have heard and noticed, you start to express what clients have not yet said for themselves. For example:

- 'Lucy, you sound torn. I understand that you feel your mother interferes. Yet she sometimes has a good idea – like her suggestion about Alan's eating. It sounds as if you are wary of going with the good ideas because that will make her think she's right about everything.'
- Maryam has spent several conversations with Amy, who is Davy's mother. Amy has wanted to talk about the local primary schools 'so that I can make a good decision', but Maryam has noticed that Amy finds something wrong with all the schools. Amy has also talked sadly about how much she will miss coming to the family centre. Maryam says warmly, 'Amy, I think that a lot of what you're feeling is about leaving here. The decision about schools is important but perhaps it would help to talk about these other feelings. You and Davy have been coming to the centre for a long time.'

Summarise disjointed information

Often clients express thoughts, describe events or give hints about personal dilemmas in a disjointed way. Even clients who are confident with their words will not necessarily present a tidy version. It is not a client's role to provide a neat flow of what they wish to communicate; it is your job to help them to sort out the various themes and issues.

Your skills in providing a summary are particularly useful when information has emerged in a fragmented way. Your summary is more extensive or deeper in terms of addressing feelings than in Stage One. For example:

- 'So, you're weighing up several issues that sound as if they are equally important to you, Helen. You want to extend your skills, particularly in information technology. You are undecided whether you get on a part-time course or give up work for a full-time one. Your husband, Robert, has been offered a job in America and you have both always wanted to go there. And neither of you wants to postpone having a family for much longer. Ideally, you would like all these things, but you know they can't all happen at once.'

Under these circumstances it can sometimes help to write down the main points. Offer the client this possibility before you pick up a pen or offer one to the client. Writing down can shift the atmosphere of the exchange, so be sure that it is suitable for the topic and stage of the conversation. For example:

- Saira has been helping Paresh with his study skills in general and with his upcoming student project in particular. Paresh has found it especially difficult to organise all the separate parts of his project. He uses phrases like, 'I'm drowning in the details', and, 'There so much that's possible, I don't know where to start.' Saira suggests that it is exactly the wealth of detail that is central to Paresh's problem at the moment. Paresh agrees they will write down the main headings to get his project into a more manageable shape.

Highlight themes and consequences

Sometimes, your attentive listening will suggest that a theme runs through experiences that the client has described. You have listened and contributed in a positive way so that you can see possible connections and consequences. At Stage Two it is time to share your observation with the client. You can be helpful so long as you remain tentative, with no sense of, 'It's obvious that . . .', or, 'I'm surprised you haven't realised that . . .'. You show respect to the client and leave him or her with space to consider when you describe any theme rather than label the client. For instance:

- You may be able to suggest tentatively, 'Do you see the possible pattern here? You've talked with me about three people: your father, your boyfriend and your colleague. You ask each of them for advice and then you argue if their view is different from yours. You seem to want confirmation of your own view but you're unwilling to volunteer it.'

On occasion, clients talk about issues that are potentially linked as if there is no connection at all. Perhaps recognising the connection may be uncomfortable or lead the client towards a need for action that she or he would rather avoid. For example:

- Sally has had a long conversation with Liam, Sean's father. Liam had wanted to talk about Sean's rough approach to the other children and Sally was pleased since the reception class team have been concerned. Liam is worried that Sean wets the bed and is very upset whenever he has to stay with his grandparents because Liam has a weekend shift. Liam then mentions almost in passing, 'Sean's mother walked out at Christmas. I thought you might wonder why you never see her now.' Sally expresses sympathy and asks a few questions about how Liam is managing with his shift work. She then offers, 'Liam, have you considered that Sean's behaviour may be a reaction to his Mum going?' Liam looks thoughtful, 'It crossed my mind but my mother said that Sean would soon forget all about his Mum if we didn't mention her'. Sally replies with, 'I wouldn't say that has been my experience. Children don't forget that easily.'

Often you can help the client to draw conclusions from what he or she is describing. For example:

- 'You've spoken about arguments with your wife, who you feel is strong and independent. You've also shared issues around working with your new female boss, and problems with your teenage daughter. Is there a general theme here of difficulties with women in general?'

These may or may not be firm conclusions but a helper can encourage the client to take the issue that bit further. On occasion this carries the sense of, 'Do you see where this approach is leading you? Is that where you want to be?' For instance:

- Moira has spent time with Wesley, whose main concern is to feel more confident. Wesley has talked in detail about how he was so disheartened by criticism from his new art teacher. Wesley dismisses this teacher as a poor artist, yet claims, 'He has destroyed my confidence.' Moira replies, 'Wesley, it sounds as if you're making the opinion of one person, whom you say you don't respect, carry more weight than your previous teacher. Let alone your family who you tell me all admire your artistic ability. Are you really prepared to stop painting because of this one man?'
- Six weeks ago Jane was mugged by someone who ran up behind her on a dark winter afternoon, grabbed her bag and sped off down the street. Jane was very shaken although otherwise unhurt. She prides herself on being able to cope and not worrying anyone else, especially her children. She has not told her daughters about the mugging but her silence has led to some problems. Her older daughter has asked why Jane is no longer using the special pen that was a birthday present from the child. (The pen was stolen with the bag.) Yesterday, Jane reacted dramatically when a jogger ran up behind her and the two girls. She yanked both daughters behind her in a protective gesture and it was impossible for her to hide her fright. In conversation with you, Jane has regularly used phrases like, 'I have to be strong for the girls', and, 'I can't possibly tell them I was mugged. They'll be frightened to go out.' You make the decision to confront some of Jane's convictions with, 'Jane, you say you "can't" tell the girls because "they'll be frightened". But from your description of what happened last night, I'd guess that they know that you're frightened, but not why. We've discussed your choice not to tell them about the mugging, what you felt were the advantages of keeping silent. Perhaps we should talk now about the downside of your silence and some reasons why your daughters need to understand what has happened to you.'

Offering other perspectives

Helping is hard work because it requires you to focus on what clients have expressed, in the way that they first wish to express it. Because you have listened, you will now have the basis for offering different views of the issue.

- Morag is trying hard to resolve competing demands: 'I want to give nothing but my best to my job but I can't bear the thought that I might neglect my own family. And I believe so strongly that women should find some time for themselves.' Perhaps it is not possible for Morag to give 100 per cent to everything, and this could be a useful perspective to offer her.
- Andrew organises his life around a goal that he has never questioned: 'I must keep any money problems to myself; I mustn't worry my wife with that.' You may offer another perspective with a comment such as, 'What makes you so certain that you must keep money worries to yourself? What leads you to be so sure that your wife wouldn't rather know? Have you checked? Perhaps she would rather help with the problem.' This intervention has to be offered as a perspective because Andrew may be right, perhaps his wife does not want to know or will panic to such a degree that he will be unable to deal with the problem. You are not saying Andrew should tell his wife; you are offering the space for him to think through the possibility of telling her.

Offering alternative views can also include checking to see whether other people share the same view as your client. For example:

- Matthew has talked extensively about how he is irritated by his dictatorial manager, Pat, and how he feels that his contribution is not rewarded. You might ask, 'Do your colleagues who report to Pat feel the same way as you?' If they do not, this can provide a helpful avenue of exploration, around differences in the way that Matthew and his colleagues work with Pat to give him a new perspective on the issue.

An example of use of skills during Stage Two

Kevin (the centre manager) is in the middle of a supervision session with Cathy (a team member).

Kevin: You say that Jon dominates team meetings and won't let you talk. But Cathy, I want you to think over yesterday's meeting. I recall at least three occasions when Jon asked you what you thought. I don't think you replied at any of those times.

Cathy: I don't think it was three times. Once at the most. Well, maybe twice.

Kevin: Okay, let's follow the theme that Jon does sometimes make space for you to talk and you choose not to speak up. What do you think is going on here?

Cathy: If he wasn't so pushy most of the time then I might. It's more his fault than mine.

Kevin: I hear what you're saying about Jon's approach but let's focus on your behaviour and your choices. It takes two to tango.

Cathy: He intimidates me.

Kevin: You're saying you feel intimidated by Jon?

Cathy: Yes, he undermines my confidence. I'm frightened to speak up.

Kevin: I saw your expression yesterday, Cathy. I wouldn't have described you as 'frightened'. To be honest, you looked rather pleased with yourself.

Cathy: (*silence*)

Kevin: Come on, Cathy. We've worked together for long enough. You looked pleased to put Jon in the hot spot.

Cathy: All right, maybe not frightened.

Kevin: Maybe not frightened. What then?

Cathy (after a short silence which Kevin deliberately does not break): You don't know what Jon was like when he first came here. He thought he knew everything! He talked over the top of everybody, wanted to reorganise everything in sight! He's just one team member like the rest of us; he was never in charge.

Kevin: So, there's some history here?

Cathy: Yes, and I suppose he has tried recently. But he was such a pain in the beginning . . .

Comment

Notice how Kevin uses skills of reflecting back Cathy's words and asking open-ended questions, but in a stronger way than in Stage One. It is possible to challenge the client in Stage Two, but this should never turn into a relentless pursuit.

This example shows an informed challenge. The way that Kevin frames his contributions communicates a feel of, 'Cathy, try looking at it this way', and, 'Hold on a minute.' Kevin does not pronounce judgement on Cathy, nor try to come across as if he can read her mind. He has shared with her what he has heard and seen. In a friendly way appropriate to their working relationship, Kevin communicates that he is not going to let Cathy avoid considering a perspective other than the one that makes her feel comfortable and faultless. He helps her to make her own view more realistic and objective. His careful challenge has been combined with support.

Informed confrontation or challenge

Many of the examples given so far for Stage Two have an element of challenge to the client, of a intervention that still shows respect because your contribution is based firmly in what the client has said so far. Sometimes you would alert clients to contradictions in what they say about the same issue or person at different times. At no point would a good helper say bluntly, 'You're defensive!', or, 'You can't make up your mind about . . .'. Your approach is a more respectful, 'I've noticed that you change the subject whenever I ask about . . .', or, 'Morag, you say that you really love your children, yet you spend most of your leisure time alone.'

Your intervention is stronger and more testing of clients than at Stage One but you should not drive clients into a corner. Sometimes, it makes sense to create space for the client by tentative phrases like, 'Does this make sense to you?', 'I suggest we look at this angle', or, 'It sounds to me like', and words like 'perhaps', 'possibly'.

Your summaries or questions may also bring to a client's attention what she or he is not saying, or almost says. For instance:

- Freddy asked to talk with you about the recent death of his father. So far, he has spent most of the conversation complaining about how the hospital phoned him in the early hours of the morning with the news of his father's death. Freddy has insisted on discussing this early hours call in an objective and logical way: why would a hospital do this, why wake people up when they can do nothing until daybreak, what do you think about this kind of practice? You have offered reflections and summaries, but your client has resolutely stayed with practical details and now returns to the phone call for the third time. You sense a rerun of the same litany as before and stop the client courteously with, 'Freddy, let's leave to one side whether the hospital should or shouldn't have called you when they did. How did you feel when the hospital sister told you your father had died?'

Respectful and informed challenge of a client, blended with support, can help him or her to think through the unthinkable in a safe environment.

- Joanne has been telling you about the practical difficulties created around her mother's recent heart attack. Bit by bit, it emerges that her mother had been estranged from Joanne in recent months. After a great deal of thought, Joanne had told her family that she was gay and that the person whom her family believed to be a flatmate was in fact her long-term partner. Joanne's father had seemed neither very surprised nor shocked by his daughter's revelation but was angry that the news had upset his wife. He and Joanne's sister have been on the phone, saying that Joanne caused her mother's heart attack and that nothing would have happened if she had had the sense to keep quiet. Joanne says to you, 'They think it's all my fault, that I put Mum in danger.' On the basis of what you have learned of Joanne so far, you sensitively put back to her, 'And what do you think?', or even the more challenging, 'And do you think this has some justification?'

A client may be very resistant to the perspective that she is making a choice, preferring to place the responsibility elsewhere. Perhaps you tried some paraphrases in Stage One (like the examples on page 137) and the client dismissed them with a firm, 'Yes but . . .'. At Stage Two, as your client circles round the same material with the same perspective, you will judge that the time has come to press her. For example:

- 'Natalie, you've told me all about how your neighbour, Rosie, wants to talk with you frequently. I understand how, if you start to say "no" to her at the door, you say Rosie just stands there and "looks pathetic" and you feel you "have to let her in". You're also concerned that your children often can't talk with you when they want and your husband says that he feels "pushed out" of his own kitchen. Perhaps we should look hard at your real choices in this situation. You say that you "have to talk with Rosie" and so she "makes you neglect your children". Let's see this as "you choose to talk with Rosie and so you choose the consequence that your children often can't talk with you because you're giving time and attention to Rosie rather than to them". These things are not isolated, they affect each other.'

Finally, confrontation can be used to help the client to recognise areas of personal strength that are not being used in this situation. For example:

- 'You have shown lots of skills in dealing with subordinates at work. Can any of these skills be used to help address the problems you're having with your nephew?'

Sharing personal experience – self-disclosure

There will be some times in helping relationships when it is appropriate for you to contribute a personal experience. You might share briefly what happened to you, how you felt or what you learned from the experience. This contribution should always be done with the objective of helping the client see that you understand their position. For example:

- 'I don't think people understand what months of broken nights are like, unless they've been there. I know I didn't really understand until I had my daughter. People are very quick to give you simple advice as if you haven't tried everything obvious.'
- You might be able to offer a personal insight in the example of Natalie and her neighbour Rosie. For instance, perhaps Natalie says, 'I'm being stupid, aren't I?', and you reply, 'No, I don't think you're being stupid, Natalie. I got myself into what sounds like a very similar situation with my neighbour. I needed to recognise that I was making a choice, not just see it as all down to her. That's one reason why I put this idea of choice to you.'
- 'Perhaps you're being hard on yourself. You're emotionally involved with your own parents, so you won't be able to stand back in the way that you can in your job. I know I had to learn that I was a different person at home from work, and that I found this difficult to manage.'
- Ciaran has been talking about problems in managing his time at the charity for which he works and his outside life. You reply, 'When I was working for another charity, I found that balancing my time between home and work was very difficult – particularly when my caseload got very high. I really felt guilty sometimes, although I knew how many hours I was working. Is that how you feel too?'

Positive self-disclosure

There is sometimes a place for contributing your own experience with clients but it will not always be appropriate to self-disclose. Sharing a personal experience will be helpful if you bear in mind the following points:

- Your contribution should be brief. Clients are there to talk about their concerns, not to listen to the details of yours.
- Your shared personal experience should bring into sharper focus what clients think or feel about their own issue and help them to consider other perspectives.
- If you speak for too long or do not link what you are saying to the client's own issue, then he or she may start to ask you about your experience: what happened, what you felt or what you did. In other words, you have moved the entire focus of the discussion inappropriately away from the client.
- Hence, if the client asks direct questions about you, answer briefly before bringing the focus back with, 'Let's explore how you feel about what's happening to you', or, 'So what does that mean for you?'
- You might introduce short personal experiences with tentative phrases like, 'I felt something similar to that when . . .', or, 'I think I had an experience that was similar.' Avoid saying, 'I know exactly how you feel', or, 'The same thing happened to me', because such phrases deny a client's individuality.
- The way that you coped or what you learned may be useful to the client but it is for him or her to see the potentially helpful links. It is not for you to assume that what worked for you will work for the client, any more than what did not work for you will be no use.

You should never make up experiences similar to those of your client. There is no need to tell untruths or even to modify your experience to sound more like that of the client. If you bend the truth, you will undermine the genuineness of the helping relationship and respect for the client. You need not have experienced the same event in order to understand and help your client.

When you have strong feelings

To be helpful to clients you need to remain alert to your own feelings. Sometimes, the experience or problem that you are talking through with a client uncomfortably stirs up your own painful memories. As a responsible helper you need to keep your own experience and any unresolved feelings clearly separate from that of the client. For instance:

- It is crucial that the client does not begin to feel burdened with your distress, confusion or unresolved feelings of anger and frustration.
- It is not the client's role to help you express your feelings; you should talk with somebody else. Keep your feelings separate from those of your client.
- Be very careful not to rerun your experience with the client, perhaps encouraging him or her to take a line of action that you wish you had followed. You should remain objective but you are not perfect and may travel this route a short way before you realise. Stop yourself and bring the client back into sharp focus.
- If all else fails, you may need to refer the client to another helper who will be able to help where you have become unable to apply your skills. Without going into great detail, you should be honest with your client about the reason for referral. Otherwise clients, especially vulnerable ones, may blame themselves for the breakdown of the helping relationship.

Immediate issues in the helping relationship

Sometimes it is important to address the relationship itself. You should carefully raise the issue if you judge that you or the client have unspoken thoughts and feelings that are blocking the helping process. You use your counselling skills to address the here and now of the situation in a way that combines elements of self-disclosure (your feelings and perceptions) and informed confrontation (an element of 'Hold on a minute').

The reasons for a client's silence, reservations or short answers will not necessarily be distress. Until you address what is happening, you can only guess. For example:

- Halfway through a careers guidance session, Sejeeven realises that his client David is scarcely talking. This situation is unusual because David usually has plenty to say. Sejeeven addresses the issue directly with, 'David, you've gone quiet. Is there something on your mind?' David pauses and replies, 'It's what you said about a gap year. I didn't realise I could take a break between my A levels and university. I thought you had to keep going. That's why I said what I did about not being sure I wanted to go to university. I said the same thing to my parents; they weren't very pleased at all.' Sejeeven needs to acknowledge David's fresh perspective, perhaps with, 'I'm sorry, David. I hadn't realised you didn't know about gap years. Perhaps that changes how you'd like to talk about your plans.'
- Over the last month, in the family centre Gareth has been helping Effie to talk through her feelings about her son, Cameron, and difficulties in handling his behaviour. Effie has seemed easy with Gareth until the last two sessions, when she started to talk about Cameron's birth and the long-term consequences of her post-natal depression. Gareth feels that Effie is far less happy talking with him on these topics and she does not seem to be getting any more at ease. She has made several comments about it's being 'different for men!' So today he raises the issue by saying, 'Effie, I've noticed that recently it seems harder for you to talk with me. You've looked less comfortable since you started to explain about Cameron's birth and what happened to you. Would you rather talk with a female worker, perhaps Melissa? I wouldn't be upset if you'd prefer that, I'd understand.'

Addressing immediate issues within the helping relationship is placed within Stage Two because this use of your skills will often be more confronting. However, there will be times when talking with a client about the here and now will be appropriate within Stage One, for instance:

- The example of Sejeeven and David could easily happen within Stage One of a helpful conversation.
- You might need to address the behaviour of extremely quiet clients within Stage One, because you will not be able to progress with almost silent clients. You use all your skills to draw out the client and tolerate silences, but in the end you cannot help if you are mainly listening to silence.

An immediate issue may arise from your side of the work. For example:

- You have continued a session with a client hoping that your growing headache will be controlled by the two paracetamol you took earlier. However, you are now aware that the pounding from inside your head is making it very hard to concentrate. Under such conditions the best course will be to admit the difficulty to the client, bring the session to a close and set another time.
- A personal example comes from Jennie's experience of continuing to work with individuals and groups whilst expecting our daughter. In the second half of the pregnancy the baby's repertoire of drop kicks was sufficiently energetic to cause visible winces. Clients needed to be told, briefly, that painful expressions were internally caused and had nothing to do with what they had just said.

Setting goals

Stage Two opens out as you encourage clients to consider new perspectives on the issues they first raised with you. This stage reaches a closing-down phase and a new focus when you have helped clients to explore their issues in detail and they have reached a more extensive understanding. Now you and your client need to work towards setting goals that will provide the basis for the client to act on the problem or confusion.

This model of helping enables clients to move beyond new ideas or insights and towards what they want to do and can do on the basis of those new perspectives. The client still retains the choice; at no point do you insist that she or he does something and some issues are more oriented to possible action than others. Goal-setting is covered in the following Chapter 8.

▼ 8 Goal setting and action planning

8.1 From problems to realistic goals

Moving towards 'What shall I do?'

You help clients to set specific goals at the end of Stage Two (what they will achieve), when they are motivated to move towards Stage Three of action-planning (how they will achieve it). Vague plans will not help a client move on. For instance, there is not much practical future in an approach of, 'Now I understand why I get so angry with my colleague. I'll be more patient, starting tomorrow.' The client will benefit from time to discuss possible ways of dealing with the strong emotions that are provoked by the colleague under particular conditions and how the client will deal with these feelings when they arise.

You are looking for a willingness from the client to act and some focus for that action. For example:

- Delroy has spent some time with Nancy, whose twin sons attend the family centre. Nancy's initial approach to her problems with her sons was, 'It's hopeless. They run all over me. If only I'd been tougher when they were younger. It's too late now; I can't control them.' Delroy has helped Nancy to focus on the present, not the past, and to recognise some real positives in her time with the boys (some 'can's' and not only the 'can'ts'). Nancy most wants to manage the chaotic evenings, when she finds it so difficult to get her sons to bed, and she is keen to talk over possible ways to handle this time.
- Kitty has gained insight into her difficulties within the team. She explains to you, 'I can see now that what I claimed was helpful was exactly what drove people mad. I would do something for a colleague because I wanted to feel needed and I wouldn't even listen if they said not to do it. Then I'd want them to be grateful for all my effort, when it was me that had insisted. I'll never forget that phrase you used, that it was a case of, "Watch out! Here comes the help!" [Kitty laughs]. I have this picture in my mind, that people duck when I throw my help at them. But I've also realised that I'm going to find it hard to stop; I'm not sure what to do instead.'

Clearing the way for clients to set goals

In order to set workable goals, you have to identify and clarify the problems and issues faced by the client. Most of this work should have been covered within Stage

Two so far, but clients also need to view their problems in such a way that they can see it is actually possible to do something positive. It is crucial that clients:

- Have been enabled to describe the situation in such a way that it is possible for it to be solved, or at least improved. Goals have to be worded so that it is possible to achieve them. Some clients may see a benefit in holding on to the problem. For example, other people are sympathetic to them and it gives them something to talk about. If you have explored the issues and the client resolutely does not want to solve the problem, you should respectfully end the counselling process (see page 170).
- Own their problem or can sort out which parts of a problem they are prepared to own. Clients cannot set goals and resolve any issues that they still insist on locating with somebody else.
- Are able to describe their problem in concrete terms so that the goals can be made specific.
- Work with you to break any large problem into smaller, more manageable units on which you can work together to produce realistic goals.

Problems become soluble

Some clients may create harder work for themselves because they actively block any possible route forward. Clients create blockages in different ways, and for understandable reasons, but in order to help you need to use Stage Two skills to bring the blockages into the open. For instance:

- Brian feels he has no way out of applying to train as a lawyer. He says, 'It's been part of my childhood. I'm the bright one, my sister isn't academic at all, so she's off the hook. My father always wanted to be a lawyer but his parents couldn't afford it. Then he got married and we were born. So he gave up his dream so that we could have the best possible education. Gran keeps on about how guilty she feels but I'm going to make it all right. It's no good, I don't have a choice. They're all depending on me.'

There is no way out as Brian describes his situation. The helper will need to bring out the different parts of the problem and highlight Brian's possible choices while acknowledging how he feels about the blocks. Brian will also need to get in touch with what he would like to do, given a choice, and the helper will be important in supporting him beyond 'Ah but . . .'. You will find more on page 160 about dealing with apparently insoluble dilemmas.

Some clients will seek to avoid working towards achievable goals on one problem through the tactic of introducing another concern. You should respect clients' wishes to explore broadly but you will realise with some clients that an interjection of 'Before we do that, I'd really like to talk about . . .' now looks like a pattern of avoidance. Use your counselling skills to confront the client with the pattern, for instance:

- The example of Amy from page 145 might reach this point before Maryam as a helper fully realises the pattern. Amy finds different strategies to avoid Maryam's help in deciding on schools for Davy. Without putting her feelings into words, Amy is postponing her leave-taking from the family centre where she has been so happy. Her goal cannot be finding a way to freeze time because it is not possible. She needs to face goals in two areas: to make an informed decision about her son's school and to find ways to meet her own emotional needs that have so far been met through involvement in the centre.

Some clients may resist discussing a problem in ways that make it open to resolution because they want to avoid the consequences that will follow. For instance:

- Perhaps Wesley (page 147) has enjoyed the attention of Moira's helping him with his lack of confidence. It is the first time for Wesley that anyone has given him this kind of non-judgemental attention. He feels that if his problem with confidence is resolved, there will be no more reason to talk with Moira. A respectful helper would not label Wesley as 'attention-seeking'. Moira needs to address the issue in the here and now of her helping relationship with Wesley and explore the extent to which he needs other goals to address his social and emotional needs.
- Parents, sometimes whole families, strongly resist specific goals about handling one child's behaviour. You may realise that the child's problematic behaviour is the front of other family dynamics. The focus on this child as a difficult and dramatic 'case' gives family members a focus that distracts everyone from other serious problems in the family.

Problems can also be presented in an insoluble way if clients resist owning their problem or insist on keeping the description vague; these are discussed in the next two sections.

Problems are owned by the client

Some clients are resistant to moving from what may be a long-standing way of coping, sometimes because of their fear of the unknown. For example:

- Graham recognises that his pattern of being aggressive disrupts his relationships with friends and at work. However, he has experience of dealing with the consequences of being aggressive; the situation feels familiar to him. Graham has no experience of the likely consequences of acting in an assertive way, and he finds this uncertainty scary. In this case you would need to work through specific issues for Graham in choosing assertion rather than aggression and be ready to help him to own the feelings that block a new option.

Some clients have coped so far by placing responsibility or blame with other people. For instance:

- Perhaps Lucy (pages 140 and 145) has continued difficulty in talking about specific examples of how her mother 'interferes' in the upbringing of the children. Lucy appears happier describing her domestic difficulties as something that her mother should solve, as shown by repeated phrases like, 'Mum should realise that I feel . . .', and, 'If she wasn't such a busybody, all these problems wouldn't arise.' An effective helper has to use Stage Two skills to confront Lucy over her unwillingness to focus on her own behaviour – the resistance to talking with her mother and preference that the latter should read her mind – and then on how Lucy behaves in the fraught situations.

You may need to stress with clients like Lucy that your focus on their reactions and possible actions are not an attempt to shift fault and blame. Perhaps the client comes back with, 'So, you think my marriage problems are all down to me then?', and you need to reply, 'No, I'm not saying it's your fault rather than his. I am saying that there are two of you in this situation and so far you seem to be much happier talking about what Jim does.'

Clients may be able to lever a problematic situation through changes in their own behaviour, once they have accepted their area of responsibility.

Problems are described in concrete terms

Clients cannot tackle a problem that remains intangible without examples and specific descriptions on which to base goals and then some actions. For instance:

● Paresh (from page 146) does not only have problems with his current project but describes his study problems on a very general level as, 'I'm disorganised. There's so much to do and never enough time and you need some life outside study, don't you? I've never been a good timekeeper. I guess I'm just not a natural student.' Along with possible issues about Paresh owning his study difficulties, Saira may need to work with him towards a more concrete description of how the problem arises. There might be several aspects. Paresh has a chaotic filing system in which it is genuinely difficult to work out what piece of work is due when. He has gone to sixth form college from an all-boys' school, is thoroughly enjoying the company of girls and does not want to turn down even one invitation for social events. He is someone on whom watches stop working and he has never developed the habit of asking others for the time or looking at clocks.

Some clients take a broad perspective that makes it harder to home in on what they personally could develop as goals. For example:

● Miriam is enthusiastic about what she has gained through involvement in the disability rights movement. 'It's changed my life. I used to feel apologetic about asking for help with my wheelchair and now I think, "Well! This building ought to be changed so that I have easy access!" People see the wheelchair and not me, like I'm invisible. I used to get upset, but now I get angry because they've got no business seeing me as an extension to my wheels; I'm a real person. I say I'm disabled, yes, but disabled by society, not by the cerebral palsy. Society does the disabling and that's what we have to fight. That's what I want to do – change people's attitudes, change society.' As Miriam's helper, you should acknowledge the strength and confidence that she has found. However, you need to work with her on goals more concrete, realistic and relevant to her situation than tackling 'people' as a general mass or the whole society.

Divide large problem areas into manageable units

It is impossible to tackle a problem with clients if it is so large and general that nobody could cope effectively with all the issues.

- Simon (from page 119) might present a large and worrying problem of, 'My home life is falling apart.' Through your use of counselling skills in Stages One and Two you may have an overall view of the different parts, although Simon still views the problem as an undifferentiated mass. You can use the skills of summarising to alert Simon to the themes you have identified, checking as you speak that this summary makes sense to him. Simon is unhappy that he and his wife do not talk together as they used to do. He fears that he does not spend enough time with his children and does not know how to deal with their complaints about Granny. He wants his wife and his mother to get along better, but does not know how to make this happen. He wishes that he had not invited his mother to live with the family and guilty about even having such regrets. Each element can then be dealt with specifically, and in turn.

Some clients will be clear about the problem which they want to resolve. However, when clients have several problems and they are possibly motivated to work on any of them, you will need to help the client to make a choice. The process has similarities to decisions made with some clients at the end of Stage One over which of several problems they would like to discuss further. You help the client to make a choice, bearing in mind these broad guidelines for alternatives:

- Choose a problem over which the client has some control.
- Give priority to pressing problems or a crisis situation.
- Choose problems that could be solved fairly easily and can therefore increase the clients sense of competence.
- Choose a problem that, if it was resolved, could bring about a substantial improvement in the client's life.
- Start with the less severe problems and move on as the client gains in confidence.

Choose the focus that makes sense to the client, as well as to you in the light of your understanding of this client.

Goals are not in themselves a programme of action; they are the detailed objectives that will guide the actions. There will often be different potential programmes of action that could resolve a problem and those possibilities are explored in Stage Three (page 164).

Steps to helping clients set goals

If they are to be of any real use to clients, goals have to include the following characteristics. Goals are:

- Expressed in terms of what the client will do. Some clients may have goals about feeling but even these need to result in some action.
- Related to the problem as described and defined by the client.

- Realistic, that is, they are likely to be achieved by this client, allowing for his or her capabilities and situation.
- Under the direct control of the client, not someone or something else.
- Valued by the client as helpful and useful. In other words, the client is committed to achieving the goal.
- Able to be measured in some way. For instance, goals are described in specific terms so that someone, perhaps only the client, can tell if the goal has been achieved or not.
- Time-bound – in other words the goal includes some element of 'by when . . .' it will be achieved, or a sequence of steps taken. How long might this realistically take? Goals with a long time-span can be disheartening. Perhaps the goal needs to be broken down into manageable steps. Similarly ambitious clients may need to be cautioned that solving the problem is likely to take longer than they anticipate.

You are likely to go through the following steps to help clients to reach specific, realistic and useful goals.

- You summarise the problem, with the client's help, including what she or he has learned so far within this helping relationship.
- You undertake any necessary work with the client to ensure that the problem is solvable and manageable.
- You invite the client to explore possible goals, which may at first be vague, such as, 'Become more organised' (Paresh, page 158), 'Stop worrying to myself and start doing something' (Simon, page 159), or, 'Develop my assertive side' (Miriam, page 158).
- You encourage the client to become more specific. For instance, Paresh agrees, 'I want to reorganise how I time my college work. I don't want to miss another deadline.' Simon decides, 'I want to really listen to my wife and understand how she feels about the situation. And I want to do this within the next week – no later.' Miriam focuses on, 'I want to find a way to deal with unhelpful strangers, so that they are more likely to think of me as a person.'
- Explore some aspects of the goal with clients: is it specific enough or do they need a different time deadline (some clients may need a tighter limit than others)? How will clients know they have achieved their goal: what will they have done, how will they feel, what kind of changes do they expect, will anyone else be able to see the changes?
- Check that clients definitely value this goal and are personally committed. They need to own this goal, not go along with it to please you. What do clients believe they will gain, what is important to them, what difference will achieving the goal make to them? Check that they have considered the consequences – of either going for the goal or doing nothing.

8.2 Dealing with dilemmas

Some clients describe problems that seem to have no way out. These situations are dilemmas in which it is easy for you to become as blocked as the client.

Dilemmas involve two, or more, equally positive alternatives or at least two equally negative alternatives. Clients express their difficulties in terms like, 'I could do . . . but then that would mean . . . and that's no use', or, 'I really want to . . . but then I couldn't bear it if I missed out on . . .'. Occasionally dilemmas can involve both a positive outcome, 'I will be able to spend more time with my family', and a negative one, 'I am unlikely to be promoted if I spend less time at work.'

People talk about being stuck on 'the horns of a dilemma' and the image created by this phrase evokes the feelings of being trapped and entangled. You may identify the existence of a dilemma by the client's use of words. Sometimes, two parts of the sentence are joined by 'but' which highlights the client's conviction that she or he must meet the requirements of both parts of the sentence, but this is impossible and so the circle continues. For instance:

- Gemma tells you, 'I've had a fantastic invitation to join Rory in a trip to the Far East but I've landed the holiday job that I really wanted. I worked so hard to get this job and it'll look good on my c.v., but I'll never get another chance to go to the Far East and Rory really wants me to go with him.'
- Ayesha and Winston are due to get married in two months' time. They are both having doubts and last night had their first really serious row. They are not sure about getting married, but their families are all excited about the wedding and arrangements are well advanced. Both Ayesha and Winston dread the upheaval and recriminations from the families if they say they are no longer sure about being married, but it seems wrong to take such an important step without being certain.

In the first example, Gemma is facing a dilemma between two equally positive alternatives and, in the second, Ayesha and Winston feel torn between two equally negative possibilities. As a helper, you will have listened to the various elements in the dilemma; your role is now to help clients to tease out those elements in a logical way and to explore each one specifically. You encourage clients through a logical process and you still completely acknowledge that feelings are both involved and fully legitimate. You help clients step back from the strength of feelings and to talk around and through the blocks that have been created in an objective 'facts and information' way. The example of Ayesha and Winston will be used to illustrate these logical steps. You can practise the same process with examples on page 163.

An example: the horns of a dilemma

Imagine that Ayesha and Winston talk over their worries with you. Through a relatively short Stage One and Two in helping, you are clear about the complex and impossible situation, as they both see it. You realise that a detailed analysis of the options is the most useful route forward now. There are five parts to the dilemma and you encourage Ayesha and Winston to talk about each aspect in turn. You reassure them that you are not trying to persuade them to follow any particular option, but to explore everything thoroughly and get all the assumptions out in the open. Ayesha and Winston work through their options as follows:

1 First option: cancel our wedding.
2 The negative consequences we believe will follow this option are: our parents will be upset and cross, our friends will think we're stupid and they'll take sides, it will be so embarrassing and we'll feel we have to pay our parents back for the money they'll lose by cancelling the arrangements.
3 Second option: go through with our wedding.
4 The negative consequences we believe will follow this option are: our rows will get worse, we'll feel trapped and we'll hate each other, we'll end up getting divorced, we'll feel like failures and our mothers will be heartbroken.
5 Our dilemma: we have to do something, we don't have the choice of doing nothing. Whatever we do will be awful; there is no right thing to do.

You now talk through each part of the dilemma, encouraging Ayesha and Winston to test out their assumptions and judgements. You acknowledge their worries about the expected consequences of cancelling the wedding and encourage them to think further, on the basis of what they have told you earlier in the conversation. With your help the pair allow for other possibilities.

1 First option: cancel our wedding.
2 The consequences we believe will follow this option may not be all negative and we might be able to reduce the negatives. For instance, our parents are kind people, they love us and we are letting them stay ignorant of our worries. They might be sad, they might even be cross with us, but they might also soon be pleased that we are being honest and responsible about a serious decision like marriage. Perhaps we should focus on the marriage part rather than just the wedding day. Perhaps our friends won't think we're stupid; they might think we have courage. We could take some steps, like sticking together and not blaming each other, to stop our friends taking sides. Perhaps the money is less important than our happiness, but we could still find out how much it would actually cost to cancel the arrangements.
3 Second option: go through with our wedding.
4 The consequences we believe will follow this option may not be all negative. We have only started arguing recently and all our rows have been about the wedding arrangements. We can talk together, we have done it today without shouting and we have both become very sad at the prospect of breaking up. We don't want to have a failed marriage, but will that really happen when we want so much to be together?
5 Our dilemma may not be to choose between two equally awful alternatives. Is our problem more about this big wedding that has got out of control rather than getting married? We were very happy together until both families started to take over our wedding day. Do we want to postpone the wedding rather than cancel it completely? Or would we feel happier about cancelling this big wedding and scaling it down to something we would enjoy? Do we want to set up home together without getting married, how do we feel about that, how would our families feel?

By encouraging the exploration of possibilities you have helped Ayesha and Winston to bring in a range of other perspectives and possible goals that can lead to action. Their dilemma is not yet resolved but they have a much greater feeling of control and see much more room for manoeuvre than previously. They have been able to focus far more on themselves, what they feel and would prefer. They can then begin to focus on setting appropriate goals for them and move forward to how they can achieve them.

Activity

Practise teasing out the logical steps of dilemmas with these examples:

- The example of Gemma and Rory from page 161.
- Patrick tells you, 'I've been headhunted for this really good job. It's in the area that I want to be in, it's more money and I like the people I've met so far. But I've worked very hard to get where I am with my current firm. We're just about to break through from being a small operator to big success. I want to see it happen; I want to be part of what I've set up. If this offer had been in maybe a year's time, it would be ideal. And yet it seems too good to let go. I wish they'd never headhunted me, then I wouldn't know what I could be missing!'
- In your day centre for older clients, you are talking with a less experienced colleague who says, 'Rachel has asked to speak with me, I'm seeing her on Friday. I'm worried because she said, "I can trust you, can't I? What I say will stay just between the two of us." But you know we've been concerned about Rachel's elderly mother and all the bruises. Supposing Rachel tells me she's been hitting her mother; the old lady isn't the easiest of people. In my job description it says I must pass on serious concerns. But if I tell Rachel that, she'll probably clam up. And if I let her think I'll keep anything secret and I pass it on to my senior, Rachel is sure to find out and all hell will break loose. But then if I keep quiet and Rachel really hurts her mother, I'd never forgive myself.'
- You are offering support to a day nursery team. One team member voices the concerns of all of them with, 'In our day nursery we've made such a strong commitment to partnership with parents, and I really support that, but we've also worked so hard to give good quality care to the babies and toddlers, to make a close relationship with them like they need. Now some of the parents are saying that they don't want us to get close to their babies. They say that they chose a day nursery because they didn't want their babies to get attached to other people. If they'd wanted that to happen, they'd employ a nanny. I don't see how we can win. If we go with what these parents want, I really believe that young children will be emotionally damaged. But, if we continue to make close relationships with the babies, then the parents will say we lied about being ready to listen to them and wanting to work in partnership.'
- Do you have a personal dilemma that you are currently facing? Try working it through in a logical way, step by step.

8.3 Stage Three: action planning

A range of possible ways forward

Stage Two of the helping model closes with a definite goal or goals to which clients are committed. They are motivated to bring about some change in their life and are prepared to give energy to making this change happen. Your work in Stage Three is to help clients explore possibilities for action in order to achieve their goal(s) – in other words how to achieve the goal(s) set. Stage Three cannot progress unless clients are committed to do something.

Some clients may choose to end the helping relationship at the close of Stage Two, because they feel able to plan action on their own. This is a reasonable position at which the counselling can end, so long as you have explored, briefly, that they are able to move forward alone.

By the end of Stage Two most clients should know what they want to achieve, even if they do not yet know how to achieve that goal. You then help them through a systematic discussion to test action possibilities, rather than a haphazard approach. Many people have not experienced a systematic problem-solving approach. So, it is important that you explain the need to open up more, rather than fewer, possibilities of how to achieve their goal and not run with the first idea or with one that worked for someone else. All the skills used within Stages One and Two of the helping model are still highly relevant. Some clients may generate ideas more easily than others and your help will support others who need assistance to get beyond the first few ideas. Clients may have tried an approach unsuccessfully in the past but that is not necessarily a reason to abandon the idea. They may now have a greater understanding and be able to take the approach through properly. It may be useful for you or the client to write down the options as you discuss them – maybe even on a flip chart. Your role is to help clients to generate ideas but the final choice of what to use must remain with the client. Any course of action will have to be consistent with the client's values. People will not follow through an idea that leaves them feeling ill at ease or which requires them to go against deeply held beliefs.

This section describes some ways of encouraging ideas for action from clients. Select what you use on the basis of your knowledge of individual clients; it would be very rare to use all the possibilities with a single client. Many of the approaches are also useful in working with groups (see Chapters 9 and 10).

Creative exploration

Brainstorming

The objective of brainstorming is to encourage plenty of ideas before looking at practicalities and moving towards any decision. Some people call this approach quicklisting. The key features of this method are as follows:

- Suspend your judgement for a while and encourage the client to back away from, 'Ah, but . . .', or, 'It'll never work.' Neither you nor the client should try to judge the quality of the ideas yet. Realism and practical issues come later.

- Encourage quantity, as many options as possible, because it is easier to reach a practical short list when you start with a longer one.
- Relax and help the client to enjoy generating the ideas. Even wild ideas are to be welcomed. Odd suggestions may lead to something more realistic in the end. One idea may 'piggyback' on to another. Clarify ideas with the client in order to reach definite proposals. Do not criticise ideas, just make them clear and not vague notions.

You then work on the resulting list of ideas with the client (reverse brainstorm) to discuss real possibilities Which ideas might be more practicable? Does one funny or bizarre idea lead to something that is a real option? Perhaps two ideas might be combined together?

Some ideas can also reveal strong feelings about the situation that the client has still not quite expressed. For instance, Natalie (who had a long-running problem with her neighbour, page 150) may surprise herself by generating a few violent solutions to her neighbour's intrusions. Obviously, you should never encourage clients to put irresponsible solutions into action but their expression can sometimes confirm for a client, 'Yes! I do feel that strongly about what has happened.'

Positive imagination

The aim of encouraging a step into fantasy is to free clients from blocks such as, 'I couldn't possibly', or, 'It's all too difficult, what's the point?' This technique is not a rush from reality, rather it can be a useful way to move some clients from an all-too-firm grip on the exact current situation.

You guide the client to talk out loud with themes like:

- 'I would really like to walk into work one day and find that . . .'.
- 'In five years time I would love to be . . .'.
- 'If I had a magic wand, I would . . .'.
- 'What I really want is . . .'.

You do not leave clients with unrealistic hopes; the fantasy is just the beginning. You and the client then discuss the practical possibilities that can follow from recognising the message of the imaginary scene. You may also invite the client to draw a picture of what a solution might look like. This option can be particularly useful with less verbally fluent clients, and gives a good opportunity to explore the relationships between the elements and the images themselves as a possible way forward.

Prompting

Through this approach you take a more active role by using open-ended questions to direct clients' attention to particular possibilities. You do not answer the questions you pose, it is the client who answers. Prompting is useful with clients who have a narrow view of who or what might be useful to them. You might encourage the client to consider any of the following:

- Who might help in some way?
- Is there anyone who is already managing what this client wants to do? Can this other person, or observation of his or her behaviour, help and how?
- Are there particular places, environments or circumstances that are more helpful, or could support the client to achieve the goal? For example, a discussion with a colleague with whom the client has difficulty may feel less formal or confrontational in the canteen than in the office.
- What about any organisations, self-help groups or sources of useful information that can help?

You can prompt clients to list their own personal resources, abilities or successful experiences. Some clients may need a further friendly push to step back from negative views or perfectionist standards. Some clients may especially need to recognise their own strengths rather than a long list of failings, to acknowledge what they do well rather than when they fall short of their own tough standards.

Overcoming blocks

In Stages One and Two, clients may be able to talk about their situation in a detached way as a 'problem'. Stage Three stands on the verge of action and some clients develop a strong resistance to change when actually doing something becomes the focus of attention. Instead of being a theoretical possibility and just a pleasant discussion, the focus becomes more real and tangible.

Clients' outlook on risk

Some clients will be especially fearful of taking risks, believing that, 'If I do this, then there's one chance of success but nine chances of failure.' Such 'catastrophic expectations' are quite common, and often result from thinking too much about possible consequences rather than real ones. In contrast, some clients are willing to 'go excessively boldly' and to take on an action plan which has a very high chance of failure. They may find it hard to let ideas settle and to think matters over before a final decision. As a helper, you need to explore the reality of this balance. Some clients may demand a level of certainty with, 'This will definitely work, won't it?', that is incompatible with the need to take even small risks. On the other hand, some clients are more willing to hazard themselves, perhaps because they genuinely take the view that, 'At least I'll know I tried.'

Choices and rejection of choices

Phrases like 'I can't' sum up a perspective that blocks clients from seeing action as a choice. If the action is theoretically possible, then clients have chosen to turn down the option. You can help by encouraging clients to explore the reasons they have rejected an option and to make those reasons conscious. At no point do you insist that clients take the option, you are effectively saying, 'Let's at least explore this before you reject the idea straightaway.'

Clients' general view of problem-solving

Clients may have fixed expectations about how situations develop and what anyone can do. Some clients may still have trouble in nailing a problem and return to the safety of vagueness, for instance that, 'My life is just in such a mess.' Alternatively some clients may have difficulty in acknowledging the bigger picture and insist on addressing just one part of a problem with, 'No, no. If I can just beat this insomnia, everything else will be fine', as if that is all there is to consider.

Social and cultural background

Everyone learns continually from their environment, including their childhood. Some clients will be more aware than others of how experience has shaped their outlook: what they believe is possible or not really an option, what they feel is normal or out of the ordinary. You, of course, will also be carrying this kind of baggage from your own early and later experiences. Clients may experience general blocks, such as:

- Fantasy or playfulness is for children, not adults, as shown by phrases like, 'Don't be childish!', and, 'Do grow up!' This may get in the way of their exploring creative possibilities, and so limits their options and freedom of action.
- Logic and practicality are positive, intuition and fun are negative.
- Traditional ways are the best, change is risky and possibly bad.
- The echo of family phrases like, 'If anything can go wrong, it will!'

Clients' background and beliefs may also create limits to options with which they can feel at ease. For instance:

- Clients from some cultural and social backgrounds will place a strong emphasis on family loyalty or duty. Any options will have to respect this concern.
- Clients with strong religious beliefs may feel unable to contemplate some options. You may be able to work through, for instance, with a Christian client the consequences of her view that, 'This is the cross that I have to bear', or, 'I must be seen to turn the other cheek.' But any final decisions about action have to respect her beliefs.
- Young people with strong allegiance to their friends may need options that fit well into the shared set of beliefs and priorities of their social group.

During Stages One and Two you should have gained an understanding of the clients' concerns and convictions and you may have worked hard to understand a perspective that is different from your own. Your aim is not to force clients to abandon their beliefs but to encourage them to acknowledge how a belief is blocking action and help them to make a more informed and conscious choice. Clients may then decide to live with the consequences of their beliefs and to choose from a more narrow range of options. They have made their own choice, with an improved awareness of both what they are doing and why.

Helping the client towards action

The opening-out phase of Stage Three happens as you and the client consider a wide range of options. The closing-down or focusing phase helps the client to choose the best course of action to achieve the goal. Using the counselling skills described for Stages One and Two, typically you discuss the following kinds of issues:

- Will this course of action be likely to achieve the goal? Here, you can share experience about the likelihood of success from your informed understanding of this client and your experiences of others.
- Perhaps a different course of action might bring encouraging changes more swiftly, or the actions need to be broken down into smaller, manageable steps so that the client will experience some success without a disheartening, long wait.
- What level of uncertainty or risk can this client tolerate?
- Are possible courses of action realistic, given clients' circumstances?
- What factors, both personal and from outside (like other people, organisations or resources), might support this action and how can the client make the most of these positive forces?
- What might work against the client and achieving the goal through this course of action? In what ways can the client anticipate and minimise the negative forces?

The close of Stage Three is the client's agreement to a plan of action. Your helping relationship need not end yet, since it can be useful to clients to meet you after they have put their plan into action. You can support and encourage their efforts and offer help if needed. However, just as at the close of the preceding stages, it is the client's right to choose to act alone.

8.4 Stage Four: plans into action

Learning from action

When clients meet you again after putting a plan into action, your role is to support them in learning from what they have done:

- Praise clients for what they have achieved in meeting or making progress towards their goal, be pleased with them. Highlight how far they have moved from where they started to where they are now.
- Help clients recognise how much they have learned and to take pride in their achievements, rather than viewing you as the person who has brought about all the changes.
- Explore any setbacks that arose and unexpected difficulties in a positive light. Support clients towards what they can now do rather than looking on the negative side of how 'it all went wrong'.
- Help clients to explore what happened, to take the credit for what they have managed and to find constructive lessons in what did not go as they hoped.

You may need to return to some issues that were covered in Stage Three or even Stage Two if it emerges that such issues were relevant to how the plan went awry. A logical approach called force field analysis is often valuable within Stage Three as well. The earlier points about building positive forces (both within the client and in her environment) and reducing the negative forces are central to force field analysis.

Force field analysis

This logical problem-solving approach passes through four steps. With some clients you might focus on only one or two steps, since you realise these are the likely source of the disappointment in putting a plan into action. You use all the counselling skills to explore with clients the details of what happened this time and how to plan better for next time.

1 Identify and clarify the issue.
   - Have any difficulties arisen or been overlooked?
2 Establish priorities for remedial action.
   - Has the client tried to tackle too many problems at once or lost sight of priorities?
   - Has the partial success of what sounded like a wise programme of action only now thrown up other perspectives? Talk these through with the client.
3 Establish more realistic objectives.
   - Is it now clear that a goal was not concrete enough, that the client was not really committed or that the goal as stated was too unwieldy?
   - Perhaps you need to return to a Stage Two discussion with clients. What was their real level of commitment to this goal? What did they really mean when they put the goal into words? Is it now clear that this goal is in conflict with other goals in their life?
   - Perhaps when clients came very close to action they realised that achieving this goal would bring a mix of consequences, some of which they were not yet ready to face.
4 Choose revised actions to achieve the goal. Perhaps you and the client now realise with hindsight that parts of the discussion were rushed. You need to return to consider the possible actions and choose the best in light of the changed circumstances.
   - Are possible actions within an appropriate time-frame or is the deadline part of the problem?
   - Has the client, or you, overestimated the level of risk that is comfortable for him or her?
   - Are there blocks (see page 166) that were not resolved effectively or which are only now clear?
   - Have you and the client properly explored the positive and negative forces operating for this individual client on this problem situation? Have you worked through how best to maximise the positives and minimise the negatives? If not, what can you now do?

On the basis of this discussion you can support the client in a revised plan of action. Clients feel enabled to continue to work on the change they want to make, so long as this conversation is couched in what can be learned and made better rather than focusing on what went wrong.

8.5 The end of a helping relationship

The helping relationship will conclude whether you have offered your skills in a single conversation or a series of sessions to a client. If you use your skills within supervision of other workers, then the relationship does not end, but you move on to other issues.

A helping relationship ends when clients feel any of the following. They:

- Feel that their needs have been met. They have been able to follow through the course of action and have dealt effectively with the problem. Alternatively, they have been able to find a way to live with the difficulty and to cope with it more positively.
- Have decided that they can take control of the issue and the actions needed and no longer want your support.
- Choose to stop, whether or not progress has been made. You would then ideally summarise what you feel the relationship has achieved and leave the option for the client to return, if wished.

If the helping relationship has not worked, it can be useful to explore some reasons at least briefly with the client. You may be able to learn about your style and approach or clients may acknowledge that they were expecting a different kind of help or are not yet ready to face this issue.

A helping relationship will also stop if you:

- Feel unable to offer any further help. This feeling may result from blocks put forward by the client, which you have been unable to address effectively. This can happen at any time within the stages.
- Judge that the client needs specialist input that is outside your experience or ability. Typically this is most likely in Stage Three, or at the end of Stage Two.

A sense of closure

It is important that a helping relationship does not just stop abruptly. Clients, and you too, need to experience a positive closure and a review of what has been learned and achieved. This kind of closure may still be possible even if you, or the client, feel that not as much has been achieved as either of you hoped. You can use the skill of accurate summarising to alert clients to how far they have come. This message can be especially important when clients lack confidence or attribute changes or success to your ability and not their own. You may need to stress, 'You've done some hard work', 'Remember how you felt when we started', or, 'You were sitting right on top of the problem. It wasn't easy to stand back but you did it.'

A helping relationship should not finish only with a rational summary. Clients may have regrets about ending their time with you that need to be expressed.

Feelings may be communicated of warmth and appreciation. Sometimes it will be appropriate for you to express warm feelings, still within the professional relationship with the client. It is important that you give some thought and attention to endings.

If you refer a client

At some point you will work with a client whose needs, when these become obvious, fall outside your expertise. It is a responsible course to admit to yourself that you are unlikely to be able to help and to explain the situation to the client. Ideally, you should ease your client's transition to another person who will offer the specialist help:

- Gather your thoughts and some information about who could be an appropriate referral. If necessary, contact individuals or agencies with general questions that will help you decide if they are an appropriate referral. Keep confidential any details of your client.
- You may be able to explain the limits to your help in the same conversation that you offer the client some suggestions about people or organisations that are likely to be of more direct help. Sometimes, there might be a break in which you realise the client's needs go beyond your capability and you gather ideas to bring to the next session.
- It will be the client's choice whether to accept any of your suggestions but you need to be honest when they do not have the choice to continue talking with you.
- Depending on the circumstances, you might offer names and telephone numbers with whom the client makes direct contact. Sometimes, it will be appropriate that you introduce the client personally or by referral to another individual, perhaps within your own organisation or well-known to you.
- Of course, you may continue to have informal contact with some clients and to support them in a general way. Check that any referral has been useful, since the client may appreciate other suggestions if the first has not worked. However, it would not be appropriate to encourage clients to talk with you about the work they are doing with the new helper.

☑ 9 Helping through group work

9.1 The nature of group work

Some background

With the strong emphasis in society on help offered to individuals, it can be easy to overlook just how much helping is offered in groups rather than one to one. Group work was relatively rare until the 1960s when unstructured sensitivity groups developed in the United States. By the late 1960s and 1970s such groups were increasingly used as a method of personal exploration in Britain. This development brought varied reactions throughout the 1970s, with some wariness based on the very unstructured American model. However, approaches to working with groups have diversified and there is now a great variety in how groups are set up and run.

This chapter and Chapter 10 provide a practical framework for working with groups, covering some opportunities and predictable difficulties. Counselling skills are equally valuable for group work, but the dynamics of a group are more complicated than in one-to-one conversation. The ideas here will support you to set up, plan and run relatively straightforward groups. However, group work, like counselling, is often very challenging, especially if you are involved with a client group experiencing complex life problems. Specific training will be necessary to run such groups.

Why run groups?

The majority of people spend a great deal of time in groups: family, school and work, religious and other belief groups, chosen social and leisure groups. Groups can:

- Support and help individuals, affirm their sense of identity and acceptance by others and satisfy social needs.
- Create a sense of consistency in individual lives, of predictability.
- Provide individuals with a context in which to be themselves, to learn and sometimes to relax.
- Also exert negative pressures, making individuals doubt themselves or feel coerced into saying or doing what they would not alone.

All groups have to deal with three major elements:

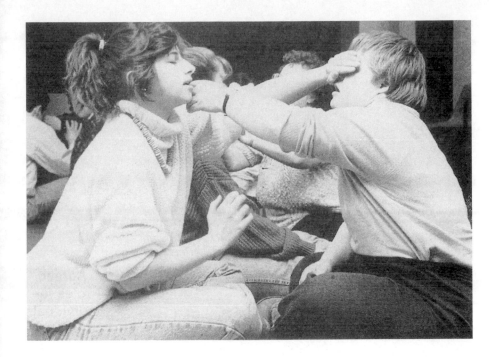

- The demands of the tasks to be done: what the objectives are, the level of support or opposition to these and the tasks required. Such needs have to be met within the group structure.
- The needs of the individuals in the group: to be included and not rejected, the satisfaction of personal aims and motivations.
- The needs of the whole group itself: the dynamics that make the group work well or badly. These include the level of participation, willingness to listen, use of assertiveness and how the group conducts itself.

The group leader needs to manage these three themes to satisfy group members and to work effectively to achieve the aims agreed. These themes affect each other and the emphasis of the group on one or other focus will change over time. Typically groups are most concerned about individual needs early on, and more concerned with achieving the goals later (see also Chapter 10). These themes are shown in the diagram at p. 174.

Activity

List all the social and other groups to which you belong.

- To what extent do the groups overlap?
- In what way do different interests or sides to your personality emerge more in some groups than others? How do you think that happens?

Themes and outcomes in work teams

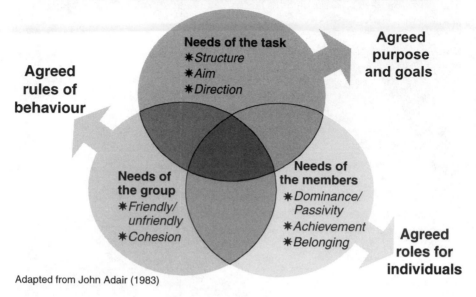

Adapted from John Adair (1983)

Different kinds of groups

People come together in groups, or are brought together, because they share a focus: similar objectives, beliefs, experiences or concerns. Groups develop an identity of their own, additional to the separate personal identities of their members. Groups come together to achieve an aim. They share some common characteristics, although their reasons for meeting are varied.

To make contact with people who share similar experiences

Individuals appreciate spending time with people who are now, or have been, in a very similar situation. The objective is to have time to talk, listen and offer support and informed advice through shared experiences. Some groups come together in order to enjoy an activity. So groups may form to play football, share their passion for steam locomotives or go rambling. In the professional context, some examples are:

- Groups of professionals in a minority at work: black workers' groups, male early years workers or women in male-dominated professions.
- Young people or adults who have been abused at some point in their lives.
- Parents who have disabled or very sick children and welcome the support of people who understand the reality of their daily life.
- The National Childbirth Trust which brings together new parents, mainly mothers, with parents of slightly older children. The aim is to build local networks for isolated new parents and offer informal support and advice.
- Support groups for the families of prisoners who face practical and emotional problems arising from the imprisonment of a family member.

Self-help in a support group

Some groups focus on individual self-help with support from other group members who share a very similar difficulty. The aim is to change group members' outlook and behaviour, sometimes by harnessing the challenge from group members who have or have had very similar problems. Examples include:

- Groups for people coping with addiction: either chemical, for instance, alcohol and drugs, or behavioural addictions like gambling, eating disorders and self-harm.
- Juvenile or other offenders who wish to avoid reoffending.
- Groups for people of any age who have very limited social contacts. The group itself provides social links and an opportunity for learning social skills.

To gain skills and knowledge

Other groups focus on the development of skills. Examples include:

- Sessions for parents and other carers on parenting skills.
- Assertiveness for young people or adults.
- Developing the skills of self-care and independence for young people about to leave residential care.
- Physical exercise and health for older people whose situation has led them to be sedentary and out of condition.
- Groups for prospective foster or adoptive parents to help them to understand what is involved in their plans to foster or adopt.

To bring about change

Some groups come together with an action plan specifically for change. They want to make something happen, for instance:

- A job club for unemployed people who want to find ways to improve their prospects.
- A residents' or neighbourhood group that wants to bring about a local change such as better street lighting or a pedestrian crossing.
- A parents' group that wants better play or child-care facilities locally.
- Minority groups of professionals (as mentioned on page 174) may also have the objective to improve their treatment or enhance their status in addition to networking and sharing experiences.

9.2 Planning a group

Identifying a need

You should be clear about your reasons for developing group work for clients.

What do you believe a group could achieve?

- What makes you think a group will be helpful? To whom? To what ends?
- What will the group experience offer to the potential members? What are they likely to gain that would not happen without the group?
- What would be the purpose of the group? With an unclear purpose, a group can be chaotic and members regularly return to questions about, 'What are we here for?', 'Why are talking about this?', or, 'But weren't we going to . . . ?'
- Which potential members should be included? How will you find out if people are likely to be enthusiastic about the kind of group that you envisage?

How do you talk about the group?

Even at the early stages of thinking about a group, be thoughtful about what the planned group is called and the way it is discussed.

- Is there is a possibility that group membership could create a stigma for members?
- In what way could this negative feature be avoided or minimised?

For instance, parenting groups may be linked in people's mind with 'bad' parents and anti-crime initiatives. Young people who are absent from school may consider a self-help group that is known as 'The Tuesday Group' but avoid one that has become known as 'The Truanting Group'.

Is there a request for a group?

- Do potential members ask for a group? You may have direct requests for a group with a particular focus if you work in a centre with an existing client base. For instance, young people in a residential home may want a chance to prepare for the day they have to leave or a primary school may have requests from parents for informative groups about helping children with reading or maths.
- How do the potential group members see this group working? Regardless of what they call the group, what do they expect will happen in group time and what do they hope the group will achieve? How realistic are their expectations?

Case study

A primary school head sounded out a few parents about what she described as 'groups to help parents get more involved in their children's school learning'. The reaction was enthusiastic and, without further consultation, the head set up a series of monthly evening meetings on themes like 'Home–school links for reading', 'Maths nowadays' and 'Healthy eating'.

Many parents attended the first meeting, less came as the term progressed and very few were at the final meeting. The head sent a letter to all parents saying how much work the teachers had put into the meetings and how disappointed she was that so few parents had bothered to come. Some parents were so insulted by the tone of the head's letter that they wrote back angrily. The deputy started to gather further reactions by talking with many parents in the playground. Several key issues emerged:

- Many parents had expected smaller, more focused, groups in which they could discuss the work that their own children were doing and details of how they could help at home.
- Parents felt there was little give and take. Teachers and invited speakers behaved as if parents were there to be told what to do. The final blow had been a very patronising speaker for the healthy eating topic followed, ironically, by refreshments of squash and biscuits.
- The parents confirmed that they would welcome the kind of group that they believed had been offered. They were offended by the head's letter, which effectively accused them of disinterest in their children's education.

Questions

- What went wrong here? How might the proposed groups have been better researched and planned?
- What do you think might be done to retrieve the situation?

Will the group be open or closed?

Closed groups start and finish with the same group members and are usually run for a pre-agreed number of sessions. If members drop out for some reason, they are not replaced. Individuals who are keen to become involved wait for the start of another group with a new set of members.

In contrast, open groups work on the understanding that members can come and go. The open group may also work for a fixed number of sessions or continue, with reviews of the work, for an indefinite period of time.

There is no simple answer that a closed group is better than an open one, or vice versa. You need to make the decision, sometimes with group members, based on the membership and objectives of the group. Some considerations are:

- Some advantages of open groups are that new members can bring in fresh ideas and perspectives and a different range of skills. They may constructively challenge the habits that have grown in the existing group.
- Like closed groups, open groups can still have subgroups and cliques, perhaps between 'old' members and the 'new' ones. Recent arrivals may become frustrated with the old clique or be cold-shouldered on the grounds that they do not really understand nor have committed to the original purpose of the group.
- An open, and therefore changing, membership is not suitable for groups in which members are working to share deep personal experiences. Trust has to built over time and new members will not be immediately admitted to this trust. New arrivals therefore, by no fault of their own, unbalance the previous

group atmosphere. Personal work at depth is not likely to be possible in an open group.

- Closed groups can undoubtedly become inward-looking and may develop favourite ways of dealing with more difficult situations, such as conflict, in a group, or develop habits and assumptions about group members. A group leader has to be alert to this disadvantage of a closed group, including the possibility that he or she has also fallen into these habits.
- Closed groups can become very cohesive and intimate, offering considerable support in an atmosphere of trust. The downside is that closed groups are likely to have more difficulty and sadness about the ending of a group, because of the significance of the relationships that have grown over time. The group leader has to be ready and prepare the group for ending and moving on.

Note on terms

We are using the words 'group leader' to cover anyone who takes primary responsibility for the life of a group. People use different phrases to describe this position and undoubtedly 'leading' has some different connotations, depending with whom you speak. The leader is basically responsible for helping the group to meet its goals through facilitation and structure of activities. See page 181 for a specific discussion of the role of group leader.

To think about

In your opinion, what are the issues that arise in the following three groups? How would you resolve the difficulties?

- In an all-girls' secondary school, with many different clubs and societies, permission has been given for Muslim students to have a closed group to explore cultural and religious traditions and issues about being a young Muslim woman. Some other students, who are interested in cultural diversity, have challenged the fact that the group is closed to non-Muslims. They ask the teacher who plans to lead the group, 'Would you let us have just a white European group? We think not; you'd call us racist.'
- An open group on health issues for young people in residential care has reached the maximum numbers. Recent additions to the group have made the balance three-quarters male and the girls feel in a minority. They say, 'The boys mess about and want to talk about different things.' The girls request that the group be made open only to girls until natural turnover evens up the sex balance.
- An informal drop-in group for childminders meets every Tuesday at a community centre. The under-eights adviser had always envisaged

the drop-in as an open group, but on a recent visit she realises that circumstances have changed. Four minders, who have attended since the start and are active in organising events, appear to have closed the group to new arrivals. Nothing explicit is said to the adviser, but she hears along the grapevine that several new childminders had felt very unwelcome in the group and did not return after a first visit.

How do people join the group?

You need to consider how prospective group members are likely to hear about and join a group. Some possibilities are:

- Group members are active themselves in starting up the group.
- They hear about the group and contact the group leader or existing members.
- Someone, either inside or outside it, recommends the group.
- Group members bring along a friend.
- Someone encourages or persuades individuals to join the group. In this case, members may not feel they had a genuine choice.

As a group leader, you need to know about the routes taken to the group by members, whether they are much the same or diverse. Some routes may encourage subgroups and any reluctant group members need to have their wariness acknowledged. There may not be serious problems, but an understanding of how the group has developed will help you to work well with the group dynamics.

Restrictions on membership?

Apart from the issue of closed or open groups, there will be other issues about the composition of the group. A good rule of thumb is that groups need to have members similar enough to have a level of shared interests, motivations and concerns, yet different enough to bring varied perspectives to help each other.

The composition of the group will have to be related to the group's objective, which in turn needs to be openly expressed. Almost certainly you will have some limits on who is suitable to join a group. If the interests, skills or concerns of the group membership are too diverse, then it will be practically impossible to have a clear group purpose and at least some of the group will be disappointed in their experience.

Case study

A day centre group for promoting physical fitness for older people was set up to involve the regular carers of the members. The group objective was to develop appropriate physical exercises to maintain muscle strength and emotional well-being. The rationale for inviting the carers was that they could better support their relatives in continuing the exercises at home.

By the end of the third session this situation was challenged by several of the older group members. Their rationale was that they preferred to exercise privately with the person they now regarded as their group personal trainer. They asked why nobody had bothered to invite their opinions and felt that this implied they were incapable of showing their carers what they had learned in each session. They also objected to some carers who 'highjack our training session to moan about their problems with social services'.

Questions

- What in your opinion has happened with this group? What assumptions appear to be at work?
- What would be positive steps now? For the physical training session? For the needs expressed by some carers?

Size of the group

You need to decide how large the group can become. Size will be an issue at the planning stage, but can also arise with an open group that becomes more successful than expected. Size is partly determined by the purpose of the group, but groups of over 25 become unwieldy whatever the purpose. Once a group grows beyond eight members, it is very difficult to attend in detail to individuals, and in groups focused on discussion some members will feel it difficult, if not impossible, to contribute.

- Groups therefore need to be kept small when the purpose is for members to talk about personal experiences and seek support for what may be distressing events. Such a group cannot function if membership rises beyond seven or eight members. The atmosphere becomes less personal and each individual has considerably less time for expressing his or her own concerns.
- An activity group with a shared purpose might work well with up to 11–15 members. The group work is less personal and so less likely to raise intimate feelings or personal pain. The larger membership then brings the advantage of greater variety in experiences, skills and ideas.
- A group with an educational purpose can function well with up to 25 members. The group leader becomes more responsible for the balance of activity, for ensuring that everyone is enabled to contribute and for managing the subgroups which are almost certain to develop.

How long does each session last?

Again the final decision here needs to be based on the purpose of the group and on the variety and size of group membership.

- Some group members, with family or other obligations, may only be able to organise to attend for a couple of hours at the most.
- Groups will not gather much momentum unless each session has a reasonable amount of time to develop. Between 60 and 90 minutes is usually the

minimum time allowed, while some groups work well in sessions of two to three hours.

- Some members may become tired or their attention may wander in longer sessions. It will be the task of a group leader to help members to refocus and to maintain attention through changes in activities. Groups often appreciate and need a short refreshment or comfort break.

9.3 The role of group leader

Individual style and temperament affects the way that a group leader operates and there is no absolute set of rules to follow. However, it is a leadership role and the leader has to accept that she or he is in a different position from the other group members. Groups can become very frustrated with leaders who insist that they are 'just another member of the group', when this claim is clearly untrue, or with leaders who give out conflicting messages about how they exercise authority in the group.

Rights and responsibilities

Group leaders, whether they are called by this term or not, have obligations to provide direction, boundaries and a safe situation for the group. Groups have a right to expect that their leader should be a legitimate source of authority and that he or she should:

- Be consistent, fair and honest with the group.
- Treat all members equally and neither have favourites nor form subgroups with individuals.
- Focus on the needs of the group and of individual members and not on the group as a means for the leader to achieve personal goals.
- Be aware of the needs of all members and alert to their welfare and feelings.
- Offer new experiences or activities, appropriate to the group purpose and the members' skills, interests and past experience.
- Offer objective feedback and comment equally to all members.
- Provide and help the group to hold to boundaries and to ensure that the group is a safe and positive experience for group members.

Leadership style

Depending on the nature of the group, a leader may be:

Directive or structuring

The leader takes a major responsibility for organising what will happen, guiding the group and stimulating ideas and expression of views or feelings. This role of leadership may be important when group members are very low in confidence or have limited experience of organising their time to a purpose. When the group purpose is educational, the leader has a definite responsibility to create and guide a group programme of learning. Typically this leader's primary focus is to fulfil the objectives of the group.

Coaching

The leader still has authority; he or she does not simply sit back and do nothing. However, the leader is less directive and gives the group more scope to plan, make decisions and agree a clear purpose. In some groups, the leader's aim may be to support members as they move to a point where they have far less need for leadership. This leadership style works best when members have some experience of working in a group and show willingness to share responsibility with the leader.

Facilitative or encouraging

The group leader brings expertise to the group and an alertness to the group process but works to support the responsibility of group members for what happens within the group. The leader offers encouragement and is involved, but with a different role to group members. A facilitative role is usually appropriate in groups where the purpose is for individuals to explore feelings and experiences, and there is not a clear group aim to achieve a defined collective result.

Delegative

Here the group leader takes a low profile, perhaps merely arranging sessions, to enable an established group to work in ways that they see fit. The delegative leader's prime role is to monitor what occurs and to ensure that the group continues to fulfil the needs of all the members. This leadership style works best with competent, experienced and motivated group members who can be trusted to make good decisions without interference.

Flexible – a combination of styles

None of the above styles is likely to work consistently all the time. As groups develop, a less structured style is typically more productive than in the early days of the group. Hence the work in most groups requires that the leader is flexible and takes up the directive, coaching or facilitating styles in response to events in the group. Flexibility definitely should not mean unpredictability. Groups resent a leader who directs when it suits and stays well back when the group would appreciate some direction. The key is to flex your style to match the needs of the group and the objectives set, and particularly the needs of the members which will change over time. You need to be fully aware of what you are doing in terms of your leadership style and why.

Skills

As a group leader you will use your skills towards four broad objectives: the creation of the group, maintenance of the group as a whole, the achievement of group tasks and the development of a positive group culture.

Creation

Groups do not simply happen; their creation and development requires work. As a group leader you need to:

- Make initial contacts and research the need for a group. What should it achieve? Who should be invited? What are its boundaries?
- Work out the practical details of the group. When should it meet? For how long? How frequently? Should it be open or closed?
- Establish a suitable and positive role as group leader and start to develop working relationships with the group, either as a new group or one that already exists but where you are a new leader. What do the members seek from the leader? What are you able, and willing, to do?

Maintenance

You apply your skills to support and maintain the existence of this group. You need to:

- Communicate your commitment to the group and optimism about what the group will do.
- Talk and listen equally with all group members and find out what each individual within the group wants and can contribute.
- Help group members to communicate with each other and deal with any blocks that arise within the group that affect the group's objectives or the well-being of individuals.
- Be aware of all levels of group working: what happens in the sessions, the emotional dimension, different relationships and subgroups. Use your observational and counselling skills to deal with events within the group and any outside issues that become part of the group's interaction.

Achievement of group tasks

All groups should have a purpose, honestly expressed, and a key focus for commitment of all the group members. The purpose is what the group is formed to achieve. Leaders need to:

- Remember and restate the group purpose as necessary, and what this means in terms of specific objectives and tasks to complete.
- Act so as to help the group contribute to the purpose and perform the tasks that need doing.
- Guide the group within agreed boundaries, values and standards for the work. Leaders need to ensure that practical issues such as timekeeping, feedback and follow-up on group tasks are completed. The group may be happy for the leader to delegate some areas for others to do but the leader still has overall responsibility that they are done.

Group culture or atmosphere

Groups should operate within some boundaries of behaviour. The expectations of how people will behave may be part of an explicit contract or result from more informal encouragement, or illustration, from the group leader. You need to:

- Develop group rules with the group and remind them of the rules when necessary. These can involve timekeeping, confidentiality and processes for ensuring that everyone gets a chance to contribute.
- Make sure that you behave as a good example of the group contract and any ground rules (see page 199). For instance, a rule in a group undertaking physical activities may be that individuals are allowed to refuse an activity or to determine their preferred level of risk. The leader has to ensure that nobody is made to feel foolish or bullied for saying no.
- Model positive interaction, for instance, on listening, accepting feedback in a constructive way, being honest about your feelings when appropriate or dealing well with confrontation or distress in the group.
- Behave appropriately for the kind of group with whom you work. For instance, a self-help group needs to be gently dissuaded from looking to you as an expert. A group in which members share personal feelings and doubts will understandably look to the leader to share something of her or himself as well, not just act as an onlooker.

Joint or co-leadership

Sometimes co-leadership – two leaders working together – makes sense for the content and purpose of a group. Co-leading is not necessarily easier than leading a group on your own, and in some ways it can become more difficult. The joint leaders need to work together in an integrated way and not compete for the group's attention. Each of the co-leaders' roles needs to be carefully agreed.

Co-leadership for a reason

Co-leadership should be decided for clear reasons, linked to the purpose of the group. Two leaders may work well in a large group, when the tasks can be shared between the leaders. Two pairs of eyes and ears increase the chance that no group member will be overlooked. However, it is unwise to take on a second leader just because the group has expanded. Two leaders will not offset the disadvantages of having too many people for the work and purpose of this particular group.

Visible differences between the co-leaders may be an advantage for the purpose of some groups: perhaps one male and one female, they may show differences in ethnic group or one leader is disabled. Male and female co-leaders can act deliberately to cross gender stereotypes. Or it may be very important for a group to see a competent and disabled leader in action. Be clear between yourselves as co-leaders, particularly if your differences are intended to promote a particular message. Be wary for a group that takes more than you intend from the difference. Sometimes, co-leaders will simply be different, with no agenda linked to the group purpose. Co-leaders should be seen as equal within the group and any differences in status from outside need to be anticipated and handled constructively.

Plan and talk together

Two leaders must plan together, so you face the first and subsequent groups clear between yourselves about what will happen, why and how you will deal with some predictable events of group life, such as conflict, expressions of strong feelings or group boundaries.

Co-leaders need to talk together outside the group during the group's life. You need to discuss what is happening in the group, any issues in the dynamics between group members and how these will be handled. You also need to discuss in an open way the dynamics between yourselves as co-leaders and the relationships between you and individual group members. Does one or both co-leaders feel that subgroups are developing, that one leader is being manoeuvred into supporting a stance that is not appropriate? Are there issues about boundaries or discipline in the group that one leader feels fall disproportionately to her or him?

Joint leaders may have different roles in the group. For example, one may focus on helping the group to achieve the tasks set, whilst the other focuses on ensuring that members are working well together and addresses issues of how tasks are being done. This division is quite appropriate, but both the co-leaders and the group need to be clear of the differences and boundaries to the distinct leadership roles.

Work positively together in the group

Co-leaders need to value, trust and respect each other. Some differences in approach or style can be a positive addition to group life, so long as the leaders respect each other. Sometimes it can be appropriate for co-leaders to discuss options or uncertainties within the group. You both have an opportunity to model, in a natural way, how to manage disagreements, misunderstandings and expression of feelings.

Constructive feedback between co-leaders

If you are to work well with your co-leader, you will both need to draw on the skills of constructive feedback as you talk outside the group. When you wish to discuss issues of your work with your co-leader, the conversation will be more productive if you follow the guidelines on feedback described on page 39. In brief you need to:

- Describe what happened rather than label or blame your co-leader.
- Express your feelings honestly rather than trying to put them onto your co-leader.
- Be even-handed and share what you felt went well in a session, not just what you think went wrong.
- Make positive suggestions about what you would rather have happen, if appropriate.

- When the feedback comes from your co-leader, listen and make sure you understand his or her perspective. Ask for clarification, if necessary, and consider what you have been told and how you might make positive changes in your style or reactions.

Examples

Think about what is happening in these groups and between the co-leaders? Do you believe the issue(s) should be addressed and, if so, in what way? How might feedback between the co-leaders be made constructive?

- Tricia and Roy are co-leading a group for 16–18-year-olds on the skills of independent living. Tricia has become increasingly annoyed with what she sees as Roy's tendency to bond unhelpfully with the boys. She expects Roy to challenge remarks from the boys like, 'Why should we learn to cook? We'll just pull some soft girl to cook for us!', but he does not. After one meeting, Tricia starts to take issue with her co-leader's behaviour. Roy's reaction is, 'I'm glad you've brought this up. I wanted to talk to you about what you're doing. You're lining up with the girls against me. I'm supposed to take cracks about "men who can't even sew on a button" as a joke, am I?'
- Shireen and Fazila are jointly running a support group for lone parents. Fazila has a more expressive style than Shireen, who feels pushed into the background with her quieter style with far fewer gestures. Matters come to a head in one session when Fazila's burst of energy leads her to get to her feet and address the group standing up. Shireen is angry that Fazila stood directly in front of her, so that she is now physically blocked from the group. Shireen hisses to Fazila, 'Sit down! For goodness' sake!'
- Joseph and Owen jointly run a neighbourhood action group. Over the last few weeks Owen has almost imperceptibly moved into the discipline role: keeping time, bringing the group back to task and reminding members of commitments made to the group earlier. Owen acknowledges that he is better at this role than his co-leader, but Joseph seems to be having all the fun. The last straw for Owen is when one group member calls him 'Owen-the-time' and everyone laughs, including Joseph.
- A paediatrician and a researcher are jointly running a series of sessions for parents on positive ways to deal with young children's behaviour. The nursery head who organised the practical arrangements for the group introduces the two group leaders as 'Dr Cartwright and Sarah'. Sarah, the researcher, is not pleased about this inequality and expects her co-leader to intervene with 'Please call me Nadia'. Her co-leader says nothing and Sarah becomes progressively more uneasy and annoyed. The group members appear to listen with more attention to the paediatrician and to ask her more questions than they address to Sarah.

- Tim and Clare are co-leaders on an assertiveness skills group. They organised six sessions and group members have a copy of the programme. After two sessions Tim has become frustrated with Clare's tendency to take the group off at a tangent, with the consequence that they are now behind in the agreed programme of activities. Tim tackles Clare before the third session and she agrees to keep to their plan. However, halfway through this session, Clare says in response to a comment from one group member, 'That's a great idea, let's see where that leads us. You'd all like that, wouldn't you?' She glances at Tim and laughs, 'Except my esteemed co-leader. He doesn't like me being spontaneous.'

9.4 Learning in the group

Planning

Group leaders need to plan for group work. You can leave some flexibility and no plan should be so tight that you are unable to respond at all to group members' wishes. However, you do need to think ahead to what will happen in each session.

- If you are taking on a group that was previously run by a colleague, then part of your preparation is to find out about the work of the group so far.
- If you are not responsible for the practical arrangements then make contact with the person who is. Practical issues include times and dates, the room you will use, enough chairs for the size of group, any equipment, possible refreshments and advance communication with group members.
- Some groups, for instance those where there is a clear learning purpose, will need detailed planning about activities (see page 212) and some outline plan to be sent to group members to manage their expectations.

The physical setting

You may have limited choice over where you run the group, but it is definitely worthwhile to choose or create as welcoming and physically comfortable an environment as possible. A group leader has responsibilities towards the group's physical needs as well as other aspects of group life. A leader who seems unaware of physical comfort or unwilling to address issues for the group appears uncaring.

Practical issues

- Have a room with sufficient, ideally natural light, not harsh artificial lighting.
- You need to be able to create an environment at an appropriate temperature for the time of year. Overwarm or airless settings tend to make people dozy, even send them to sleep, whilst chilly rooms leave people more concerned

about how to keep warm than what the group is doing. Remove all the distractions that you can.

- Have seats that will be comfortable for the duration of a normal group session. Consider seating and access issues for any disabled group members.
- Would the group appreciate refreshments? If so, then these need to be organised in advance. Is it appropriate to plan for some non-structured chat time?
- If group members are likely to be very tired, then you need to consider the length of any session and suitable activities. One of us worked with a group of young mothers who were suffering broken nights, and at least one person fell asleep during each session. It was important to be tolerant, since the behaviour arose from exhaustion and not criticism of what the group was doing.

Some groups may be composed of strangers or people who scarcely know each other. However, some groups include members who know each other well outside the group. The physical setting and its practical details may be especially important for such groups. You have the chance to make this group distinct from the rest of the members' working or personal daily life. For example:

- If you want to encourage a health clinic team to talk openly, with less awareness of the usual status hierarchy, then have the group meet somewhere other than the clinic. Perhaps prepare name badges that only give a first name and no titles. You might want to seat people apart from those with whom they normally work.
- You might want to boost the self-esteem of a group of primary school helpers who feel unappreciated. You can start by taking trouble over the comfort of the group setting: perhaps get a vase of flowers and organise some decent refreshments. If the group must happen in the school, then be firm that you are not interrupted by teachers who 'just want a word about . . .'.

Privacy and security

Individuals need to feel safe both in the group and in the surroundings. If group members feel physically or emotionally threatened within or around a group, they will not be as committed.

- Groups cannot work well unless they are ensured some privacy. Avoid rooms in which group discussion is disturbed by people knocking on a window or staring in on the group.
- You may have to use a room that is a throughway to some other part of the building or doubles as the resource centre for your organisation. Negotiate with the rest of your team, and put up a notice for any service users, that the room is closed for the duration of the group. You need to tackle any colleagues who treat group time as open to interruption.
- Some groups run in buildings where members have to leave through empty corridors or a badly lit car park. Group members may be positive about the group experience but seriously worried about arriving and leaving. Consider practical arrangements to provide company for the times or areas that people find intimidating.

Learning is best when active and through doing

Fundamentally all groups are designed to help the members learn something: how to cope better, ways of expressing feelings, what to do, or some new knowledge or skill.

Experiential learning – learning through experience

The main ideas underlying experiential learning are that:

- Everyone learns more effectively by doing actively rather than simply being told and listening passively.
- People learn best when they are personally involved in the learning experience.
- Learning is sometimes painful, particularly if it involves unlearning established and unproductive habits or coming to grips with a deep personal issue.
- People really need to discover knowledge and insights for themselves if these are to have meaning. Group leaders therefore primarily support and enable. They do not just tell. Look also at page 117 about the unhelpfulness of telling in a one-to-one helping relationship.
- People are more committed to learning when they can set their own goals within a framework that they help to determine.

Effective learning involves four phases that repeat within a cycle. These ideas were developed by D. A. Kolb and R. Fry (first presented in Cooper C. L. (ed.) *Theories of group processes*, Wiley, 1975).

- Concrete, personal experience (CE) – something happens in which you are directly involved. For example, your car breaks down.
- Reflective observation (RO) – you think about what has happened. If you know something about the workings of a car, you may open the bonnet (to use your Abstract Conceptualisation of the workings of the engine). If you know nothing, this is pointless, so you call an expert, perhaps the Automobile Association.
- Abstract Conceptualisation (AC) – you (or the representative from the Automobile Association) use knowledge of the workings of a car engine to do . . .
- Active experimentation (AE) – and tinker with the car.
- Concrete Experience (CE) – the car starts (end of cycle) or it does not, at which point further reflection occurs. For instance, the manual may be used to help with alternative ways of experimenting, until the car does start.

Additional learning may have been acquired by reflecting on this complete experience. It may be that the fanbelt was the problem and, as the AA representative said this often breaks, you determine to carry a spare in the future. Through watching the expert, your reflection tells you that the repair was straightforward and you could save the lost hour. You are willing to experiment actively with this new strategy next time.

You may start at any point in the cycle, but for best learning to result, you must go through all elements. For instance, a group exploring assertiveness skills may do short interviews with each other (CE). Following the interviews, group members are encouraged to reflect on their own current style and situations in which they find it most hard to be assertive (RO). The leader then briefs the group on how to be more assertive, and gives them a handout (AC). Individuals develop plans for how to behave in new ways and practise alternative ways in the group (AE). They experiment in a safe environment by doing another interview (CE) and so on. Alternatively, you may begin the learning process by a briefing from an expert on the behaviour associated with assertiveness (AC). You then plan your practice (AE) and do it (CE) before reflecting on the experience (RO) as the springboard for additional tips from the trainer in response (AC).

Individual differences

Some people are more comfortable in one phase of the learning cycle than others and may have difficulty in moving on to less preferred aspects of learning. For instance, some people may relish trying out new options for action and experimenting but are less keen to reflect on what they have learned. Others may enjoy the discussion of ideas and building theories but are far less enthusiastic to do anything as a result.

Group leaders will also have personal preferences. Become aware of your own inclinations and how these may affect both your choice of activities and how you use these to help the group to learn. Perhaps you value discussion and find it relatively easy to express your feelings. However, some or most of this group may not share your comfort at all. On the other hand perhaps you are enthusiastic about physical games and are confident that such activities always generate energy and throw group dynamics into sharp relief. You need to be aware that some group members may not share your enthusiasm, especially if they feel there is no choice or feelings of physical insecurity are not acknowledged. The cycle must be completed for learning to be most effective, and this means inevitably that both the leaders and group members will experience some aspects which they enjoy less than others.

Plan activities

Some groups may spend most of their time talking and listening together. Then the role of the group leader is to support discussion using counselling skills. Further suggestions about talking in the group are made from page 203 onwards. However, some groups do not find it easy to talk fluently about issues or else the purpose of the group leads to other activities besides talking. You will need to plan ahead, at least to the extent of having ideas up your sleeve, and to prepare activities, some of which will need materials. You will find suggestions for activities from page 212. In planning to use activities, consider the following:

- A planned activity should help to focus the group and add to the learning of group members. As group leader, you should have a clear purpose in choosing one activity or a series of activities; it should never be a case of, 'We have to do something otherwise they'll get bored.'
- Sometimes a group will express themselves successfully in words but, on other occasions, even careful interventions by a leader may be met with denial or avoidance. Pushing groups to face or discuss something can be counter-productive. They need an experience which helps them to stand back and to discover for themselves, perhaps one not involving language primarily.
- An activity can provide a group with direct and shared experience which can be a focus for discussion. Working together on a common task can develop group feelings of support and achievement. Another advantage is that all group members have taken part in some way in this activity and ideas or feelings can be raised through the activity and the debriefing afterwards.

To think about

Focus on a group to which you belong now or recently. (Your notes from the activity on page 173 may remind you of groups.) Reflect on your own experience as a group member:

- What were the advantages and disadvantages of the physical setting in which you all met? What did the group leader do to overcome the negative aspects?
- What was the purpose of the group (and/or the meeting itself) and how clear was this to everyone?

- What kind of role was taken by the group leader or co-leaders (look back at page 181)?
- In your opinion, what went well in the life of the group and what did not go so well? Looking back, what would you change and for what reasons?

▼ 10 Running a group

10.1 The development of a group

Your aim in running a group is to enable the group members to interact as productively as possible to achieve the aims of the group. As such it will take longer, and more patience, to help a group share deep feelings with each other than it will to encourage them accurately to share facts or opinions. You constantly encourage members to move outside their personal zone of complete safety to learn and to grow, but should never pressurise them to move so far or so quickly that they panic or withdraw. The art is to lead, sensitively, where members wish to follow, until they are able to chart their own paths.

Phases in the life of a group

Most groups pass through similar stages in their life. Each meeting may also be a mini-version of the entire process too. An awareness of these developments helps you to recognise that some difficulties are part of the inevitable group process rather than events you should have managed to avoid. These are essentially the same as the communications hierarchy discussed in Chapter 2. Groups start with *ritual and cliché*, and over time progress through *facts and information* and so on to *emotions*.

The polite phase

Initially, as groups form, everyone is polite and communication is in the form of a lot of ritual and greeting. At the outset, nothing of any great relevance is aired or discussed.

'Why are we here?' – forming

Groups start as everyone gets to know each other and finds out how this group is going to work. It is not unusual that events occur such as:

- People are uncertain what to do and look for clues from you, the first outspoken person, their past experience of similar groups and any expectations of this kind of group. The leader's role in the early sessions is to ease people into this group.
- Group members show a mixture of scepticism and cautious commitment to the group. Individuals may wish to protect themselves from making a wrong

move, appearing bossy or being given responsibilities. At this stage, members are wary about being rejected.

- If group members do not know each other already, they need to see how they will all work together. If some people do know each other, they may be wary of how their current relationship in the group will fit with life outside. The group leader has the task of establishing this group as distinct from any groups or relationships elsewhere.
- One or two people may be keen to speak up and shape where the group will go. Some may even make a bid for formal or informal leadership.
- In groups who meet to discuss problems or feelings, someone may talk about him or herself at a deeper level than the rest of the group are yet comfortable with. That person may feel exposed or be frustrated that nobody else will follow the lead, whilst the others may feel pressured to reveal more than they wish.

The discussion may ramble and the group may look in a dependent way to you as leader for structure and control, perhaps for a clearer guide than you feel is appropriate. If you do not take an appropriate lead, some members may suspect from previous group experience that you have an agenda which you are not willing to disclose. Needless to say, any hidden agendas that you later reveal will shake the group's trust in you. Be honest with the group.

Open groups often have new members and under these circumstances there will be some re-forming whenever new people join. New arrivals have to find their place and learn how this group runs. Existing members may be welcoming yet wary that the newcomers do not push the group in ways that are contrary to established group norms. Much of the group's energy at this time is spent focused on the individual, each individual wishing to feel comfortable and not threatened.

Storming

Once members feel more at ease in the group, or judge that they have the measure of this particular group, then leaders have to deal with group events linked with individuals' needs. Individual members trying to fulfil potentially selfish needs from the group is a common characteristic of the storming phase. For instance:

- Some people will manoeuvre for position in the group, seeking a preferred role or making a bid for power in some way.
- Group members may voice objections: that they did not really want to come to this group in the first place, that it is not the kind of group they expected or that nothing useful is happening.
- High hopes that the group task might be easy can move towards disappointment, perhaps that the group leader does not tell everyone what to do or that members are expected to do some work themselves. Some members may become frustrated or angry with the behaviour of others in the group. You have to manage any conflict and balance a constructive confrontation with support. Expectations of the group must be managed constantly: why the group is here, what it is aiming to do, and how it behaves.
- Some members may be torn between wanting to belong to and work with the group and yet also retaining their own individuality. Some people may already face conflicts arising from their current group membership, or previous experiences in groups, as well as their relationships or responsibilities outside the group.

A time of reaction and rebellion is very normal in group life and will usually help the group to move on. Instead of being polite, now that group members have better information, they begin to make judgements about what the group should do, how it should be run and by whom. As group leader, you need to communicate clearly what seems to be happening in the group, and explore and bring out the key issues. You should try very hard not to see the events as a direct attack on your own competence or self-worth, even if some members make personal remarks. The group are growing in confidence and are telling you what they think. You need to create an atmosphere where you remain in control of the group but still leave space for disagreements to be expressed and handled.

Storming is the most risky and potentially disruptive time for the group and sometimes a group disbands at this point. The storming phase certainly may result in some people leaving. Some group members may now understand much better, through the honest and sometimes conflictful sharing of perceptions, that the group is not right for them. The benefit of storming is that the level of honesty has increased in the group, and the improved candour enables the group to move to agree improved ways of working together to reach their goals, ways which hopefully will prevent storming in the future.

Norming

With the help of the leader, groups should be able to work through the issues raised at the storming phase.

- The discussion and group activities should have helped to develop greater trust, cohesion in the group and a sense of group identity, of 'our group'.
- Stronger norms develop about the way of working in this group. These norms may be formal or informal useful ground rules of communication and support. However norms can also be disruptive or impose on some of the group, for example, prevailing on one person to take on unwanted group responsibilities or making another the butt of unpleasant jokes. A group leader has to remain aware of these patterns and step in, even at the cost of possible disharmony in the group (see page 206).
- Your aim is to harness the group's motivation, their energy, skills and commitment to work towards the group's task. At this stage, people are more ready to take responsibility as individuals and as a whole group.
- During norming, the group devotes quite a lot of time to sorting out issues of functioning as a group, the processes and patterns of behaviour and interaction. Only when this discussion is largely completed will the group be able to devote its energy to doing the tasks for which it was formed.

Performing

The group settles to work on the agreed objectives. Some groups may have very specific tasks to achieve or actions to complete. Others may have definite learning objectives and yet another kind of group may aim for personal exploration and resolution for individual problems and concerns. The idea of stages in the life of a group does not imply a fixed, forward movement. Many groups have setbacks, unexpected problems or crises. Issues, that you thought had been resolved earlier in the group, reemerge and have to be faced.

As group leader you need both to keep the group on task and also to manage the processes that will support their work. You can help by reviewing progress, guiding the group to learn from mistakes and reassess norms as needed. In some groups, an important role will also be to remind people why they are there and why it is important. You may need to stress how group work links with outside life as a means to an end.

In some groups, leaders remain central and help by assigning tasks, helping with problem-solving and supporting members in difficulty. In other groups, the leader may become less and less necessary until the point at which the group manages alone, and the leader becomes fully delegative.

Esprit

If you are lucky, sometimes groups experience esprit, in which they reach higher goals than were initially sought, and group members develop very high levels of pride in and commitment to each other. This phase is both wonderful when it happens and rare.

Ending

Some theoretical discussions about group life fail to cover endings. Some groups may run with a clear end time fixed at the beginning but many groups are more flexible and under review. Some groups end prematurely, often through being unable to resolve a storming period. Group members and the leader benefit from a clear end to the life of a group and a review of what has been achieved (see page 218). The ending needs to be recognised, as well as the feelings of loss that this may engender.

10.2 The first session

The opening session of any group is important because it sets the pattern of how the group may well continue. First sessions can be awkward, with long silences. Group members often look to the leader for direction and there is usually uneven participation between group members, some talking considerably more than others. Group members begin to get to know each other or, if they are already familiar, to establish how they will relate in this context. They form their first impressions of the group leader and how this group is likely to work.

Jarlath Benson, in *Working more creatively with groups* (Tavistock, 1987), stresses the three Cs, key messages for a group leader to communicate in the first session and afterwards:

- Competency: the group leader communicates, through words and non-verbal behaviour, that she or he is prepared and can be relied upon by the group. Leaders do not imply that they are utterly in control and certain about the group; this would be unrealistic. Show you are competent to deal with the group's natural concerns at the start.
- Compassion: the leader should act in a way that helps members to feel safe and included. You should show, from the very beginning of the group, a willingness to be considerate of everyone present and to adjust what happens in response to the input of the group. Care and concern will be shown through how you manage expectations and give space to each group member. However, it is not genuine to imply deep feelings for individuals whom you do not yet know.
- Commitment: you show through your words and actions that you are ready to give time and energy to this group, that the development of the work of the group matters to you.

Welcome to the group

Relate to members as individuals

Be at the venue in good time to welcome people personally as they arrive. Greet them by name, if you know it, or ask their name after you have introduced yourself. Simple refreshments help to show a welcome and give members some informal time to adjust to the new environment without pressure. It also gives new members something to do while waiting for others to arrive.

Promote good communication

Work to even out striking differences in participation between group members. Some may talk a great deal or want to shape the group in a direction that makes sense to them. Others may be very quiet and contribute little, although they may show resentment of individuals who are very prominent. Particularly quieter people need to be asked to contribute, but not pressurised. (See page 202 on helping groups to listen.)

Communicate clearly and in straightforward language. Avoid professional jargon and any phrases that are unlikely to be part of this group's usual language. However it is unwise to change your way of speaking significantly in order to appear to be more like the group. You will not appear genuine and anyone who knows you in a different context will probably comment on the discrepancy.

Be aware of your body language

Make your voice, tone of voice, gestures and body posture communicate interest in the group, warmth towards them and a level of your own comfort in being here. Hold an attentive and open posture, whether you are talking or listening. Avoid hunching up, firmly crossed legs or folded arms and any distracting body gestures. Your aim is to model openness and attention to the group (see also Chapter 2).

Consider how you dress since this too carries a message. Do not make yourself uncomfortable, but generally aim to make your dress in tune with the group. For instance, you should not be dressed very formally, in a business suit, if most or all of this group is dressed casually. The difference will create distance between you; members may even think you are trying to be superior. On the other hand, you would give an equally discordant message if you insisted on wearing your old jeans and T-shirt when the group were in smart casual style.

Introductions

There are several ways to introduce each other. These include:

- Group members simply introducing themselves with some personal information, not necessarily serious, for instance, 'I'm Janine and my favourite film is . . .'.
- Members can talk briefly in pairs and then introduce each other.
- A soft ball or bean bag can be passed between members as one person says, 'I'm Steve and I'm passing the ball to Aaron.' A variation is to run this activity with a ball of wool or string, when everyone holds on to part of the wool but throws on the remaining ball. You create a visible network of links between the group members.

Use people's names regularly during the first session. Ask politely if you have forgotten. You will help other members of the group to learn names by repeating them and showing that you think it is important.

Expectations and contracting

All groups need to discuss the purpose and boundaries of the group. You need to explore a group contract in a similar way to the contracting process with one person (see page 124). Contracting in a group should not take up the whole first session, but the discussion will take longer than with one person. The objective is to clear away as soon as possible any issues which can get in the way of the group functioning well and to form a basis of sensibly working together. A group contract should establish the appropriate boundaries for this group. It sets out how the group will act and summarises its purpose. Group members' rights and responsibilities are sometimes covered. The contract gives something definite to which to refer later in group life. You could consider writing down the details of the group contract for all members to see. A written version will not always be appropriate, but can definitely help if there appear to be diverse views in the group or any issue has needed a lot of discussion before a conclusion is reached. In this area consensus is important. Each member must feel that they have had the chance to contribute, and that any objections have been fully explored before the contract is drawn.

The contents of the contract will vary slightly with the nature of the group but some or all of the following are often included.

The purpose of this group

- The group needs to discuss why they are all here. You can handle expectations about the group or your role much more constructively if they are expressed early. Clarify any misunderstandings about the nature and purpose of this group.
- Some groups may have specific or time-bound purposes while others are more flexible – but should still not be vague and confined to 'We'll work it out as we go along.'
- If the group purpose is left undisclosed or unclear, wishes and assumptions of individual group members will still exert an impact on behaviour. Strong individuals may push the group towards their own preferences and less confident individuals may follow, but feel resentful.

Hopes and concerns

- Have some members arrived expecting a very different kind of group or approach by the leader? However carefully you plan, there may be people who have an unrealistic idea of what the group will do and how quickly. People who have been sent to the group may be reluctant and uncertain.
- If the group is therapeutic in purpose, you should see each individual before the first group session, to clarify whether the experience will be appropriate for them. Other kinds of groups may well have gathered in such a way that the

initial session will be the first time to explore individual hopes, expectations and any concerns.

- Consider an activity that helps everyone to express their personal 'hopes and concerns for this group'. You can ask everyone to note and then express their views one by one, or they can discuss the matter in pairs or small groups and write hopes and concerns on large sheets of paper. Deal with what everyone has expressed.

How this group will work

- Cover the practical details of where, when and how often a group will meet. You can cover timekeeping, breaks and, if it is the nature of this group, the commitment of members to attend all sessions.
- Clarify your role as group leader or how you and a co-leader will work together. Give your personal commitment to attend for every session. If another person or co-leader will join only for particular sessions, then tell the group now, as well as reminding them before the relevant sessions.
- Is the group open or closed and do the members understand what this means? Are group members free to give up the group and can they return if they change their mind? If so, how does this happen?
- With regard to confidentiality rules for group members and the group leader, are there any limits to confidentiality? If so, be clear and honest about what they are. In groups where individuals are likely to share personal experiences, then make the importance of confidentiality especially strong. Ask, and get, an individual 'Yes' commitment from everyone, out loud, before moving on.
- Deal with any practical issues such as any rules on smoking, and the length or frequency of breaks. This may also include exact start and finish times. It is also wise to gain a commitment that all pagers and mobiles are switched off during group time (unless individuals are genuinely on emergency call).

Later contracts and agreements

You may need to return to issues within the group contract later on. Perhaps conflicts have arisen about confidentiality, a subgroup wants to take a different direction from that originally agreed, or a challenge has arisen to you as group leader. Over time you may also realise that this particular group needs further exploration of rights and responsibilities. For example, a very lively group in which members talk over the top of each other may need some group rules to which everyone commits:

- It may be a simple rule of 'One person speaks at a time', 'Listen, don't interrupt', or, 'Talk rather than shout'. You have to manage this process when individual members have limited experience of holding back and listening rather than raising their voice.
- Some groups need a practical rule to help them follow the general one. A group given to saying 'Yes, but . . .' to ideas has a rule of 'Say three good things'. The next speaker has to say three things in support of the previous person's comment before making their own point. An alternative is that everyone has

to summarise briefly what the previous person has said (to this person's satisfaction) before adding their bit.

- Groups where interruptions are serious may need to create better habits by passing the baton (an object that has to be held in order to speak).
- Another group may need a rule about, 'Don't assume how people feel, ask them', or some rules derived from constructive feedback (see page 39).
- Cautious and wary groups may need explicit permission, even a written notice that says, 'It's OK to make mistakes here', or, 'It's fine to say that you don't know', to help them feel able to contribute.

Introductions and warm-up games

First sessions often benefit from non-threatening activities that help a group to get started and everyone to know each other. Some suggestions are given on page 213.

To think about

Consider the following scenarios during and immediately after a first group session. What do you think may be going on in the group? What could be a positive way to handle the situation?

- The contracting phase of a group for juvenile offenders is almost finished. The group leader asks if there are any other issues to raise. One young man says, 'I want everyone to know that I hate groups like this. I didn't want to come, but my social worker said I had to. I'm not going to talk about myself and I want everyone to leave me alone. Is that clear?'
- During member introductions in a group for prospective foster parents, everyone has shared their first name and something personal about themselves. Then the last woman says, 'I'm Mrs Hardcastle and I'm sure everyone knows who I am.' Another group member comments, 'Well, I've never met you before', and is given a cold stare.
- At the end of the first session, two members tackle the group leader and one explains, 'We were told this group was our chance to talk about problems with our children. But we're not sure we can trust the others in the group. Especially Tyrone, I know him from work and he can't keep his mouth shut. How can you promise everything will be kept confidential?'
- As you are packing your bag one group member comes up to you. She spoke a great deal during the first session, encouraging other members to talk and sharing her ideas and own experience in detail. She says to you, 'That was hard work, wasn't it? They need a lot of bringing out of themselves. I think we'll make a good team, you and me.'

10.3 Working with group dynamics

Group work inevitably brings more uncertainty than using your counselling skills with one other person. In a group there are a number of people whose actions and words you cannot accurately predict, and in addition there is the further complexity of dealing with subgroups.

- An entire group may introduce a brand new topic, work hard to avoid another topic or bring a wide range of strategies for avoiding a clear focus on the agreed task.
- Group members form relationships with each other as well as with you. These allegiances may support, or undermine, the work of the group. Subgroups may involve you, or conspicuously cut you out of their contribution.
- There are many individuals who may want to talk at the same time and interrupt, ignore or misunderstand each other. Some individuals in a group may be very quiet, even making an issue out of their obvious silence. You may be faced with an entire group which regularly lapses into long silences or many short statements.
- Some group members may say or do something that you know you would not have done. In some cases, the impact will be negative on the group, or on you personally but not the group. Your skills as group leader will be important to deal with the consequences effectively.
- However, on many occasions in groups, individual members will be constructive and insightful, with the consequence that you do not have to speak. Sometimes an unexpected intervention from a group member, something you know you were very unlikely to have said or done, works out positively and you learn from what has happened.

Group work can be very exciting. It may often be the best way to work with clients but it is certainly not easy. All the counselling skills described in Chapters 7 and 8 are valuable within group work. This section provides ideas and suggestions about applying these to groups.

Listening and helping group members to listen to each other

You need all the skills of listening, reflecting back, summarising and open-ended questions (see page 43). You also use these skills to promote listening and understanding between group members.

- Encourage dialogue between members, rather than a whole series of contributions directed to you as group leader. Suggest that members talk directly to each other, rather than just through you. Invite other people into an issue with, 'What do you think?', 'How does that strike you?', or, 'Is that close to the point you were making earlier?'
- Help members to relate to each other by making links between what individuals say. Demonstrate that you value each contribution and expect that members will have some views and experiences in common.
- One way of encouraging links is to build explicitly on what individuals contribute. Help the group to explore shared themes with comments like, 'Let's see if we can build on Jof's idea about . . .', 'Supposing we add to Hamid's point by . . .', or, 'That sounds as if it links back to what Ruth said earlier

about . . .'. This approach also counteracts the tendency in early sessions for members to communicate through the medium of the group leader.

- Work to encourage an atmosphere in which it is acceptable for members to say that they do not understand what someone has said or are confused. Periodically check out that the group understands what you have said with, 'Does this make sense to you?', or, 'Are you following what I'm saying here?' Be ready also to show your own need to be clear on what a group member is saying with, 'Chloe, I'm not sure that I follow what you're saying here', 'Are you saying that . . .', or, 'I'm sorry, Ron, I got lost at . . .'.

Lively groups that have difficulty in listening to each other may benefit from some agreed ground rules as mentioned on page 200.

Helping individuals to communicate better

Your role is to help people to speak as well as to listen to each other. By your contributions, you encourage individuals to express ideas when they are cautious; to voice their feelings, hopes or expectations. You help to increase both the quality and quantity of the communication in the group.

- All groups have to develop some level of trust so that everyone, especially the less confident or more cautious members, feel able to speak.
- Help by establishing clear rules of confidentiality and dealing constructively with any individual concerns or experiences of broken confidences within this group or previous ones.
- Use the skill of reflecting back to deal with the negative reactions that can discourage honesty and sharing of ideas. The putdown of 'That's a stupid thing to feel' can be met with 'You don't understand why Kayleigh feels that way.' The block of 'That idea will never work' may be met with 'Rob, you feel that idea won't work. Tell us what you see as the problem.'

Focus on the here and now

The advantage of group life is to enable individuals to focus on what is happening now. In some groups, members may be talking about previous experiences or distress, but the role of the group is to help them to focus on how the experience affects them now, their feelings, assumptions and beliefs about themselves and what is possible.

A focus on the here and now also includes what is happening within the group itself. The discussion may be triggered by something that an individual has brought into the group from outside. Yet, what matters is how individual experiences, actions and feelings are affecting the group right now. The task of a group leader is to help everyone to focus on:

- How are you feeling now?
- What's going on in the group at the moment?
- What do you want to happen now?
- What does this experience (behaviour) mean for you (us) now?

Dealing with feelings

Some groups and individuals find it hard to talk about feelings. A group norm may develop or have been brought in from outside that feelings are irrelevant or soft. You can help by modelling how to raise and talk about feelings.

- Deal with emotions as they arise, do not store them up to be dealt with later. Make space and time to deal with people who get upset or angry. Until the feelings have been dealt with, you cannot continue with a productive session.
- Help the feelings to be expressed without pushing anyone. Recognise feelings as always valid and true for that individual. Follow individuals' use of words to describe the feelings they are willing to share and guide the rest of the group to respect how others wish to talk about them. For instance, one individual may find it easier to say that he is 'angry' rather than 'upset'; another group member may have the opposite preference. Words have quite specific meanings for different people.
- Offer a constructive challenge to group members who want to protect others from the hurt of feelings and make everything better. Their protective approach may be far more about their own needs and perceived role in the group than what someone else wants or needs.
- Challenge group members who want to speak up for how someone else is feeling or champion them against some assumed slight. It is the individual's right to defend her or himself, or not.
- Sort out the 'We all feel that . . .' into the separate individual 'I's genuinely included in the 'we' and those which are assumed to agree, but whose views have not been checked first.
- Prevent gossip within the group when members talk, or even argue, about the feelings and reactions of another member as if that person is not present. Encourage direct talk to each other, and use their names as appropriate.
- Allow people to say what they wish and no more. Avoid pressing people to share and self-disclose. A group rule may need to be established that 'Everyone has the right to say "I'm not saying any more about that".' Watch out for a group norm of pressure to give more information to satisfy the curiosity of others. Whose needs are being met by continuing?
- Avoid many 'why' questions. Stay with the more productive 'how' or 'what' questions.
- Watch out for individuals who want to take the floor for their own self-disclosure of experience or feelings, but are unwilling to allow space for others.
- Some people may insist on relating the experience of fellow group members to their own with, 'I know exactly how you feel.' You may need to confront such individuals with care, saying, 'Hold on please, I don't think Felicity has finished yet', or, 'I would like us all to listen to Felicity's own version and then we'll have a much better idea if our own experiences can help.' With serious interrupters, you may have to repeat your comment in slightly different words and with an assertive tone – even on occasion to ask them to be quiet for a while.

Your own self-disclosure

The points made on page 151 about self-disclosure in one-to-one counselling are equally applicable to the work of a group leader. You may appropriately self-disclose in several different ways:

- You share personal feelings to clarify communication within the group, for instance, 'I feel confused about . . .', or, 'I am uncomfortable over what is happening in this group about . . .'.
- You share brief, personal information to help the group forward, for example, 'Yes, I do have some understanding of how you feel. I've got a job now but a few years ago, I was made redundant and it took me 18 months to get another job.'
- You say briefly how you feel about an event in the group, for instance: 'Thank you for telling me about . . .', 'I find it pleasing when you . . .', or, 'When you say . . . I find it hard to . . .'.
- You express personal values and beliefs, when appropriate, such as, 'I don't believe we should be talking about Mina as if she wasn't here', or, 'I don't think we should do . . . without first checking with . . .'.
- You share experiences gained from running similar groups in the past, or experiences of other approaches to an issue facing group members – all with respect to boundaries of confidentiality.

The central point is that any self-disclosure by a group leader should help the group, or individual members, to achieve their goals. Your self-disclosure will not move the group forward if you:

- Have failed to listen and offer an irrelevant self-disclosure.
- Share serious feelings of unease or distress. It is not the group's role to help you with these. Share these outside the group, ideally with a trusted colleague.
- Allow your personal experience to become a focus for the group's discussion. Your professional experience may well allow the group to discuss this new perspective for some time quite appropriately.
- Present your experience or feelings as an expert view when they are not. Leaders have quite a lot of power in a group, and it is important to tell the group when you are offering an expert view and when you are not.
- Seek group time to work through your feelings or past experience.
- Seem through your self-disclosure to condone doubtful behaviour or poor practice within or outside the group.

Common difficulties in groups

Dominant individuals or subgroups

The development of groups can be swayed by the behaviour of individuals whose actions begin to dominate others. Some people may:

- Talk constantly, being the first to speak at each meeting and filling any silence. They may also interrupt and talk over people.
- Have the worst problems, the most dramatic difficulties and strive to top other members' experiences.
- Be the nicest person, the one who protects and supports other group members whether they want it or not.
- Offer assertive help or advice, pronounce on other's problems or insist on speaking up for the rest of the group with, 'We all think that . . .'.
- Act aggressively and demand attention, especially from the group leader.
- Behave in a cynical way, sceptical of the point of any ideas or the point of activities, dismissive of the enthusiasm of others in the group.
- Play the clown, joking with or about other members and perhaps refusing to take group activities seriously: 'It's not real. We're just playing games.'

People may dominate a group for a range of different reasons. Reasons are not, of course, excuses for behaviour that can disrupt a group or reduce the opportunities for other members to participate fully. However, your decision about how to intervene can be guided by keeping an open mind about what fuels the behaviour. Perhaps:

- There are problems within the group, maybe lack of trust or confidence in speaking out, and these leave a vacuum that, as group leader, you have only just recognised (perhaps a bit late!).
- The group started with unequal relationships, perhaps status differences imported from outside the group, that leave dominant members able to take a lead and others loath to challenge.
- The dominating person may be accustomed to being the centre of attention and usually behaves in this way. He or she feels more competent and superior.
- A cynic may be reacting to bad previous experiences. He or she deals with a fear of failure by not becoming involved and so avoids risk. Cynics are sometimes protecting themselves to stop anyone coming close.
- An individual feels more worthy of attention, more needy and believes that the group should sort out his or her problems as a priority.
- A person is unable to tolerate silences.

Quiet individuals or subgroups

It can be just as difficult sometimes to deal with very quiet people who may be reticent to express themselves because they:

- Have little self-confidence, or fear making mistakes or looking silly in front of other people.
- Have had bad experiences in previous groups when their contributions were belittled or dismissed and the group leader did nothing.
- Are in the habit of deferring to particular kinds of people, some of whom are represented in the group. Quiet, passive, individuals are not necessarily content; they may feel resentful and frustrated and this feeling starts to influence the group.

- Want to be noticed for their silence and to be asked to contribute to the group. People can be silent in ways that intrude, through their body language and facial expression, or heavy sighs, dismissive grunts and cynical half-laughs.

Scapegoating in groups

Some groups turn on particular individuals, or subgroups (cliques) target one or more individuals. People may be heavily teased or made the butt of jokes or unpleasant innuendo. Ideas may be proposed in a way that dismisses this person, for instance, 'If Richard can manage it, of course', or, 'I can see I've shocked our little Miss Uptight over there!' Individuals who are keen to belong to a group may tolerate, even seem to encourage, jokes made against themselves, but the pattern is disruptive of broader group working. Frequently those scapegoated are different in some way from other group members and the contrast is as likely to be behavioural, that they are quieter, or smarter, for example, as visible differences in how they look.

Ways of intervening

When you are working with a single client your choice is when and how to contribute to the conversation and whether to allow a silence to continue. In a group, you have additional choices and decisions because more people are involved, as talkers, listeners and observers of the action. The group can take a route and direction that does not directly involve you, which is acceptable as long as it does not go off-track for the group purpose. If it does you will need to decide both whether and how you intervene. You can use the counselling skills of both Stage One and Stage Two to handle confrontation within the group, to encourage group members to stand back from what is happening and observe the process of what is happening.

Do you allow the situation to continue?

There are no hard and fast rules about when you should intervene and when you should listen and watch. Use your skills to judge how you should act and remain very aware of what you are doing as well as the rest of the group.

- You can wait and watch for a short while to judge whether the situation will be handled by the group.
- You can allow a situation to continue, anticipating from experience of this group that other members will intervene in an appropriate way. You can then join and help the group to examine what has been happening.
- Be aware of your own preferred style; your non-intervention should not be just because you dislike confrontation. On the other hand, keen confronters need to learn that groups do resolve matters themselves sometimes.

Disruptive actions or uneven contribution by group members should not be allowed to continue for long. The pattern will become set and that much harder to shift. Trouble may simmer under the surface and group members will complain, either within the group or outside.

Indirect responses

Sometimes you can affect the process of how the group works through a group change or activity. For instance:

- Over-talkative or over-quiet group members may be influenced by changes in how people's contributions are managed. Perhaps suggest going round everybody one by one and courteously insist that each person has an uninterrupted turn.
- Some organised group activities (see ideas from page 212) give an opportunity to place individuals in less usual roles within the group.
- You may break up subgroups by suggesting or engineering a change in seating to make communications easier.

Direct but implicit response

You have some options to affect the group by direct intervention which does not yet identify individuals or a group pattern. You can:

- Give quieter members a chance to speak without identifying them as quiet ones. You might bring someone in with, 'Sasha, I believe you've had experience of . . .', or, 'Dafydd, you started to say something.'
- Halt a dominant person with, 'Hold on a minute, Lesley, I don't think Dafydd had finished.'
- Invite general contributions beyond the ideas of a dominant member with, 'That's a good point, let's see what other people think.'

Quieter group members usually like the opportunity to make a contribution to the group without feeling in the spotlight, or having excessive attention after their contribution.

Direct and explicit response

In some groups it becomes necessary to raise the situation as an issue or a problem within this group. You have three main verbal options. You speak:

1 *Directly to an individual* with a comment that describes the situation, 'Richard, you seem to be blamed for . . .', or, 'Lesley, you give so many ideas at once, it's hard to take them in.' Sometimes it will be appropriate, with the support of the rest of the group, to encourage constructive feedback (see page 39) between particular individuals on how they experience each other's behaviour. You might invite a cynic to express doubts more constructively so as to make her or him responsible for the cynicism. A cynic may have a useful point if expressed more positively.

2 *To the rest of the group*, the ones not directly involved, with, 'Does it concern you that Richard is accepting the blame for . . .', or, 'The rest of you are letting Lesley do most of the talking.'

3 *With the whole group* in a way that does not divide off individuals into subgroups. This option is usually preferable since difficulties will affect the entire group in some way. You can ask the group directly to talk about how they

are allowing this situation to develop or continue. For instance, 'I'm sure you've all noticed what's happening with . . . Can we explore . . . and agree a way to make the group better for everyone?'

However you proceed, your aim is to free individuals from the unhelpful role that they are taking and enable the group to move forward. Your interventions can be gentle, soft but firm, or challenging, depending on the severity of the problem requiring intervention. Your first and preferred approach should be to speak to the individual within the group. If this tactic fails to effect the change that is needed, you might have to speak privately with the person outside the group. As group leader, your commitment is to the success of the group, and this priority may mean in extreme circumstances that you ask a highly disruptive member to leave.

Exploration with the group

Your role is to help the group progress further than they would on their own. You are part of the group, yet as leader you have to offer an objective perspective as well. You choose how to approach the range of situations that can arise. These could include: a developing conflict, the scapegoating of an individual or subgroup, avoidance of an activity or topic for exploration, breaking a previously agreed rule or belittling the purpose of the group. You use skills of observation and counselling to understand what seems to be happening and how you may best intervene:

- You need to work out what is happening. By watching and listening, can you identify who is involved and when? Some variations include: one individual is in conflict with another, two group members are setting themselves against you as the leader, or subgroups have developed who are handling the situation in different ways or who are trying to take the group in different directions.
- If the group, or you, appears to have become confused and lost, you need to identify what is most important at this time. Depending on the group, it may be that you show strong leadership, protect individuals or a subgroup, or bring the group back to the agreed task or to the agreed key values.
- Without trying to second-guess individual motivations, consider the emotional needs that may underlie the actions of individual group members (see page 206). You can disapprove of actions and still appreciate the motivations that underlie them.
- Decide if it is appropriate for you to intervene and, if so, say briefly what you see happening, perhaps also what you feel or how the behaviour is affecting the group. Explain simply why you want to discuss what is happening and focus on the here and now of group life.
- Use counselling skills to make informed confrontation a shared experience, pulling back from aggressive responses or highly personal remarks about individuals. You might say, 'I'd like to tell you something I've noticed', and then explain why you feel it is important to the group and invite members to look at what is happening.

- Encourage the group to look at the issues. Perhaps there is very limited commitment at this point and you may decide not to push. However, if the same situation continues or recurs, then consider making a firmer statement, linked if appropriate to the group contract.
- Any discussion should include as many of the group members as possible. It is your role to invite contributions towards a discussion of the problem or where the group appears to be going. Keep the discussion focused on what is happening and how and do not slip into personal blame or revenge between group members. Individuals need the opportunity and encouragement to voice what they need or what they think is happening.
- You can encourage and help the group to consider the consequences of the behaviour of individuals, including those in the group who sit back and watch disapprovingly but do not risk themselves to say anything.
- Deal with the issues as belonging to the group, not just the problem of one or two members. You need to bring out the feelings of everyone involved. You can consider whether any existing or new group rules would help. Explore what all group members will do about the situation and work to establish a shared responsibility and not just that the dominant person will stop whatever he or she is doing.
- You might also need to make an intervention which changes the structure of the group temporarily to allow a more open debate, or an exercise to help throw the issue into a different light and help the group to learn.

Learn about yourself

You will continue to learn about your own behaviour in groups. You will have to deal with what, with hindsight, you believe to have been a poor judgement or a mistake. Willingness to reflect on what you did and why is part of your own development. Just as much as in one-to-one work with clients, you need to consider your own personal style and any ways in which your inclinations may support or mislead you. For instance:

- Perhaps you dislike confrontation and you become aware that this preference tempts you to smooth over conflict in the group rather than using counselling skills to bring out disagreements safely. Smoothing over is a temporary coping mechanism. It does nothing to address the reasons for the conflict and to deal with them directly so that it does not reoccur. Smoothed conflict merely festers beneath the surface.
- Alternatively, you may place a great value on honesty and expression of feelings, however uncomfortable. Your preference leads you to underestimate how raw some of the group feel about what they have been encouraged to disclose and the blunt reactions of some members. Some of the group can feel resentful and frustrated, increasing the chances of conflict later on.

Distress in the group

Sometimes someone in a group will become distressed, perhaps because of an event within the group, but possibly because of concerns that are outside the group experience. You may see this situation coming, having noticed that an individual has gone very quiet or tearful or it may arise without any warning.

- Stay calm. The rest of the group need to see that you are able to cope and are neither embarrassed, nor showing panic.
- Stop the proceedings of the group since it is inappropriate to carry on as if nothing is happening. Apart from being disrespectful, you will make no progress if you continue.
- Offer space to the person and specific comfort as appropriate. It might be a light touch, a hold or hug, depending on the relationship and circumstances. Sometimes, it may be another person in the group who offers the comfort.
- Do not rush to get drinks or do something active. Tissues may be the most that is required if someone is crying.
- Ask if the person wishes to talk, and respect his or her views. If she or he does want to talk then listen and deal briefly with what emerges.
- See if you can talk through the distress to get the group member back on track. You might say, 'Tell us what is happening to you right now', 'How can we help you with this', and reassure as appropriate, perhaps with, 'It's fine to make mistakes. No, I don't think you're stupid at all.'
- If a distressed individual feels unable to stay while distressed, then offer some time out of the group. Does he or she want or need someone with them? Consider how you will ease the entry back. It might be a brief welcome, 'I'm pleased you came back', or a smile.
- Deal with any issues with other group members who feel responsible for causing the upset and reassure if appropriate. Do not let them discuss the incident as if the distressed person is not there.
- Consider whether this person needs additional help and, if so, whether you can give this time. A serious and stressful personal issue, that is very separate from the group work, cannot be handled within the group. If you offer individual help, respect the individual's right to refuse without taking it personally.

To think about

Think through how you might handle these scenarios if you were group leader. Work through ideas of the exact words you could use. If possible, discuss some of these examples with a colleague.

- You are running a group on communication skills for reception and front desk staff. Use of video feedback is part of the learning and this was made clear in the material sent out before the first session. Martha refuses flatly to join any role play that is being videoed. You make the decision to let her sit out for this session, in the hope that she will be feel able to participate fully next week. Each role play is then followed by viewing the video and an exchange of constructive feedback. Martha is highly critical of her fellow participants and laughs out loud at one especially awkward moment. You remind Martha firmly of the agreed rules for constructive feedback. She is silent for part of the next feedback but then starts criticising once more.

- Three group members have been targeting James, a quieter individual, by making jokes about any ideas he contributes and teasing him about his dress style. James looks uncomfortable but has refused opportunities to talk about the situation with the group. He now begins any contribution with words like, 'I expect this is a pretty stupid idea', and laughs nervously at the jokes or heavy teasing. From other comments that James has made, you believe that he has learned to tolerate this kind of behaviour in order to have a role in any group.
- Ian normally contributes to the group but he has been very quiet during this session. Max, another group member, tries to bring him in with, 'You're very quiet today, Ian. Aren't we going to get any of your good ideas?' Ian looks stricken and Max follows up lightly with, 'What's the matter? You look like someone's died.' Ian immediately leaves the room. Max looks stunned and says, 'What have I said? I meant it as a joke.' Harriet speaks up, 'It's the first anniversary of the road accident. Ian's daughter was killed this time last year.'
- During the first two sessions of the group, Kamalini has been highly alert for what she judges to be sexist behaviour from any men present. None of the instances which she has confronted have been directed at Kamalini. She speaks up on behalf of other women in the group with phrases like, 'Donna doesn't seem to have noticed, but I think . . .', and, 'We all feel that . . .'. Before the third session, two female group members speak privately with you as leader. They say that they want you to stop Kamalini, they do not agree that any of her examples were sexist, they feel patronised and resent her claim to speak on their behalf.

10.4 Activities in the group

Positive use of activities

Groups spend a great deal of time talking and listening to each other but they also benefit from some activities selected in the light of the group objectives and the range of members. These can speed up learning, by placing group members in different situations and using different tools. It is worth developing your repertoire of possible activities for groups, which include work on an individual basis, in pairs or small subgroups or whole group work. Some general points about choosing and using activities include:

- Explain the purpose of any activity to the group and manage their expectations about what they will be doing and how.
- Invite but do not insist on participation. Sometimes there will be a choice between being a participant and an observer.
- Make it clear that group members who do not want to join the activity remain part of the group. Discourage unhelpful criticism or poking fun and prevent

group members from talking or behaving in ways unrelated to the group activity.

- Be positive and encouraging; expect the activity to be enjoyable and useful.
- Keep an eye on the time, but do not be restricted to a length of time that has worked before. Some groups may take longer, others less, so be guided by this group and do not prolong activities to a point where a group is bored. However, agreed time boundaries for the end of a group meeting or session should be maintained.
- It is usually valuable to review an activity afterwards. This discussion is usually quite brief. You might explore basic questions with the group like, 'What did you think of the activity?', 'What was it like for you?', or, 'What did you get out of it?' Sometimes, even activities that do not work as well as you hoped may still generate a good discussion.
- Group members often want some feedback as to how they did in an activity. You need to provide such feedback without inappropriately appearing the expert or the only person with any insight. There should never be any sense of 'gotcha', in that the leader has manoeuvred the group into experiencing something that should have been obvious at the outset.
- Activities must be suitable for the skills, interests and relevant past experience of group members. Activities can usefully stretch group members and encourage them to take an acceptable level of risk in a safe environment. However, an activity should never expose individuals or show them in a negative light. Learning from such experiences is not predictable and often limited or counter-productive to the well-being of individuals and the group.

Warm-up and energising activities

The majority of groups need some introductions at the first session (see page 198) and reminder introductions of names can be useful on subsequent sessions until everyone has learned the names.

- Some activities break the ice in a group or boost a sagging energy level. Possible games are to explore communication without words, a 'sword fight' with fingers or making statues out of each other.

Some groups need a warm-up at the beginning of each session and you can use different welcome games to practise everyone's name. A regular check-in start to each session allows everyone, including the group leader, to share something to bring the group up to date with how they are feeling, what they have done since the last session or what they are looking forward to in this session.

Creative activities

Art

There are many ways of using the group's imagination and ideas through art. You should make any such activities straightforward and stress that artistic ability is neither the point nor a necessity for involvement. Some groups express ideas and emotions through drawing or modelling better than verbally, particularly when they find it difficult to put feelings into words.

- Collages can build up an image of individuals, the group or the group as members think they are seen by others. They can help to build a vision of where the group might go, or parts of history that have affected the group. Have a substantial store of magazine pictures, scissors, paste or cellotape and large sheets of paper.
- A drawn self-portrait, personal badge, a self-designed motto, logo or a coat of arms can help people to introduce themselves to the group or to show what is important to them. Keep the materials simple, with pencils, crayons or felt tips, to avoid much cleaning up.
- Group members can show the different sides of themselves through one or more masks.
- Quick line drawings or stick people can sum up feelings of what is happening in the group.
- Drawings, photographs or sketches can be arranged in patterns or 'family trees' to explore relationships within the group or outside in individuals' work, family or friendships.

As with any activity, you should give some time to discuss and debrief any drawings, collages or models. Let people share as much as they want from what they have created and resist the temptation to over-interpret. Discourage any criticism on artistic grounds since the meaning of the creation is in what the individual wanted to say, not technical artistic competence.

Expressive writing

Some groups enjoy writing. Less outgoing people are often more comfortable with the written word.

- People might like to keep a group experience diary, either a personal, private journal or a shared group journal to which everyone contributes.
- A group poem or story can be written line by line by different individuals as a way of bringing the group experience together. Neither of these activities necessarily has to be completed within a single group session.
- Ensure that there are no technical blocks to the writing. For instance, poems do not have to rhyme and stories are for this group, not for commercial publication. A group that is uneasy about the actual writing, because of spelling and other literacy issues, can dictate what they wish to say to the group leader to note down accurately.
- Stories might also be supported by pictures from magazines, art or sculptures and presented together with a storyline.
- Personal stories can also be written as a narrative to help each member of the group understand more about everyone else's life before they joined the group. This can also help new members when joining an open group, and may be part of the contract. Group members should never be pressed to disclose more than they wish.

Music

There are a number of possibilities for music in groups:

- Consider playing some background music as the group gathers or during a refreshment break. Choose the music as suitable for this group rather than your personal favourite tape or CD.
- You can sometimes use background or break music to shift the group's mood: quieter music to calm a noisy or disruptive group, lively music to bring back some energy to a group that has sagged.
- Group members may share musical memories or pieces of music that mean a great deal to them. Individuals' musical choices should be respected just as much as any other self-disclosure.
- The use of music can also develop into dance and movement, even 'show us' by acting out a scene, or role play discussed below.

Using the imagination further

Many of the activities described in this section draw on the group's imagination but some also involve members' more personal use of images, visual descriptions and symbols to extend the work in the group.

Some groups and individuals become blocked into talking in an exclusively rational way. Tapping into the imagination can free up ideas and bring in new perspectives. Group members who place a strong value on rational discussion may be resistant to flights of imagination, so you need to choose with care. Imaginative techniques can also be very relaxing for a group and introduce some lightness and fun, whilst still tapping into the concerns and feelings of the group, sometimes with surprising depth. Additional ideas include:

- If you were a fly on the wall, that is, not part of the group at all, how would you describe what has just happened or what sense would you make of what is going on?
- What colour is the atmosphere? Pictures and images in the mind can bring out qualities of what is happening that are hard to put into words.
- If we are all animals, which animal are you, what am I? For instance, 'I'm a fox and I'm in my hole and the dogs are coming to get me.'
- If you were a cartoon character, which would you be?
- If we were all on a ship and you were the captain, what would be your first order to us?
- If you could wave a magic wand (or have three wishes about this situation), what would they be?
- If you were listening to yourself as a good friend, what would be your advice? This activity can free people up from the 'if's' and 'but's' to get to what matters most in the situation.
- How would you like people to remember you after you have died, what would please you to have live on in people's memories?
- In order to get through this difficult situation, who shall I imagine is standing by my side? A real person, someone from a favourite film or television programme, a mythical hero or heroine?

- Use imagination as part of relaxation techniques with a group. Follow a steady pattern of talking the group into a relaxed state and allow time to bring people out of relaxation.
- The activity of body sculpting is a way to encourage group members to move themselves, or to move others, into a living sculpture or live photograph. This sculpture can bring alive some issue or concern in the group, or symbolise feelings or difficulties that are hard to put into words. A body sculpture can show feelings of relative closeness or distance between individuals in the group. Sometimes it makes sense to invite the group to repeat the activity in a later session and look for any changes.

Some of the above suggestions may look like lightweight games but, in some groups, the activities can release strong feelings or trigger self-disclosures that need respectful handling. All your counselling skills remain as important as ever as you lead and guide the group.

Role play

This kind of activity can be developed in several different ways:

- You can plan and guide a briefed role play in which some of the group take on a role as a different person and may have to imagine themselves into a given situation. They are briefed for the situation and characters (if necessary). The aim of role play is to resolve a problem, reach a decision, run a meeting, practise a skill or some other clear purpose. This kind of role play is useful in training groups.
- Some groups benefit from a role play in which at least one individual is her or himself. This activity gives a chance for group members to replay a past event in a way they would prefer, perhaps to tell someone something and begin to resolve an issue. Some members find role play an easier way to show the rest of the group how they feel or behave in a given situation. This individual will need to brief the other people in his or her role play.
- Role play also works as a real life rehearsal. Perhaps individuals want to prepare for an upcoming event like an interview or to practise how to handle a situation that regularly arises, like how to avoid drinking more alcohol than is safe. Again, one or more individuals will be themselves and they will brief the support roles they want other people to play.

Role play is a flexible activity that can work well if the following points are observed:

- The details of the role play should be suited to the current needs of the group, everyone should be briefed appropriately and the role play debriefed properly.
- The main advantage of the technique is the direct involvement of everyone. So anyone not given a role to play should be briefed to be an attentive observer. Everyone should be involved in debriefing.
- Role play can increase spontaneity and free up individuals to behave in ways that they would not normally and they can learn from this experience. A group member with a passive style can sometimes learn much from

playing the role of being a highly assertive person, particularly when he or she wishes to achieve this change, and they find the role play both easy and satisfying.

- You (or the role players) can stop a role play at any point, but be aware that some groups may find it hard to restart. Ask people to exchange roles or invite individuals to step into a role to express matters differently or say something that they feel is not being expressed by the current role-holder to keep the momentum going.

It is always important to debrief a role play, to discuss what has happened after the completion:

- You need to enable individuals to step out of role and back to the present and themselves. When feelings are strong, this step may need more than a few moments.
- Invite comments from the people directly involved: how did they feel in role, what did they feel about other people, what do they now understand about the situation?
- Turn to the observers for comments. What did they notice, what have they learned?
- Encourage a general discussion of issues raised by the role play itself.

Do you record group activities?

Groups may want to keep their drawings or written thoughts. On the other hand they may be keen that these are destroyed. You should respect their wishes.

Some training groups have the option of video-recording an activity. For many groups, use of video would be inappropriate and provoke anxiety among group members. However, video-recording is useful when the group objective is for individuals to learn how they react in a given situation or to practise skills. Several issues arise over positive and responsible use of video:

- Groups should always know that they are being videoed; there should be no covert recording.
- If individuals are using video for practice and feedback, everyone who wants to practise on video should be given the opportunity in a 'round robin' fashion.
- You should allow time within the group session for the participants to watch the recording together soon after the activity. You will need at least twice the amount of time that the activity took in real time. You can stop the recording for discussion during the playback as well as exploring the issues with the participants and observers at the end. Ensure that any discussion is constructive and there is no blaming of individuals or using the recording as proof that 'You always . . .' or 'He never . . .'.
- Be ready to give time to individuals who have issues arising from how they have seen themselves.
- Wipe the recording as soon as everyone has seen it, or be explicit that the video becomes the property of the person practising, for example, if no one objects.

Further information

You will find many activities and games in the following:

- John Newstrom Scannell, *Games trainers play* and *More games trainers play* (McGraw-Hill, 1983).
- Edie West, *201 icebreakers* (McGraw-Hill, 1997).

10.5 The end of a group

Group members have a variety of feelings about ending, depending on its nature and the experience within the group. People may feel satisfied with a job well done, sad about the end of the group and the loss of relationships that have been built, relieved that an uncomfortable or painful experience is now over and so on. Group leaders also experience a range of feelings.

Groups who do not want to end may try to prolong the group's life by:

- Denying that the group can end.
- Trying to find problems or other reasons to continue.
- Dropping out before the end as a form of avoidance.
- Planning reunions rather than accepting the end.

It is usually disappointing to prolong groups artificially. You need to address directly the feelings in the group that prevent letting go. Work through the suggested ways to end the group given below and leave members a choice to continue informal social contact without the group leader.

Some groups end prematurely because:

- The group has achieved its task(s) more swiftly than anyone anticipated.
- The group has not been able to attract enough members or has experienced such variable attendance that the group cannot function.
- Serious misunderstandings about the purpose of the group or how it will run have not been resolved and the group is brought to an end.

Ideally, you need to review any progress the group has made and to understand how it has come to an early end when the reasons are anything other than the completion of the group's task.

When group leaders find it hard to end a group

Sometimes a group is ready to end and the group leader is as resistant, or more so, than the members. You need to remain alert and honest with yourself when a group strongly fulfils your needs. Perhaps you enjoy the social contact of a group that is now completely capable of continuing without you. In some groups, the entire purpose is that the group leader works him or herself out of a job. The aim of group work, as with individual counselling, is that the helper creates abilities and motivation in those who are helped, not a greater or continuing dependency. Some groups may have the confidence and honesty to tell you that your work is appreciated but no longer needed. On the other hand, you may conspire with a group that wants to continue when you, as group leader, should be helping them to review and make an end.

You may need to talk with a colleague or supervisor to come to terms with your own feelings, what this group meant to you or how you need to set yourself new goals rather than hold on to old ones.

It is a fundamental part of the role of group leaders to help groups to end in different ways:

- If appropriate, make it clear at the outset that the group is scheduled for a fixed number of sessions.
- Keep an eye on the completion of individual or group tasks as the end of group time approaches. If appropriate allow group activity to wind down somewhat, but not to the point of boredom. Avoid starting new activities and projects that cannot be completed in the time left.
- Some groups may naturally move towards relationships and links outside the group and you may encourage this shift. In some groups, external speakers may be invited to emphasise a positive movement away from group life.
- Allow the time to review and celebrate progress with the group. You can cover issues such as: 'Where did we start?', 'What was the group like for you?', 'Where are you now and where are you going now?' In some groups it will be appropriate to help members to plan their next move, perhaps through the logical steps of force field analysis (see page 169).
- Express your appreciation to the group of what has been achieved. If positive, and therefore appropriate, share with them what you have learned and enjoyed. An alert and effective group leader usually learns something with each group experience, but it is not suitable to share feelings such as, 'I've learned that I hate group work.'
- Seek to give group members a tangible memento of the group. It may be a copy of a group photograph or a group diary or a certificate of attendance.
- Individual unfinished business or needs still unmet will have to be handled outside the group, by you or through an appropriate referral.
- Some groups want and appreciate a proper ending through celebration. It may be a plate of seriously indulgent cakes, a group trip to the pub, a meal or a party.
- Whatever you do, recognise the importance of a proper ending, and for some members that means an opportunity to grieve.

Further resources

- Jarlath Benson, *Working more creatively with groups* (Tavistock, 1987).
- Allan Brown, *Groupwork* (Gower Community Care Practice Handbooks, 1989).
- Marianne Schneider Corey and Gerald Corey, *Groups: process and practice* (Brooks Cole, 1997).

☰ 11 Specific applications in brief

This chapter provides a brief review of some specific applications of counselling skills and suggestions for further resources.

11.1 Mediation or conciliation

Mediation services use a specific application of counselling skills when clients are in dispute or conflict. Mediators help other people by offering the following opportunities:

- Each person in a conflict to be heard in turn. Mediators use the skills of reflective listening and non-judgemental questioning, with support skills to enable involved individuals both to express themselves and listen to others.
- In an even-handed way, mediators create a conciliation process, in which disputants are enabled to see both sides, to acknowledge each other's feelings and to focus on the main issues.
- The parties are helped to explore possible choices and to negotiate and offer compromise between the possibilities.
- The end of the mediation process is that all involved individuals agree on a mutually acceptable way forward.

One use of mediation skills is to support couples who are in the process of separation and divorce with the aim of reducing the high levels of conflict and hostility that can arise far too easily. The skills have been successfully taught to children and young people, often as part of the personal and social element of a school curriculum. Primary school children as young as 9 and 10 years old have become effective playground supporters enabling their peers to deal with conflict in a non-aggressive way.

Further resources

- For general information about mediation, contact Mediation UK, 82a Gloucester Road, Bishopston, Bristol BS7 8BN. Tel: 0117 9046661. The project Bristol Mediation at the same address is involved with schools.
- For information about using mediation skills to help couples who separate, contact National Family Mediation, 9 Tavistock Place, London WC1H 9SN. Tel: 0207 383 5993. Fax: 0207 383 5994.

- Hilary Stacey, and Pat Robinson, *Let's mediate* (Lucky Duck Publishing, 1997. Tel: 0117 973 2881).
- Anne Rawlings, *Ways and means: conflict resolution, training, resources* (Kingston Friends Workshop Group, 1996. Tel: 0208 547 1197).

11.2 Advocacy

An advocate acts as an objective representative of an individual whose interests and concerns may not otherwise be heard. Advocacy should operate so as to empower clients to have their viewpoint heard, to exert control over their lives and to obtain their legal rights. Advocacy should not be used if it is possible for clients to deal with the situation themselves.

Advocacy on behalf of children can be a valuable addition to the mediation process for separating couples. Agreements at the end of mediation may deal with arrangements for continued contact for children with the non-resident parent. However, mediators are not usually in a position to follow through how such arrangements work in practice. Someone acting as an advocate for children can bring their perspective and their rights to the fore, helping to maintain a friendly relationship with both parents, uncomplicated by the adults' continuing frustrations with each other.

A guardian *ad litem* (GAL) is appointed to represent children, their wishes and interests, in a range of legal proceedings. GALs need to establish rapport with a child but will not form a closer relationship since their work ends with the final hearing in court. Independent visitors are appointed for children and young people in local authority care who have little or no contact with their families. The visitors may act as advocates in ensuring children's views are heard and also develop social relationships with the children.

Advocates represent adult clients when they lack the relevant expertise or language to deal with the situation. Advocates are also essential if clients are not permitted to attend the setting in which they need representation.

For advocacy to work:

- The role of the advocate and the boundaries of that role have to be very clear to all concerned. Clients need to understand both the potential benefits of and the limits to advocacy.
- Advocates must listen to clients and enable them to ask questions and to express their priorities. Advocates are professionals working under their clients' instructions and should never act so as to undermine clients or to encourage dependency.
- An advocate has to reach an agreement with a client about the terms and conditions of the advocacy and this pattern should be consistently applied across the service. As with any helping service, advocacy needs realistic aims and if the client does not agree with those aims then other avenues need to be explored.

Further resources

- There is a general discussion of advocacy in Naomi Dale, *Working with families of children with special needs: partnership and practice* (Routledge, 1996).
- The work of guardians *ad litem* is described in Susan Howard, *Guardians ad litem and reporting officers* (National Children's Bureau, Highlight, no. 147, 1997).
- The work of independent visitors is described in Abigail Knight, *Valued or forgotten? Disabled children and independent visitors* (National Children's Bureau and Joseph Rowntree Foundation, 1998).
- If you want to know more about advocacy with children and young people, contact the National Youth Advocacy Service, 1 Downham Road South, Heswall, Wirral, Merseyside L60 5RG. Tel: 0151 3427852. Fax: 0151 342 3174. Email: nyas@btconnect.com

11.3 Bereavement and loss

British society has lost many of the supportive rituals surrounding death, with the consequence that many people are uncertain how to behave towards friends or acquaintances who have experienced a loss. Individuals who have lost someone they loved can find that friends and acquaintances offer clichés that seem to diminish their pain, phrases like, 'It was a happy release', or, 'It's been a year now, surely you're getting over it.'

The 'medicalisation' of death has meant that today many people die in hospital rather than at home. Bereaved relatives sometimes have to deal with brusque reactions from health care staff which worsen their own distress. In contrast, the hospice movement has worked hard to create a caring atmosphere in which terminally ill individuals can feel respected and able to spend time with loved ones. Hospitals or units for very sick or disabled children have also developed good practice in involvement of the whole family through caring concern by staff.

Use of counselling skills with bereaved clients follows a very similar pattern to work with any client, but some issues are special to this situation:

- When individuals have lost someone very close, they often go through a phase of feeling numb, of shock at what has happened and even a sense of disbelief. It can help to alert bereaved clients that such feelings are not unusual. However, clients should never be given the impression that there are fixed stages in bereavement, nor should their individuality be undermined by comments like, 'Everyone goes through this.'
- Clients may experience a mixed range of emotions. People may feel distress along with feelings of guilt about what was done or not done, anger with other family members or the medical profession who should have done more, and even anger at the person who has died and left them. Your role is to listen in a non-judgemental way and to support your client to move forward.

- Over time clients need to reach acceptance of their loss. You may be able to help by listening as they talk out the circumstances of loss, perhaps many times. However, clients who cared deeply for a deceased partner, close friend or child may never be over that loss completely, because it has changed their life for ever.
- Help them to find their own way of coping and to grieve in a way that best supports them. What worked well for a friend will not necessarily be right for this client.
- Clients may be helped by positive remembrance. Removing all traces of the child, young person or adult who has died is certainly not the best way forward for everyone. Talking about that person can be a positive part of coming to terms with loss. Finding past happy memories can be especially important when the most recent memories of a loved one are of them in pain or fading away from illness.
- Children and young people are also bereaved and can be overlooked in the distress of adult family members. Younger children may be particularly left out because of the inaccurate belief that 'They don't understand' or 'It's better not to upset them.' Cruse (see below) has valuable material on supporting children.
- Be aware that working with bereaved clients can arouse your own feelings of loss from the past or fears about losing loved ones. It is unwise to work with bereaved clients when you are still raw from a personal loss. It is too difficult to separate the feelings and offer appropriate caring detachment.

You may work with clients who are themselves terminally ill. Clients should always have the choice whether to talk with someone or not; it should never be forced on them. Realistic goals in using counselling skills in this situation can include to:

- Help clients talk about their situation with someone who does not resort to false hopes or clichés.
- Listen to clients' feelings, preferences and choices. Perhaps help them to action some choices.
- Support clients in coming to terms with their limited time and to consider any actions they wish to take: to complete tasks, say goodbyes or make arrangements. Clients may appreciate a sense of closure and appropriate support for those they leave behind.
- Support older children and young people, who may be fully aware that they will not recover and value the respect of talking with someone just as much as a dying adult.

Further resources

- Cruse-Bereavement Care, Cruse House, 126 Sheen Road, Richmond, Surrey TW9 1UR. Tel: 0208 940 4818. Fax: 0208 940 7638.
- Colin Murray Parkes, *Bereavement: studies of grief in adult life* (Routledge, 1996).

11.4 Crisis and trauma

Life transitions and crises

Normal adult life involves periods of uncertainty and distress that can be severe enough to call life crises. Such events include the disruption created by redundancy, divorce, death in the family, children growing up and leaving home – in fact any event that requires people to readjust familiar patterns and established relationships. Counselling skills are very suitable for supporting clients in life changes. The stages described in Chapters 7 and 8 help clients to move from a full understanding of their current situation (Stage One), to an exploration of how they would prefer matters to be (Stage Two), how to make that transition (Stage Three) and making the transition (Stage Four).

- Because Stage One is exploratory, you offer clients the opportunity to tell their story to someone who will listen and contribute in a non-judgemental way. During life transitions and crises the client may be in shock, unable to take in all the events, minimising what has happened or plagued with self-doubt. Acceptance of the client and gentle exploration can be especially reassuring when clients are uncertain. They may also have experienced unhelpful, although well-meant, interventions from friends, family and other professionals.
- You build a relationship of trust and allow the client to acknowledge mixed feelings: excitement, relief, panic, paralysis. Clients can step aside from the urgency to do something or to control their feelings. You create time for the client 'to look before you leap'.
- Clients in transition can become stuck in the first phase of change, perhaps continually replaying what happened: the children have left home, there is a serious crisis in the partnership, the experience of redundancy or the final blocking of a much desired goal. By moving to Stage Two, you help clients to take stock and move on, but in a way that makes sense to them.
- In a respectful way, you identify and work on issues that will make a difference to this individual client. Clients may have had difficulty in moving on, or perhaps been driven by friends and family to an unhelpful way of trying to move on. You can help them to explore ways to adjust and move towards a feeling of recovery.

Through Stage Two, you can support clients to examine what their better future could look like. They need to accept the reality of change and that there is no going back. Goal-setting can be a watershed for clients, helping them to let go of the past and shift attention through the present to the future.

Accident and trauma

Traumatic events destabilise people for weeks, months or even years. Personal feelings of control, the ability to protect yourself and others, are undermined by accidents, assaults, and the violation of possessions through break-ins and burglaries. Even minor events can create anxieties where there had been confidence, and raise mixed feelings about what has happened and whether the situation could have been avoided.

Anyone who has experienced a potentially traumatic event should be given a choice about whether to talk with someone and when. Individuals do not always want to talk and pushing people against their will only adds to whatever distress they already feel. Counselling can offer an opportunity to talk through feelings and the impact of the event. Some issues that arise include:

- Clients who have not been physically hurt can still be unnerved by what has happened and realise that their anxiety or fear is affecting their behaviour. They want help to recognise what is happening and how best to cope.
- Clients need support when they have disturbing experiences such as flashbacks, intrusive thoughts about a traumatic event or recurrent distressing dreams. Reassurance that this is normal can be appropriate, since clients may feel they are losing their mind. Effective help then needs to move towards how to cope better.
- Children who have minor injuries from an accident can still feel great emotional distress and do not necessarily tell their parents or carers. The extent of upset becomes more obvious through their general behaviour and play. Child witnesses to accidents are sometimes just as distressed as their injured sibling or friend, whose feelings are more likely to have been addressed.
- Clients frequently express mixed feelings, not all of which are logical. They may still need to talk through whether they could have avoided what happened. Individuals often need to locate responsibility with the criminal who attacked them or the driver who caused the road accident, rather than revisiting their own actions as if they are to blame. Victims of random violence sometimes seek some rational basis for what happened, when it was just that they were in the wrong place at the wrong time.

Post-traumatic stress disorder (PTSD)

PTSD is defined as a specific collection of symptoms that have persisted for more than a month after a traumatic event. Similar symptoms that last less than a month are known as acute stress disorder. Some of the symptoms of trauma-related stress are:

- Persistent recollection of the event, through intrusive thoughts or distressing dreams.
- Reliving the event through vivid flashbacks.
- Intense psychological or physiological distress reactions to experiences that are linked to the event.
- Persistent avoidance of memories and blockage of feelings.
- Children can experience similar symptoms, although they may relive a traumatic event through repetitive play, re-enacting parts of the experience and apparently unrelated disturbed behaviour triggered by an inability to talk about or deal with the distressing feelings.

Dealing with PTSD is a specialised area of offering help and, unless you have received appropriate training, you should look towards referral of a client who, it emerges, is experiencing PTSD. (See page 171 about referral.)

Further resources

- Stephen Murgatroyd, and Ray Woolfe, *Coping with crisis: understanding and helping people in need* (Harper & Row, 1982).
- Michael Scott, and Stephen Stradling, *Counselling for post traumatic stress disorder* (Sage, 1992).
- The Child Accident Prevention Trust, 18–20 Farringdon Lane, London EC1R 3AU. Tel: 0207 608 3828. Fax: 0207 608 3674. Email: safe@capt.demon. co.uk

11.5 Helping children and young people

Good communication with children and young people has much in common with communicating well with adults. However, some points to bear in mind include:

- The younger the child, the more any helper has to adjust appropriately to his or her understanding and language skills. However, adults often underestimate children's ability to express themselves when someone listens attentively or to understand when someone explains with care.
- A child's view can be different from that of older people and you need to work that bit harder to look through children's eyes rather than assume how they feel or make sense of a situation. Children may use words differently from adults or lack the language to express subtle distinctions. Sometimes using communication through play and artwork can help. Make sure that you check your understanding and reassure the children that you want to understand clearly.
- Children are often aware of crises, such as serious illness in the family, redundancy or troubles between their parents, but are not given much information. They have to fill in the gaps. As such they may consequently gain an inaccurate idea of what is happening and their role or responsibility in a difficult situation. They may think it is their fault when it is not.
- Children experiencing troubles of their own, for instance over bullying, may not believe that their life could be different. Even more than adults facing problems, children can be burdened with the view that change is impossible and attempts to share their problem will only bring blame or more distress. Children typically do not see themselves as powerful as do adults.
- Since children are less likely than adults to construe problems as something that could be resolved, they are more likely to be referred for help because an adult is concerned about them. Supportive families and schools with an effective pastoral system are more likely to encourage children to speak out on their own behalf.

- Even more than adults, children are inclined to say what they feel is expected or what adults want to hear. This tendency is worsened by experiencing adults' leading questions or demands to know why the children have done something. Open-ended questions and reflective listening will be crucially important to establish trust that you genuinely wish to hear what children feel and think.

Further resources

- Jean Campion, *Counselling children* (Whiting & Birch, 1991).
- Jennie Lindon, *Child protection and early years work* (Hodder & Stoughton, 1998).
- Jennie and Lance Lindon, *Your child from 5–11* (Hodder & Stoughton, 1993).
- John McGuiness, *Counselling in schools: new perspectives* (Cassell, 1998).

11.6 Helping in health-care settings

Although attitudes have improved, helpers within health-care settings may still have to counteract the medical tradition of people as patients, with all the negative overtones that the term entails. Some specific issues arise with work in health care:

- Health, illness, diagnosis and treatment are not just physical and physiological processes; feelings are also involved and can often be crucial to a positive outcome.
- Ill health cannot just be seen as a person passively reacting to a condition. His or her outlook and confidence and the extent of support all have an influence on the progress and outcome. Anxiety and lack of information can worsen an individual's outlook. The disease is medically treatable, the illness is not.
- Frequently, the illness of one person has an impact on others, especially in the immediate family. Continued chronic illness of an adult or a child affects all the workings of family life.

Clients in health-care settings should not be automatically referred for counselling support. It must be a choice for the client and there should be no stigma of referral of people 'who can't cope'. The availability of such support should certainly not relieve medical staff of the responsibility to treat 'patients' well.

In health-care settings you need to allow for the often strong emotional content of information about diagnosis and possible treatment.

- Clients need information but also the time to absorb confusing or distressing facts and to ask questions.
- Encourage clients to ask questions, showing that you welcome these and will answer to the best of your knowledge.

- Clients will not necessarily absorb all the information, especially a distressing diagnosis, all at once. They often need more than one opportunity to hear something or patience and time within one conversation. Always leave the opportunity to come back after a first meeting.
- Explanations about possible courses of action need to be clear and honest so that clients can make an informed decision. Clients may be depressed by the medical conclusion that 'There's nothing we can do' and not realise that symptoms can be relieved even though the underlying condition is untreatable.
- Be aware that clients will not necessarily share the same priorities as health-care professionals. Parents, for instance, will often have obligations and concerns in addition to the child with whom you are involved. Everyone has to balance his or her life to meet different priorities.
- Be honest if the situation is one of 'We do not know yet' or 'We do not know why'.
- Consider using more than one way to communicate information about a condition or approach to treatment. Talking and listening can be supported by informative leaflets, there is the possibility of talking with people in a similar position or even a video might be available. Clients need to decide for themselves what is best and on what kind of time-scale.

Further resources

- V. Aitken and H. Jellicoe (eds), *Behavioural sciences for health professionals* (W. B. Saunders, 1996).
- Robert Bor, Riva Millar, Martha Latz and Heather Salt, *Counselling in health care settings* (Cassell, 1998).
- The *Telephone Helplines Directory* is a valuable source of information on organisations with a specific health focus. (See page 107 for full reference.)

Support for children and young people

If you work within health care, you need to take account of the age and understanding of young clients and remain sensitive to individual reactions. Normally confident adults are not at their best when worried or confused and in unfamiliar surroundings. Adults may hide the depth of their feelings or find strategies to cope. In contrast, children will often express their distress, panic or pain without any reservations. Children experience embarrassment and loss of dignity in a similar way to adults or teenagers and dismissive or rude treatment can greatly complicate any health procedure. The feelings are the same, but what children do about them is often different from adult reactions.

Children and young people may appreciate and need the company of a familiar adult, but you should not talk only to the adult as if the child is not there. Parents will be in a better position to help and support their children if they are given information about a service or a condition. It is less effective to depend only on talking; advice is probably best given in written form as well as spoken.

Further resources

- Action for Sick Children, 300 Kingston Road, Wimbledon Chase, London SW20 8LX. Tel: 0208 542 4848. Fax: 0208 542 2424.
- Richard Lansdown, *Children in hospital: a guide for families and carers* (Oxford University Press, 1996).

11.7 Disability and chronic health conditions

Working with clients with disabilities or chronic health conditions raises some issues additional to usual good practice in use of counselling skills. You may need to examine your own attitudes – especially when first working with disabled clients. The general concerns raised in Section 1.6 on anti-discriminatory practice apply but some further, more specific issues include:

- You need a respectful balance between inappropriately ignoring a client's disability or condition and overreacting so that you fail to see the individual person past the disability.
- Be wary of stereotypes of disabled adults or children that persist in society, whether these are backhanded compliments about being 'brave' or 'special', or negative views such that parents of disabled children are 'overprotective'.
- It is crucial to challenge any of your own unquestioned assumptions that somehow disability is incompatible with intelligence, emotional strength or the ability to make important choices.
- It is dishonest, and often unhelpful, to insist on treating disabled or chronically sick clients 'just like anyone else'. Acknowledge the situation in a straightforward way. Some clients may specifically want to talk about how their disability or illness makes an impact on their daily life.

Action planning with disabled clients has to take relevant account of the disability and not create unrealistic hopes or plans. Even if you share your client's condition, you may still experience different levels of severity in that condition. The usual caution must apply about assuming a similar experience means that clients will share your perspective and priorities.

Clients may need attention relevant to their disability:

- Always inquire what a client would like or will find helpful. You can ask, 'How can I help you with . . . ?', or, 'How would you prefer to handle . . . ?' Some disabled people may be used to being touched as part of receiving assistance but be careful to offer such help with respect.
- Clients with limited mobility may need assistance within your building or it may be considerate to rearrange your work setting or meeting place.
- Clients with visual disabilities may also appreciate help in finding their way around an unknown environment. In conversation, bear in mind that visually disabled clients will not be able to see your body language and the extent of the loss of information will depend on their visual disability. Your words and tone of voice have to carry the message, rather like com-

munication over the telephone, even though you and your client are physically together.

- Clients with hearing disabilities need appropriate communication adjustments from you. The organisation Hearing Concern publishes a useful leaflet, *Break the sound barrier*, which explains simple ways for hearing people to improve their communication with individuals who are hard of hearing or deaf. Hearing Concern are at 7–11 Armstrong Road, London W3 7JL. Tel: 0208 743 1110.

Clients will not benefit from an overprotective attitude from a helper:

- Disabled or sick clients may need to be challenged constructively about their behaviour through Stage Two counselling skills.
- Clients may need to recognise the consequences of their care of themselves, for example, mismanagement of a diabetic regime which brings serious health risks.
- Unreasonable behaviour towards friends and family is not made reasonable by the client's condition. If you work with the parents of disabled or very sick children, you may well help parents to establish a better balance. The children deserve attention to their special needs but still benefit, like any children, from clear boundaries.
- Some clients, and parents on behalf of their children, become of necessity experts in the disability or condition. Their expertise can easily coexist with yours so long as you have not tried inappropriately to establish yourself as an all-round expert.

Further resources

- Richard Lansdown, *More than sympathy* (Tavistock, 1980).
- Naomi Dale, *Working with families of children with special needs: partnership and practice* (Routledge, 1996).
- Peggy Dalton, *Counselling people with communication problems* (Sage, 1994).
- Hilton Davis, *Counselling parents of children with chronic illness or disability* (British Psychological Society Books, 1993).

HIV–Aids

A helping relationship may be established with the adult who has been diagnosed HIV-positive or with the parent or carer of a child or young person with the condition. Working in this area raises particular concerns:

- Clients who are HIV-positive may have many years of healthy living but still face social difficulties because of their condition. Confidentiality is key here, and clients may want support in discussing whether to disclose their condition.
- HIV–Aids brings inevitable uncertainty about the best treatment, contradictory advice, and likely side-effects in known or experimental medication. The area is unusual in that medical professionals have not retained control

over facts, options and research. Possibilities are extensively discussed and information disseminated through activist groups, publications and the Internet.

- Individuals, and their loved ones, will face at some point all the problems of chronic ill health and impending death.

Counselling skills are typically offered to clients at different points in the process:

- Before an HIV test takes place.
- While clients are waiting for the result.
- When they receive the result.
- During the healthy period before any symptoms appear, as well as when physical symptoms are apparent, when clients may wish to discuss possible courses of treatment.
- When clients want to discuss possible disclosure of their condition and any issues arising from relationships, family or work.
- Coping with the terminal stage of the condition and preparing for death.

Counselling may also be offered to clients' partners, family or to anyone who fears they may be at risk.

Further resources

- Terrence Higgins Trust, 52–4 Gray's Inn Road, London WC1X 8JU. Tel: 0207 242 1010.

11.8 Work with couples or families

Clients may seek help as a couple because they recognise that problems are rooted in their relationship. Alternatively, an individual may want to talk about difficulties in an intimate relationship but his or her partner never becomes involved in the sessions. Relevant organisations often started as agencies focused on saving marriages; now most have developed towards a more general use of counselling to help relationships and to ease separation if necessary.

Working with couples or families is complex:

- Remaining an objective helper can be hard work as individuals encourage you to take sides. Working with a colleague can help but needs just as much care, and discussion outside the situation, as co-leading a group (see page 184).
- It takes effort to work through what is happening and to make clear distinctions between what the parties believe to be happening. It is easy to be pulled into the dynamics of a couple or a family.
- Change in either a couple or a whole family has a series of consequences. The change in behaviour of one partner, or family member, usually requires adjustments from others which are not always welcome. Habits are developed in a relationship and how a family runs, and such habits are hard to change.

- You can be provoked, uncomfortably sometimes, into looking at your own close relationships with a partner or within your family.

   An understanding of couple relationships and families can be important in the use of counselling skills described within this book. However, specific work with couples or families needs further training.

Further resources

- Stephen Murgatroyd and Ray Woolfe, *Helping families in distress: an introduction to family focussed helping* (Harper & Row, 1985).
- Mary Pipher, *The shelter of each other: rebuilding our families to enrich our lives* (Vermilion, 1996).
- John Gottman, *The heart of parenting: how to raise an emotionally intelligent child* (Bloomsbury, 1997).

11.9 Work with elderly clients

Apart from the wide range of concerns that any clients bring to you, elderly clients may also have difficulties or issues that arise specifically from age. It is important for you to remain aware of anti-discriminatory practice because:

- Elderly clients often experience patronising attitudes from others during their daily life, with disrespectful assumptions that older people are unable to make choices, to learn or even to understand unless people raise their voice. Your practice should affirm older clients as individuals and avoid unchecked assumptions based only on age.
- Clients can be very aware of their own failing health and are frustrated over enforced changes to their lifestyle. Some may have difficulty in coming to terms with illness or frailty. Others will appreciate the chance to talk through practical issues such as achieving independent mobility without a car.
- Clients in their 70s and 80s often face the ill health and loss of partners and many friends. A shrinking social circle can lead to loneliness – even for the more outgoing clients.
- Some elderly clients will have carers, either within the family or in a residential home. You may work with elderly people themselves, with carers or both. You need to focus clearly on who is the client in your relationships with different individuals in the situation. Be careful not to conspire in a situation where elderly clients are marginalised or talked about as if they were absent from the session.

Further resources

- Age Concern, Astral House, 1268 London Road, London SW16 4ER. Tel: 0208 679 8000. Fax: 0208 679 6069.
- Age Concern publish a Carers Handbook Series with a range of practical titles.

11.10 General resources

The following books cover use of counselling skills with a wide range of clients.

- Tim Bond, *Standards and ethics for counselling in action* (Sage, 1993).
- Patricia d'Ardenne and Aruna Mahtani, *Transcultural counselling in action* (Sage, 1989).
- Windy Dryden (ed.), *Key issues for counselling in action* (Sage, 1988).
- Windy Dryden and Brian Thorne (eds), *Training and supervision for counselling in action* (Sage, 1991).
- Gerard Egan, *The skilled helper: a problem management approach to helping,* 5th edn (Brooks Cole, 1994).
- John McLeod, *An introduction to counselling* (Open University, 1993).
- Stephen Murgatroyd, *Counselling and helping* (BPS Books and Methuen, 1985).
- Richard Nelson-Jones, *Practical counselling and helping skills,* 4th edn (Cassell, 1997).
- Stephen Palmer with Gladeana McMahon (eds), *Handbook of counselling,* 2nd edn (Routledge, 1997). This book includes full details of the British Association for Counselling's Codes of Ethics and Practice for counsellors, counselling skills, supervisors of counsellors and trainers of counsellors.

The following publishers have series on counselling which offer a wide range of titles. These series are worth checking if you want to explore specific applications of the skills:

- British Psychological Society: *Communication and counselling in health care settings.*
- Macmillan: *Basic texts in counselling and psychotherapy.*
- PCCS Books: *Incomplete guides* (the series title indicates that the books are good for basic skills rather than unfinished!).
- Sage: *Counselling practice.*
- Sage: *Counselling in action.*
- Sage: *Professional skills for counsellors.*
- Sheldon Press: *Overcoming common problems.* The books in this series are written directly to people experiencing the problem but will also be a source of information and insight if you are in a helping role.

☑ 12 Safe practice for yourself, your team and your clients

12.1 Health and safety issues

Policy and practice

Health and safety in the workplace is covered by legislation and enforced by your local authority Environmental Health and Safety Officers or the Health and Safety Executive (HSE). The officers can inspect any workplace premises following a request from an employee, a union representative or a member of the public. If officers identify health and safety problems, they can issue an Improvement or Prohibition Notice that requires some action to be taken. Failure to comply with the notice can lead to substantial fines.

You will find suggested further reading on page 235 but the broad issues include:

- Any organisation should have an easily available, written, Health and Safety Policy. This policy should take account of volunteers and trainees as well as paid employees.
- Organisations and services should have carried out a risk assessment to identify specific areas where there may be hazards to workers or clients. The results should be available and any necessary actions clear.
- Health and safety is everyone's responsibility. Within this there should also be named individuals within the team who take particular responsibility and to whom concerns should first be raised.
- All the relevant insurance should be up to date.
- There should be an easily available Accident Book.
- First aid equipment and facilities should be adequate and there should be someone trained in first aid.
- Fire precautions should be adequate, the Fire Certificate up to date and fire extinguishers and electrical equipment regularly checked by someone who is sufficiently qualified to identify any problems.
- Attention should be paid to health and safety issues specific to the kind of work undertaken. There should be proper work breaks and eye tests for staff who regularly use visual display units (VDUs). Hygiene issues arise when helpline teams pass telephones and headsets between them. Comfortable seating is important when workers sit for long amounts of time, at a VDU or on a helpline. Stress should also be recognised as a potential risk in helping services.

Possible further reading

- *Management of health and safety at work regulations: the approved code of practice* (HSE Books, 1992).
- *Workplace (Health, Safety and Welfare) Regulations: approved code of practice* (HSE Books, 1992).
- *Writing a safety policy: advice for employers* (a free leaflet from HSE Books).

You can also contact the HSE InfoLine on 0541 545500.

Safety with clients

Even the best-run helping services will sometimes encounter difficulties. A responsible team avoids the assumption that difficulties always arise from what clients do, or do not do. You need a sense of even-handedness and a willingness to look constructively at your own behaviour. Some problems can be calmed and handled by good use of communication skills (see Section 3.3 on dealing with complaints and mistakes). This section focuses on difficulties that worsen and safety issues arising.

Clients whom you find difficult

Positive self-talk

You need to work to achieve a sense of 'I can' rather than 'I can't'. Negative self-talk seeps into your body language and contributes to an exchange going wrong. On the other hand, positive self-talk can help you avoid being pushed to and fro by other people's reactions. Your internal dialogue can support or undermine your overall attitude and therefore your behaviour. You may need to say to yourself:

- 'I will be able to handle this', rather than, 'Oh no, here we go again.'
- 'I can help this woman in some way', rather than, 'It's that impossible woman again!'

Focus on what you can do, rather than viewing the situation as one in which clients are imposing on you.

- Be realistic about your ability to control a situation. Avoid negative internal dialogue such as, 'I can't let her get away with this', or, 'I must cope; I mustn't ask for help.'
- It is unhelpful to go on about, 'They have no right to treat me like dirt!', or, 'They shouldn't . . .' and 'They ought to . . .'. Talk these feelings through with a colleague, vent them and lose them rather than leaving them to fester.
- You can only deal with what is and not with a list of 'should's' and 'ought's' that focus on other people's behaviour.
- You have choices over your own behaviour; you cannot make people behave in different ways. Your reactions can nudge clients in a positive direction.

- Take hold of your own feelings; they are yours. You give other people permission to 'make me feel angry/upset/useless'. You do the feeling and most usefully can explore how these feelings are provoked in you, and then how to address them.

A balance in discussion about clients

Teams in helping services need to work to be fair and balanced with clients. It is far too easy to emphasise those clients with whom you find it harder to work, to call them 'difficult clients' and treat them as difficult which then encourages them to be difficult. You need to be aware about how your team talks about the clients of your service:

- Which clients stick in your mind?
- Whom do you talk over most in team meetings or supervision?
- Does a team or individual members thrive on the drama and story-telling potential of the awkward clients?
- Do people ever talk about exchanges with clients that went well?
- Has the team developed an unhelpful stereotype of the 'good client', against which everyone is then measured? Does this mean that some patterns of behaviour, for instance, persistence in asking questions or even a mild challenge, are judged to be evidence of a 'bad' client who is causing trouble?
- Is there a risk that the team conspires in negative outlooks on clients? Are there discussions with comments like, 'You daren't let them get away with anything or else they think they've won', often followed by disrespectful phrases like, 'I know these people!'

In a team you need to spend time on being pleased about clients you have helped, happy with those that are not difficult, and potentially tough situations that you handled well. This kind of discussion is just as important – if not more important – than working through outstanding problems.

Consider the clients' perspective

It is far too easy for any team to focus on a situation only as they see it and to label clients in a negative way. So-called 'inadequate clients' may have learned that this service requires clients to have problems in order to receive help; it does not reward their coping skills. 'Demanding clients' may just want the best for their child or family and have been previously frustrated by a series of unhelpful helping professionals before coming to your service. A genuinely helpful service makes an effort to go beyond the solely professional perspective. For instance:

- The limited professional viewpoint may be that this is a 'hostile client'.
- The client's perspective is, 'I don't feel valued or respected.'
- A more rounded professional view is to ask yourself, 'What is it about me as the professional, what I represent or the network of which I am a part that makes this client feel threatened or belittled?'

You can then address your part of the relationship to help clients. You are not necessarily to blame for clients' previous bad experiences with helping services, but it is your responsibility to work on the situation as it now is.

Activity

Explore the ways in which you and your colleagues may need to allow for clients' perspectives as well as your own professional viewpoint. For instance:

- The professional perspective is that this client is 'manipulative'. But the perspective of the client may well be that, 'I don't feel in control of what is happening to me or to my family.'
- You need to reflect on, 'What is it about me as a person, me as the professional, what I represent or the network of which I am a part that makes this client feel that she or he has to wrestle back some control?'

Take some common labels that are used about clients in your team. Work them through in an open-minded way following the pattern given above. Discuss with colleagues the ideas that emerge.

Angry or frustrated clients

Some clients may well be angry. However, in any service a proportion of clients become angry because their calmer and more courteous comments were ignored. Some reasons include:

- Their feelings have been directly provoked by the behaviour of people in your organisation towards clients. Specific actions may be worsened by an unwelcoming setting, unorganised waiting systems or a lack of information about how priorities are handled. For instance the triage system in medical settings like an Accident and Emergency Department is a way of establishing priorities that is not always explained to waiting 'patients'.
- Clients may not feel valued. You are there; they can tell you what they are feeling. But those feelings have been provoked by a series of other frustrating experiences and discourteous treatment.
- Some individuals have a habitually angry or aggressive approach to life. It has been learned from childhood, perhaps from parents who dealt with problems through anger and argument. Fury and bluster can cover up a basic lack of confidence, but it has worked in getting clients their way in the past. It may never have occurred to these clients that a courteous approach will gain attention from people in authority, or previous attempts at courtesy were in their view less effective than confrontation.

Dealing with strong emotions from clients

It is important that you acknowledge clients' feelings (including anger) and the strength of these emotions. It is unhelpful to answer emotion with only logic and rational information, because these do not fit (remember the communications ladder on page 26). You need to recognise that these feelings are present and that the client has the right to feel them. Communicate to clients that you appreciate their feelings and perhaps that you understand how they can have them.

You can mirror the intensity of a client's emotion, not the emotion itself. As such, adjust your response to a situation in which a client is angry or distressed, but do not show anger or distress yourself. If you start to show anger, the situation will worsen. If you show distress, then the client may be unable to continue to tell you about what has happened or be distracted into feeling anxious because, 'Now I've upset you too.'

If a client feels strong emotions, she or he can be irritated or annoyed by someone who remains apparently unmoved by the emotions shown, very calm or speaking very quietly. Use your words, tone of voice and firm expression to say with a positive feel comments like:

- 'I can see that you are very concerned about this.'
- 'You have every right to feel that way. I'd feel like that too if that had happened to me.'
- 'I can hear that this has been very frustrating for you.'
- 'I'm glad that you are telling me about this.'

Clients will not believe that you have understood or care, if your emotional intensity is very different to theirs. However, you must remain calm, and in control. Single words like 'obviously', 'exactly', 'of course' or 'absolutely' can be delivered with a positive quality of firmness and respect. Used poorly, they can of course come across as patronising or critical.

Clients who are angry will probably need more personal space than usual, so be prepared to sit or stand less close than you might usually. If clients want to leave the area or the room, then do not try to stop them through misplaced beliefs that you have to control the situation or have failed if they leave. Certainly make no attempt to counsel or problem-solve until the client is calm.

Activity

With a partner, experiment with saying phrases such as those given in the section above.
- Try saying them with different levels of emotion: from very calm and unmoved through to very emotional yourself.
- Explore how to say the words and phrases with a positive quality of firmness but not too emotional.
- Discuss the exercise together.

Potential violence

Much of the rest of the book, including particularly Chapters 1–3, describes good practice that will encourage clients and help them to feel empowered in your setting. Good use of communication skills, attention to the impact of your setting and changes in rigid, client-unfriendly practices will reduce the risk of aggression, but not always to zero. You may work where service users are more likely to be unpredictable, for example, when their inhibitions are reduced by the impact of alcohol or drugs. Several practical issues are important:

- Your organisation should act so as to protect you. This protection should partly take the form of safety measures within your setting (see the later points). However, support is also given through a value position that nobody should have to accept verbal or physical aggression or have it excused as an 'occupational hazard' in your line of work.
- Everyone should have a range of skills to cope, but they should still have the right to remove themselves from a potentially dangerous situation, for instance, in a home visit to a client, or to summon help within the work setting.
- You need to balance safe practices for personal security with not making your setting look too intimidating, as if you expect trouble from clients. If you have security doors, a reception desk that screens callers, safety glass at windows or other similar measures, then counter these with welcoming messages.

If your client base or the physical setting creates vulnerability to violence, then seriously consider some practical safety measures.

- Nobody works late on their own or sees clients when the rest of the team has gone home.
- A system of buzzers and alarm calls.
- Ensure that the whole team is ready to react constructively at the sound of raised voices or to unusual or worrying events. It is better for one or two team members to make a discrete check than to leave a colleague facing a rapidly deteriorating situation.
- Keep track of team members who go out to visits and their expected return time. Perhaps you accept that some areas of your patch are only visited by workers in pairs.
- Some self-defence skills may help, but should certainly not be seen as an alternative to the measures described so far. The confidence you feel through being able to defend yourself can communicate itself assertively through your body language and so help to calm a situation.

Create proper boundaries between work and personal life. Do not give clients your personal phone number or address. In some services it is wise that everyone has an ex-directory home telephone number. Helpers have sometimes been harassed at home over the telephone, but directories also give your address, so you may be troubled by callers on the doorstep.

Dealing afterwards with an incident

The worst sometimes happens, and you need to address an incident in your service in which a team member was threatened or actually attacked.

- Offer support to the individual through informal contact and the supervision system.
- Use counselling skills with the individual to work through the feelings aroused by the incident. As well as feeling angry about threat or attack, helpers can also

face some sense of guilt: 'Did I do something wrong?', or, 'Would it have made a difference if I . . . ?'

- There may be lessons to learn from the incident; equally sometimes helpers have to accept that they could not have anticipated what happened.

Groups of workers may discuss events immediately following an incident, however, it is also useful to explore, probably in a meeting, what could be learned for the whole team.

- This discussion must be constructive and, while recognising what has happened to one team member, not leave that person feeling uncomfortably in the spotlight.
- Watch out for criticisms from colleagues such as, 'Why on earth did you . . . ?', or implications of, 'I certainly wouldn't have . . .'. Violent episodes unnerve everyone and even colleagues are sometimes unhelpfully self-protective. If you decide that your team member was foolish in a way that you never would be, then you feel safer, but at the cost of undermining your colleague. If the worker was at fault, then this is an issue for supervisory help later.
- Look for what can be learned for the whole team. Useful lessons are not always about what must be changed. Perhaps your safety measures worked well.

Possible further reading

- Glynis Breakwell, *Facing physical violence* (BPS Books and Routledge, 1989).

12.2 Handling stress

Stress and burn-out

Working within helping services can provide a great deal of job satisfaction but the work also requires a high commitment that draws on your physical, intellectual and emotional resources.

A manageable level of stress is not negative. When you successfully cope with new issues or difficulties in work with a client or group, the temporary stress can be a source of learning and a boost to your self-confidence. However, excessive pressure and unrelenting demands can lead to accumulative experience of strain and distress. The consequences of this experience on professional competence is known as 'burn-out'.

In the helping relationships covered in this book, helpers give a great deal to clients in terms of support, empathy, full attention and counselling skills. Clients can work very hard too, but that is not an effort that necessarily replenishes your own energy as a helper. It is not your clients' responsibility to support or take care of you; that is a responsibility shared by you and your organisation. You are responsible for ensuring that you manage your life to achieve a positive balance in giving and receiving, so that your personal energy and emotion account does not slip into the red.

Consider the following warnings that can let you know that burn-out may be approaching:

- You are about to attend a case conference or a similar important meeting on your client. You feel depressed and think desperately if there is anyone who could go instead of you.
- You are halfway through a session with an individual client and you realise that he or she is looking directly at you. You have no recall of what the client has said in the last few minutes.
- In a group that you lead, you increasingly have intrusive thoughts about the pointlessness of the group's problems and your ability to make any difference to them.
- Increasingly you find yourself thinking, 'Here we go again', and, 'Been here before', when clients start to explain their individual issues and problems.

You are in danger of losing any freshness in your approach and respect for your clients, because you are too overloaded yourself.

Excessive demands on your time, energy and emotional commitment will drain your personal resources. This overload may arise because of unrealistic demands of your organisation about how many clients you can see, in how short a time or how many groups you can effectively run within your working week. However, some helping professionals, whether paid or voluntary, conspire in their own dangerous overload because they are unwilling to place limits on their work, to ask for support or to delegate to colleagues. In short, helpers often find it hard to say 'No' or to seek help themselves.

Continued stress damages your health and, even if you are beyond caring about yourself (in itself a serious warning sign of burn-out), you must recognise that stressed helpers are ineffective in their work, perhaps as seriously as to pose a risk to their clients. There are three phases of burn-out, each more damaging than the previous one: physical, psychological and spiritual fatigue.

Physical signs of overload

If you are continually tired or lethargic, you must take this condition as a warning sign. Everyone gets tired sometimes or has a dip in the working day, but if you keep going despite exhaustion, you will never allow yourself to replenish your energy. A good night's sleep will no longer be enough and you will catch any minor illnesses that are doing the rounds. Everyone in a team may be expected to keep going through very minor illness, but it is in nobody's interest if you stagger on with the insistence of, 'I can take it. I won't let my clients down.' You are also overriding stress, if you increasingly take over-the-counter medication just to get through your day. You may have personal and familiar physical signs of stress like mouth ulcers, breaking nails, trembling limbs, difficulty in sleeping or breathlessness.

Psychological signs

You may start with physical signs, but your emotions will soon also reflect the overload you currently experience. You may think to yourself or express out loud feelings like, 'It's all too much', or, 'What's the point anyway?' Helpers under stress sometimes begin to look towards their clients for personal support or explicit gratitude for the helper's efforts. Your increasing emotional strain will start to lead to mistakes in your work and to lack of attention. Increasingly you will have difficulty thinking around problems, and see them more as stark choices, absolutes of right and wrong or even as impossible dilemmas. Attending and listening in particular become harder and harder. Job satisfaction and enjoyment decrease markedly and you will no longer feel that you 'want to go' to work, but that you 'have to'. Your life becomes increasingly seen as all duties and responsibilities, with few apparent choices. You feel alone and unsupported, perhaps even rejecting support that colleagues or friends try to offer. You feel disconnected, low in confidence and competence and you slide easily into the next phase.

Spiritual fatigue

You become less and less able to give to others and feel increasingly threatened by legitimate requests for help or attention. Your energy, interest and health worsen and you think about escape, either through unhealthy habits or by leaving a job that previously gave you so much satisfaction. You doubt your own effectiveness, values or even the ethics of what you do. However, this is not a normal, positive self-examination but a self-attack that can see no light at the end of the tunnel. Work, and life itself, begin to seem pointless and meaningless. All fun and laughter disappear, tears seem near for no reason, and, apart from anger and irritation, your emotions shut down. Active caring vanishes.

This combination of serious physical, psychological and spiritual effects of stress leads on to a downward spiral in which you are increasingly unable to cope and you will become a serious liability to yourself, your colleagues and your clients.

Take care of yourself

Recognise your warning signs

There is no magical solution that will ensure that you do not experience serious stress and move towards burn-out as a helper. You can, however, take positive and sensible steps to take care of yourself, and therefore also of your value to your clients.

Recognise the phases of burn-out as you tend to experience them and take note of what is happening before it goes too far. Be ready to learn from your personal warning signs of overload:

- Perhaps a self-indulgent habit like eating chocolate, smoking or drinking increases markedly as you try to give yourself some compensation.
- In burn-out your perceptions move to a view that work seems increasingly endless, and clients increasingly ungrateful and grasping.
- Some people react to excessive stress by adding on even more pressure to demonstrate that they can really cope, for instance, taking up a highly energetic physical exercise regime or new work responsibilities.
- Highly stressed working parents sometimes add another organised activity to their time with their children, when those children would much rather the parent just sat with them and relaxed.
- You may notice that you even have particular phrases that you are far more likely to say when you feel seriously under stress.

Create boundaries around your work

Address the main reasons for your overload:

- Work for that crucial blend of caring and detachment. (Look again at the discussion on page 113.) Remember that clients own their problems and you will not help them by trying to take responsibility for matters outside your control.
- You may need to reflect on personal beliefs, philosophical or religious, that make you resistant to creating a safe emotional distance from clients or which make it harder for you to say 'No' to further excessive demands on your time.
- Keep a perspective on clients' problems. Focus on what you can do and the difference you have made, and not on what is still left and out of your control. Look back to page 4 on common myths about helping, since some of these are a source of undue stress on helpers.
- Be ready to ask for help yourself, in brief conversations with colleagues and through proper supervision time. Recognise when the problems of a client

have hit you hard. Perhaps their experience has touched raw or unresolved emotions within your own life.

- Keep a realistic schedule in terms of the level of your work and the number of sessions with individuals or groups. Make sure you take breaks and create some time to recover, to reflect and write up notes. Learn to say 'No' within work and to calls on your time outside working hours.
- Leave clients' problems behind when you leave work and try not to continue turning them over in your mind.
- Take holidays without fail. It is a serious warning sign when you refuse to take time off, and perhaps also disrupt valuable shared leisure time with a partner, friends or family because you feel your work cannot do without you for a single day.
- If you work from home, create as clear a division as possible between work and personal life. Ideally have a room that is dedicated to work and do not let it spread throughout the rest of your home. Have a work-dedicated telephone line and put on the answer phone out of working hours.
- If you work hard, play hard. If necessary, schedule activities into your diary that you enjoy and help to recharge your batteries. See friends, go on a walk, go out to dinner, give yourself permission just to sit, read or watch television.
- Watch out for your health, with good food, enough sleep and a sensible level of exercise. Have other sources of self-esteem besides your work; it is risky to live only for the buzz of helping.

Burn-out can be positive, if worked through effectively. It helps you to empathise better with what many of your clients experience and, through learning to manage stress better, you can be better equipped to help them.

The responsibility of your organisation

Helping services and organisations should support you in taking care, with a working atmosphere in which you feel able to limit the amount of work that you accept. Helping services can develop a culture of macho caring in which nobody feels able to say, 'This is too much.' This negative atmosphere can also be fuelled by an understandable reluctance to turn any-one away. However, services or individuals who stretch themselves way beyond their capacity to cope will not only have a much more conflictful working environment, they will also provide an increasingly poor service to their clients.

Responsible senior workers in a helping organisation must be alert to signs of stress, such as individuals who see matters as absolutely right or wrong or a general increase in impatience. As a good manager, you should:

- React sooner rather than later to improve the situation, without assuming that a stressed worker is weak or incompetent.
- Help by being aware of signs of stress in yourself, rather than assuming that stress only happens to other people.
- Model positive behaviour, such as admitting that you are under stress and intend to take action to relieve the situation. Basic actions can be significant.

For instance, your team will feel unable to admit to being overloaded, if you, as their manager, insist on working through the flu, keeping very long hours, or never taking a holiday.

Possible further reading

- Cary L. Cooper, Rachel D. Cooper and Lynn H. Eaker, *Living with stress* (Penguin Books, 1988).
- Jane Cranwell-Ward, *Managing stress* (Pan Books, 1987).

Can you use helping skills in your personal life?

Communication and counselling skills can be very positive within friendships and informal help. So the simple answer is that you can use these skills to improve your own personal relationships and help people you know and those whom you care for deeply. However, the additional answer has to be that help will be given in a different way than in your professional life. Blurring work–life boundaries can be a source of stress.

Family, friends, acquaintances or neighbours are not your clients. You may not want to see them that way, nor are they likely to wish to be viewed with professional detachment. You need to be cautious if you offer or agree to help, because both practical and ethical issues can arise. You also need to be ready to reflect on what is happening and reevaluate the direction that any help is taking.

Impartiality and detachment

To be an effective helper and use counselling skills to the full, you have to retain some level of detachment. You should be impartial in a way that is unlikely to be appropriate with your family or friends. If you attempt to run a conversation in much the same way as you would in your paid or voluntary work, you may be pulled up by comments such as, 'Don't act the professional with me! I'm your brother, I know you!', 'But surely you're on my side. You're my friend!', or, 'Mum, don't go all cool and logical on me. I'm upset!'

You can draw on your counselling skills, and may be able to help a friend or family member to step back from the problem, so long as you are not seen to step back from the personal relationship. When your close friends or family are involved, you will often have a vested interest. It is appropriate that you have an emotional commitment that a situation is resolved and in how it is resolved. In a sense, you tend to interact with friends in the spirit of Stage Two (see page 144), and often appropriately use self-disclosure more, and are more confronting. It can be right to say in ways that would not be appropriate in a professional relationship, 'The horrible girls! I'm really cross that they're bullying you', or, 'I know your wife's a pain in the rear end, but . . .'.

Priorities and choices

An important issue in your personal life is how you balance all of your responsibilities and priorities. If you allow a friend or neighbour to call on your time with increasing frequency, then you may have very little time or emotional energy left for your partner or your children, let alone yourself. You may feel the pressure of, 'But I must give her time, she's so distressed', or, 'He needs to talk, how can I say no?' It can help to reframe what you are doing in terms of stark choices through self-talk. Try telling yourself, 'I chose to talk with Janie on the phone and to make us late for the cinema', or, 'I chose to walk round the common talking with Stefan rather than help my son with his homework.' Often it is helpful to give yourself permission to do what is best for you and your family. You have the right to help yourself too.

Confidences and confidentiality

Relationships with close friends frequently involve issues of confidentiality and trust. Personal experiences or problems are usually confided in the expectation that good friends do not gossip about what has been said. If you offer counselling skills to acquaintances or neighbours, you may hear confidences that are highly personal and may involve other friends as well.

The anticipated problem may be because you will face the friend's partner in social situations. On the other hand, a helping conversation may take you into far more intimate territory than you wish, with someone who is otherwise an acquaintance or neighbour. There are times to say, 'Are you sure you want tell me this?', or the more assertive, 'I don't want to hear this because . . .'.

Boundaries and saying 'No'

Even people who are skilled in setting up and holding to boundaries in their professional work can be unwary in their personal life. Within your work setting you will have hours of work, perhaps someone who answers the phone or deals initially with callers at reception and you will have a working atmosphere that communicates the other professional calls on your time. In contrast, help offered informally in your personal life can incur greater demands than you either planned or wanted. People may knock on your door or phone you at inconvenient times. What you hoped would be a short conversation stretches on and on. People whom you do not know well may turn out to be very needy or to have complex emotional problems that you cannot possibly resolve in this personal sphere even if you would like to.

Assertiveness is key to handling these types of situations, and is important for your own well-being and peaceful personal life. You need to learn to say 'No' courteously and in different ways appropriate to the circumstances. However, it is also a matter of courtesy to friends and acquaintances to be honest with them as soon as you can to avoid their feeling uncomfortable or guilty when it becomes clear that they have disrupted your other commitments.

With assertive responses, you take responsibility for your position, while respecting the other person's right to theirs. It is not shifting all the responsibility, or blame, to the other person. Unless you tell them your real constraints, friends and acquaintances may assume that their requests are fine; you have given them no reason to think otherwise. So, instead of thinking, 'She should stop asking me', or, 'He ought to know this is a thoughtless time to phone me', you need to offer honest, firm responses. If you have agreed to help, to some extent, consider managing the contact with responses such as:

- 'It's not a good time to talk, I could call you back at [time]. Shall I do that?' Keep your promise to return the call and consider addressing issues about times you are happy for this friend to call. Persistent callers may need to be told, 'Sachin, I said before that I can't talk like this in the evening. I want to give time to the children. Please don't call again at this time.'
- You also need to be fair, and firm, about face-to-face requests for a helpful conversation. If you are happy to talk, then alert a friend or neighbour with, 'That's fine, but I have to leave the house in half an hour', or, 'We'll have to stop talking very soon. I must pick the children up from school.'
- Ideally, you want to avoid reaching the point when you dread the sight of an acquaintance or neighbour arriving to talk or their voice over the telephone. Try to anticipate the situation and be honest with, 'I'm sorry, I have no time to talk.'

It is natural to want to be generous with your time and effort to close friends and family, but there are limits to even strong emotional commitments. You may need to consider and then say, with care for the other person:

- 'I'm sorry you still feel so unhappy about . . . but I don't feel able to talk with you about it any more.'
- 'I'm too close to this situation. I'll support you in whatever choice you make, but I think you should talk with someone else about what you might do. I can't stand back enough to help you.'
- 'I don't feel able to talk about this any more. To be honest, I find it too distressing. And I can't help you when I'm so upset.'
- 'I really think we've circled round this enough. I'll help you when you're ready to do something.'
- 'Debbie, I am uncomfortable working professionally with a friend. I'd much prefer to keep our relationship just as friends. If you'd like me to recommend someone that could help, I would be happy to.'

Without setting some limits to what you give, it is as possible to overload on stress within your personal life as in your professional life. There should be colleagues with an eye on your welfare at work; in your personal life your number one, and maybe only, protector is you.

12.3 Working well together

Teamwork and communication

The quality of relationships within a team affects the work with service users, positively or negatively. Respect for clients is central to an effective help-

ing service, so your organisation must develop a work culture that supports this outlook. Teams feel much more able to respect clients when they feel respected themselves. It is the responsibility of senior workers to ensure that everyone within a team is respected. Some teams operate as if volunteers do not count or that the reception staff are less important. Dangerous cracks can appear in the service to clients when people in the team are ignored or undervalued.

When teams, or parts of a team, feel ill-used or overworked, the result is that:

- The team may shift those feelings on to clients: that it is the clients who ask too much, or are impatient or ungrateful.
- New developments in work with a client group may be seen by a team in a competitive way, with remarks like, 'Never mind the clients' rights, what about ours?'
- A team may start to protect themselves by stopping seeing clients as individuals and seeing them as examples of a problem, as a list of demands on their time or as incompetent and inadequate.
- Problems within the team may even be discussed with sympathetic clients. The proper helping relationship has then been distorted, because the team looks inappropriately towards outsiders rather than colleagues as a source of support for themselves.

Problems of this kind need to be tackled sooner rather than later. As a new team leader you may take over disaffected workers. Communication and counselling skills will be important as you, and committed team members, work to reestablish the boundaries of the work and to address the team's legitimate wish for their skills to be affirmed and needs recognised. It is the responsibility of senior team members to ensure time for thorough discussions and expression of feelings within the team as well as a renewed focus on obligations to clients and the service.

Support and supervision

Informal support

Ideally, any helping organisation has a positive network of informal support between colleagues. Perhaps you all:

- Share ideas with each other, within the bounds of confidentiality to clients.
- Pass on useful information about contacts and helpful resources.
- Give attention to colleagues who look overloaded, puzzled or distressed.
- Support each other so that you are all more able to support clients.

Being busy makes this less easy, but even so some helping organisations fall far short of this ideal. You may be subject to an unrealistic workload which leaves no time for reflection and exchange of ideas. You are also very unlikely to ask for or accept help from colleagues if the culture of your organisation does not tolerate admission of doubt or mistakes. Again it is the responsibility of senior members to ensure that everyone is enabled to talk appropriately about their work and that an atmosphere of learning is created within any service. Time may need to be created to ensure that this happens.

Supervision sessions

Regular supervision is especially important when you use counselling skills within your job:

- To ensure that your work, and that of your colleagues, is consistent with the values and objectives of the overall organisation. This kind of supervision can be crucial when individual team workers are dispersed between sites or shifts and do not regularly meet each other.
- You need and deserve some personal support for yourself. Helping services, especially counselling and group work, make considerable demands on your energy and creativity.
- Supervision is needed by everyone, not just new trainees and not only when there is a problem. There should never be a sense that supervision is only for those helpers who cannot cope. Helpers may also need to retain some humility, that they can benefit from help, rather than feeling that, 'I'm the one who does the helping.'
- You need to be able to talk over your work with a colleague within the appropriate boundaries of confidentiality. You will have many ideas yourself but it also helps to use someone else as a sounding board.
- Helpers who do not have an opportunity to talk within supervision will either keep all their concerns to themselves or may be tempted to talk with friends or family which raises further issues about confidentiality.
- In supervision you may often want to talk through the difficulties or uncertainties in your work. A good supervisor should also call your attention to what you have done well and learned through your practice.
- In some organisations, for instance on a telephone helpline, a team of workers might be contacted by the same clients. Supervision and discussion of issues

raised by clients might then take place better in a meeting of a group of helpers.

- Supervisors should offer an understanding of the work you undertake and the skills you use as well as providing a degree of independence, to enable you to be more objective about your work. Ideally supervisors are not your line manager as well, but in practice the two roles are often combined.

The skills of supervision

Good supervision draws on the communication and counselling skills described in earlier chapters of this book, although there are differences between supervision and working with a client. Supervisors have an obligation to ensure that your work is consistent with the values of the organisation, productive and ethical. So, supervisors may sometimes be more directive than you would be with a client.

It is certainly important to recognise when there is a difficulty with a team member's practice. Counselling skills are appropriate for potential problem-solving and for helpers who are open to learning and change. If the serious problem continues, it may become a disciplinary matter. Following the procedures of your organisation for such situations is crucial as well as communicating clearly and unambiguously.

Possible further reading

These suggestions, especially our book and that of John Hayes address the different kinds of supervision given from a managerial position.

- Michael Carroll, *Counselling supervision: theory, skills and practice* (Cassell, 1996).
- John Hayes, *Developing the manager as a helper* (Routledge, 1996).
- Jennie and Lance Lindon, *Working together for young children* (Macmillan, 1997).
- Warren Redman, *Counselling your staff* (Kogan Page, 1995).

Professional networks

It is important to develop and maintain an effective network with other services and professionals, since these contacts can help to extend your information base (page 68) and support effective referrals (page 87).

Contributions to inter-professional discussion

If you are in the position to contribute to a discussion or consultation with other helping professionals, then it is crucial that you value your own contribution. It often helps to prepare what you will say. This is essential if you are giving a report, or contributing a summary of your own work when several different individuals or agencies are involved. However, it will often be enough to list for yourself the key points that you wish to make, without detailing every word.

You may experience established differences of status within some meetings and, difficult as it can be, you need to make your own contribution with confidence. Offer your experience and perspective, rather than waiting passively to be asked. Otherwise, you may continue to support some unhelpful traditions that underestimate the value of your contribution to the helping services.

A coordinating role

Several professionals or services are sometimes involved with the same individual or family. Unless one key person takes responsibility to coordinate the various contributions, the client can become understandably confused. For example, parents of sick or disabled children frequently find themselves trying to relate to many professionals and services. Their differing advice is not always compatible and may not allow for others' recommendations. Parents can appreciate the kind of support that affirms the importance of their role as parents. This helps them to weigh up conflicting priorities, assess any confusing advice and find out more information as they need it.

Several general issues can arise in coordination:

- Are you in the role of formal or informal coordinator?
- Informality can be appropriate if the client is coping well with different agencies and appreciates discussion with you to clarify any confusions or to weigh up possible courses of action. Someone who is in regular contact with a client, and his or her family, may be the best person to help that client to coordinate different relationships with helping agencies.
- You will probably need a more formal role if clients need you to contact other agencies on their behalf and certainly will do if you are acting as an advocate for clients (see page 221).
- Is your client present at discussions with other agencies? Good practice is to have clients present and there should be a very good reason if clients are not with you. If clients lack confidence in speaking up, then you may speak for them. They still need to be actively involved and no discussion should proceed as if they are not in the room. Work towards enabling your client to ask the questions and to comment.

12.4 Personal development

Preparation and training

Workers in any kind of helping service, including a telephone helpline, should have the opportunity for:

- Basic training or preparation before they start to relate to clients.
- Further training and development.
- A system of support and supervision so that helpers can discuss the kind of inquiries with which they deal and the responses that are needed.

The nature of the preparation and training that is appropriate will vary depending on the exact service but many skills are in common:

- All helpers should have a basic preparation in the skills of greeting clients, listening and asking open-ended questions.
- Information services need helpers who are well-informed about the topic(s) covered, able to judge when they do not know an answer and able to find out or refer as appropriate.
- Helpers need further preparation in counselling skills when services, including telephone helplines, invite clients who are likely to have emotional as well as practical issues.
- Some services and charitable organisations select helpers and volunteers because of their personal experience. This is valuable but helpers must be able to place their own experience in perspective.

Personal learning

Most skills are learned while doing the job, not through formal training. Competent helping professionals remain open to learning, however experienced they have become, and are willing to reflect on what they have done and why. This outlook is sometimes called the 'reflective practitioner'. An effective system of supervision and support (see page 249) should help as you work with individuals or groups. It is also valuable learning to think through, or discuss, work that has been completed.

Review for yourself how the sessions with an individual or work with a group progressed:

- Make sure that you consider the strengths of your practice as well as your weaker points. What have you learned about what you do well? How could you develop these strengths further?
- With hindsight, would you now handle particular events or individuals in a different way? What guided your decisions at the time and what can you learn to improve in the future?
- Admitting mistakes to yourself helps you to learn; it is not saying that you are a poor helper. Check that you are not being too hard on yourself. Is a different choice of action only obvious with hindsight?
- Accept feedback in a constructive way. You may be given feedback by the individuals or groups with whom you work, or by colleagues who observe you or work as a co-leader. Ask directly for feedback if you do not receive enough reaction to how you work. Look at page 39 for a discussion on giving and receiving feedback.

Your practice will improve with both experience and your willingness to reflect on what happened. It will not help to strive for unrealistically high standards that do not allow you to make mistakes. Are you:

- Trying to be perfect, refusing to tolerate your own mistakes, even when you encourage an individual or group members to recognise that mistakes happen?
- Aiming to take complete and personal responsibility for your work as the source of all insights and positive interventions? However, you are successful when your clients reach new perspectives, notice events or generate ideas.

- Seeking to take an individual or group in a direction further or faster than they are currently ready to accept?
- Accepting the individual or group as they are at the moment? It is usually unhelpful to compare one individual or group with others that you found easier, friendlier or readier to affirm your skills.

Activity

Explore your own learning from a recent experience working with an individual or as a group leader. Ideally, with the support of a colleague in discussion:

- Identify a specific area in which you would like to modify how you work. Describe to yourself, or to a colleague, the concrete details of what you would like to do. Focus on your own behaviour, feelings or beliefs, as appropriate.
- Develop a realistic goal about the change you want to make in how you work. Plan for this change and consider what will help you and what may hinder. (Look at page 155 on goal-setting.)
- Prepare to apply this change, appropriately, to your next work with an individual or group.
- Evaluate afterwards what has happened and what you have learned.

▣ ⍌ 13 Final thoughts

A considerable number of people in Britain are employed in one way or another in helping others. Apart from the many paid professionals involved in help, advice and support, there are a considerable number of people working in a voluntary capacity in organisations and centres, many taking their turn giving information or running helplines.

The considered application of good communication skills makes a huge difference to the experience of clients. Being alert to the importance of non-verbal behaviour and use of language is crucial to the effectiveness of any service, not least the important yet often overlooked reception desk or first telephone response. Within our personal and professional experience, we have been struck by the considerable difference brought about in a service when the whole team genuinely recognise that their clients really matter.

A crucial first step is to acknowledge and behave to clients as deserving the kind of courtesy and respect that we all prefer to receive ourselves in inter-actions with others. This attitude is crucial, yet typically is most useful when important skills are both in place and visibly supported by the organisation. Courteous communication at its most basic and essential level is not tech-nically difficult and is not indeed about 'techniques' as such: it is about caring for, and respecting, clients. This informs and underwrites the practice often needed to communicate well, and to ensure that skills such as reflective listening become part of what soon seems like the 'natural and obvious way' to approach clients.

Some job roles benefit from applying more detailed helping skills, which we covered in the context of counselling skills both in interaction with indi-viduals and in the related skills of working with groups. However, these more detailed applied areas work best for clients when use of counselling skills is grounded in the context of wider communication skills. Particularly people with concerns or in crisis deserve a respectful approach that treats them as individuals and does not try to simplify matters by fitting unique concerns into preshaped problem categories or current solutions. The counselling approach enables clients to learn from their experience and to emerge feeling more competent in their daily life and better able to resolve or cope with difficulties themselves.

In many different settings, and with very different professional groups, we have seen over and over again the approaches that we describe in this book work-ing in practice. The difference between those clients emerging from a service, even from a short exchange, feeling affirmed and respected and those feeling dismissed or left with inappropriate help is simply staggering – and is reflected in the relative success of the helping organisations. Often the greatest pleasure for professionals in a helping position is to feel that they have made a difference to clients and this feeling of satisfaction is far more likely to happen regularly in a climate of mutual respect and open communications. Not only does such an experience cheer you, it also helps to reduce your stress, and hence to release more energy to help your clients. It is a truly virtuous, fulfilling, circle.

◪ Appendix

This book will support your practice and study on a wide range of counselling courses offered in colleges, by hospital trusts or counselling organisations in order to gain the following qualifications:

- The RSA Certificate in Counselling Skills in the Development of Learning.
- NVQs in Advice and Guidance from CAMPAG.
- The AEB Certificate in Counselling Theory, the AEB Certificate in Counselling Skills, the AEB Advanced Certificate in Counselling Skills and Theory, and the AEB Diploma in Therapeutic Counselling (Humanistic or Psychodynamic).
- BTEC Counselling Skills and Caring Services (Counselling).

Most programmes of study in the field of early years care and education and for playwork include units on working with parents and carers, on running groups and supportive working relationships within a team. This book will support study linked with units in:

- Levels 2 and 3 S/NVQs in Early Years Care and Education.
- Levels 2 and 3 S/NVQs in Playwork.
- CACHE Certificate (CCE), NNEB Diploma and Advanced Diploma (ADCE).
- BTEC Childhood Studies (Nursery Nursing).

∇ Index

A

access
  to buildings   22, 58, 188
  of clients to own records   18–19
  to service   70–2, 94, 96
accidents   79, 134, 224
action plans   164ff, 229
advanced understanding in counselling
    144ff
advice   2, 4, 9, 30, 83, 84ff, 98
advocacy   3, 221–2
Aids/HIV   84, 230–1
angry clients   65–6, 237–8
anti-discriminatory   20ff, 232
assumptions   9, 20, 23, 60, 68, 73,
    126–7, 133
attention   29ff, 97, 132–4
attitudes towards clients   14ff, 35,
    106–7
audit of service   7
automatic referral   88, 227

B

barriers to listening   33–5
basic understanding in counselling
    118, 130ff
behaviourist tradition   108
bereavement   36, 78, 111, 132, 150,
    212, 222–3
bilingual clients   47–9, 71, 80
blocks to action plans   156, 166
body language   30, 32, 29ff, 65, 94,
    133, 198, 229, 243–4
boundaries   5, 10, 11, 21, 68, 84, 93,
    181, 183, 221, 239, 246
brainstorming   164
British Association for Counselling
    109, 233
burn-out   240ff

C

careers guidance   1, 3, 50, 70, 84,
    85
caring detachment   113–4, 243, 245
challenge   18, 67, 149–51, 204, 210,
    229
child protection   11, 92, 227

children and young people   4, 5, 8, 11,
    15, 41, 42, 48–9, 79, 91, 99, 220, 221,
    223, 226ff
chronic illness   227, 229ff
clichés   27, 56, 75, 77, 78, 111, 223
codes of practice   9, 109, 233
co-leadership   184–7, 200, 231
complaints section   3.3
computers
  information on   68, 70, 72
  records on   13, 18–9
conciliation   3, 220
confidentiality   7, 10–3, 81–2, 126–7,
    200
contracting
  with groups   199, 200
  with individual clients   122, 124–9
coordinating role   251
couples   112, 220, 221, 231ff
courtesy   55, 61, 64, 99, 254
cultural tradition   3, 27, 40, 61, 62, 90,
    108, 110, 112, 119, 167
customer charters   8, 14, 124

D

dependency   90, 118, 218
dilemmas   160ff
disability   7, 21, 22–3, 42, 48, 58, 75,
    90, 96, 184, 222, 229ff, 251
distressed
  clients   10, 74, 210–11
  helpers   52, 152, 205, 240ff
dominant group members   204, 205–6
dyslexia   23, 63, 73

E

Egan, Gerard   109, 121
elderly clients   48, 50, 61, 63, 90, 175,
    232ff
email   29, 69, 80ff, 86
empathy   26, 59, 107, 108, 109, 130
ending of
  counselling sessions   170–1
  group   197, 218–9
  short contact   63–4, 66
  telephone conversation   103–4
ethical issues   9ff
ethnic group   7, 21–3, 78, 93, 99, 113

experiential learning   189–91
eye contact   32, 37, 41, 49

F
families   113, 157, 231ff
feedback from
   clients   8, 39, 78–9, 90, 211, 252
   colleagues   23, 39, 78, 185–6, 252
feelings
   clients'   49ff, 65, 73–4, 95, 98, 102–3,
     165, 171, 203–4, 222, 237–8
   helpers'   52, 107, 114, 152, 171, 205,
     218, 235–6, 240ff
first-contact person   54, 56, 64, 71
first impressions   54ff
force field analysis   169, 219

G
gay men   24, 105
gender   7, 20, 41, 110, 184
genuineness   108, 109, 113
goal-setting   154, 155ff, 224
greetings   55–6, 98, 197
group
   activities   191, 198, 212ff
   dynamics   193–7, 201ff

H
health and safety   234ff
health-care settings   1, 14, 15, 61, 74,
   85, 222, 227ff
here-and-now focus   153, 203
humanistic tradition   108

I
imagination   165, 215
inappropriate telephone calls   99,
   105–6
information   2, 12, Chapter 4 *passim*
informed consent   12, 17, 88, 227
Internet   68, 80, 82–3
interruptions   33, 34, 55, 125, 188
intervention in groups   207–10

L
leadership style in group   172, 131ff,
   200, 207
leaflets   25, 69
legislation   19–21, 234–5
lesbians   105, 150
letters   29, 86
life crisis   224ff
listening   4, 29ff, 43–4, 64, 98, 121, 202

M
mediation   3, 220
Minicom   22, 96
mistakes   64ff, 252
misunderstandings   4, 28
monitoring a service   6, 7–8, 69, 85

N
names   60–2, 104
networks   250–1
notes, personal   19, 134

O
objectives of
   group   172–7, 183, 199
   service   5ff
open or closed groups   177–8, 180,
   183

P
paraphrasing   45, 134–5
parents   113, 157, 163, 175, 176, 230,
   251
personal experience   118, 144, 151–2
personal learning   39, 52–3, 115ff, 210,
   251ff
personal life of helpers   10, 115, 244,
   245–7
personal style in helping   115ff, 141
persuasion   87, 113
phases of group life   193–7
physical setting   22, 34, 54, 58, 187–8
post-traumatic stress disorder   225–6
priorities   111, 142, 159, 237, 245
privacy   95, 97, 125, 188–9
prompting   165
psychodynamic tradition   108

Q
quality assurance   7
questions   17, 44–7, 67, 73–4, 99, 115,
   139–41, 204, 227
quiet clients   153, 198, 206–7, 208

R
reception staff   36, 54, 211
records of
   clients   17ff
   groups   19, 217
redundancy   74, 110, 226
referrals   60, 69, 87ff, 101, 128, 152,
   171, 226, 250
reflecting back   50, 134–6, 203, 227
religious beliefs   62, 107, 110, 167, 243
reluctant clients   128, 179, 201

respect   13, 30, 36, 64, 88, 99, 108, 113,
    123, 254
Rogers, Carl   108
role play   216

S
safety with clients   238–40
scapegoating   207, 212
schools   1, 12, 14, 15, 85, 94, 124
secrets   11, 127, 163
security measures   58–9, 188–9
self-disclosure   118, 144, 151–2, 204–5,
    215, 216, 245
self-help   3, 175
self-talk   235, 246
silence   43, 97, 98, 153, 202
staged model of helping   121ff
stress   234, 240ff
summarising   45, 138–9, 141, 145
supervision   11, 15, 123, 249–50
sympathy   130

T
teamwork   15, 240, 247ff
telephone helplines   9, 35, Chapter 5
    passim, 111, 249
terminal illness   85, 223
text telephones   82, 96
therapy   3, 5, 14, 109, 199
three-way communication   48
training   226, 251ff
trauma   224ff
trust   9, 27, 51, 113, 121, 123, 224

V
video-recording   13, 39, 217
violence   59, 88, 111, 238–9

W
warmth   106, 108, 109, 113
web site   68, 80, 82–3
words, use of   41ff, 99, 136–8
writing original material   75ff, 214